EAST TENNESSEE STATE UNIVERSITY FOOTBALL

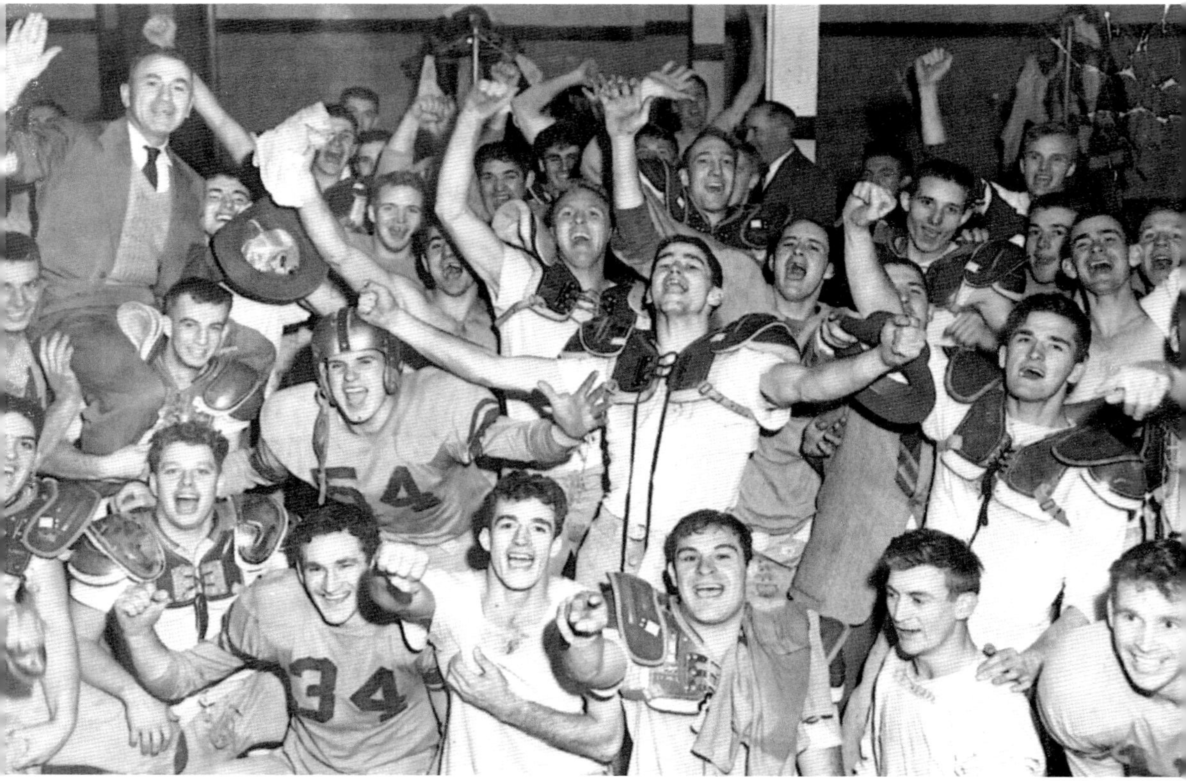

The background image from the front cover is worth repeating in all of its unadulterated glory. The joy on the faces of the players and coaches has been repeated by victorious competitors throughout the ages. (Photograph courtesy of A. G. Dawson.)

FRONT COVER: Hal Morrison, East Tennessee State University's first genuine All-American (first team Little All-American 1954), is the only football player to have his number retired. He is shown in the inset. In 1953, he established an NCAA record for catching 11 touchdown passes in a single season. He served as an assistant football and basketball coach during the 1950s and 1960s, and he was the first and only golf coach from 1957 to 1984. During his tenure, he brought the golf team and university national recognition. (Photograph courtesy Buc Football and Friends Foundation.)
COVER BACKGROUND: The background image on the front cover is the locker room celebration of State's 1952 Burley Bowl victory over the Emory and Henry Wasps by a score of 34-16. (Photograph courtesy Buc Football and Friends Foundation.)
BACK COVER: In this image, ETSU makes what is to date its last entrance into the Dome prior to their final game of the 2003 season, a victory against the Citadel. (Photograph courtesy ETSU Photo Lab.)

EAST TENNESSEE STATE UNIVERSITY FOOTBALL

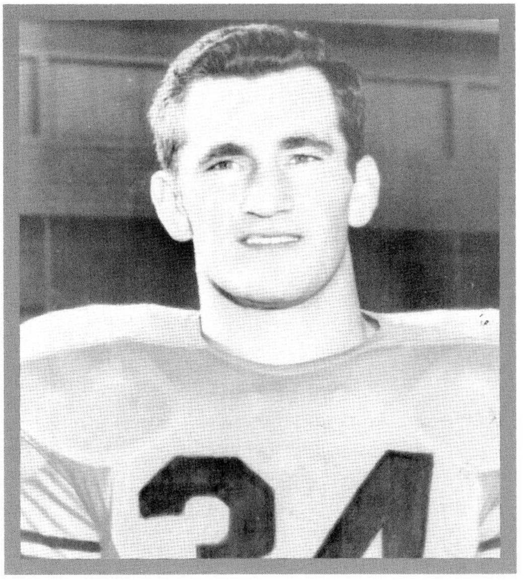

L. Thomas Roberts, Jerry Robertson,
and the Buc Football and Friends Foundation
Foreword by Jack Higgs

ARCADIA PUBLISHING

ISBN 978-0-7385-4424-3

Published by Arcadia Publishing
Charleston SC, Chicago IL, Portsmouth NH, San Francisco CA

Printed in the United States of America

Library of Congress Catalog Card Number: 2006938813

For all general information contact Arcadia Publishing at:
Telephone 843-853-2070
Fax 843-853-0044
E-mail sales@arcadiapublishing.com
For customer service and orders:
Toll-Free 1-888-313-2665

Visit us on the Internet at www.arcadiapublishing.com

Dedicated to the glory of God through Whom all things are possible!

—L. Thomas Roberts

Dedicated to past (and hopefully future) ETSU football players, cheerleaders,

band members, coaches, trainers, equipment managers, secretaries, team physicians, fans,

and especially Jeanie, Jo Lynn, and Josh!

—Jerry Robertson

In memory of Loyd T. "Preacher" Roberts, Dr. Howell H. Sherrod,

and Berney Burleson.

CONTENTS

ACKNOWLEDGMENTS

Many people volunteered their time and talents when needed to make this book come to fruition. We will try to recognize each of them, and we apologize ahead of time for anyone who may be unintentionally overlooked and for not being able to include all the material provided to us. First and foremost, thanks are due our families for allowing much time away from them to complete this project—with no complaint! The following people graciously looked through their family papers and photograph albums, generously providing copies/scans of their materials and stories to complement them: Hal Morrison, L. T. Helton, Jan Burleson, Johnny Russaw, Hal Littleford, Tim Jones, the Cathey family, Aaron Fenimore, Pete Wilson, Jimmy "Wink" Baker, A. B. Clevenger, the Trawick family, A. G. Dawson, and Barbara Hundley. The staff of the Archives of Appalachia were cheerfully accommodating with requests for help, especially Georgia Greer and Ned Irwin. We appreciate the time Dr. Paul Stanton took to review and approve of this project and the help and advice of other university staff, Michael White and Bob Plummer. Many thanks are due to Dr. Jack Higgs for his expert advice and for providing the foreword to this book. Finally, we are indebted to Larry Smith, director of ETSU's Photo Lab, for taking time to dig through his archives to provide photographs. The story of ETSU football would not have been nearly as complete without these people.

FOREWORD

East Tennessee State University Football by Tom Roberts and Jerry Robertson is the second important book published recently about the game in East Tennessee. The first—*Football as a War Game: The Annotated Notebooks of General R. R. Neyland* (Falcon Press 2002) by former University of Tennessee (UT) All-American Andy Kozar—is an argument inviting by its title an opposite view. Is football like war? Yes. Is it different from war? Indeed. Roberts's and Robertson's book is equally valuable, offering not a thesis to debate but just the facts, which they present in graceful narrative with fascinating photographs of teams and coaches.

Every page conveys the stamp of verity characterized by accuracy and honesty. It is a book not just for alumni of the university and sports fans but also for the historians of sports in America, especially in Appalachia. In the 1920s, when college football was just getting started, a common problem was finding a level, well-drained place for teams to play. The authors recount, "The first athletic field was said to be hard and uneven. Early in his presidency, Dr. Sherrod had the field leveled and graded with teams of mules." A few years earlier (1921) in Knoxville, the university was dealing with a similar situation in building Shields Watkins field without the help of mules but with the help of the student body using picks and shovels.

The compelling picture that unfolds in this history is a story of those who coached and played the game (see the index for these familiar names). Victories, changing team names and conferences, and hardships and reversals faced are all recorded here. It is also the story of renewal after the Great Depression and World War II when the program was closed. Note for example the caption under the photograph of the "Barefoot Boys:"

> Coach McMurray finished his tenure at State with a 7-1 record in 1946. . . . Returning veterans came back to a poorly funded and ill-equipped team that would be dubbed "The Barefoot Boys" because half of the 70 members trying out for the team had no shoes. It was only three days prior to the first game with Brevard that enough shoes had been repaired, borrowed, and purchased to outfit the 40 remaining players.

One of the high points of Buccaneer football was the win in the Grantland Rice Bowl over Louisiana Tech and Terry Bradshaw in 1969 on the 100th anniversary of college football. Roberts, appropriately, devotes a chapter to this event. What Grantland Rice, a Tennessee native and arguably the greatest of American sports journalists, admired was not whether one won nor lost but how the game was played. To him this was the sign of what he called the "uphill heart." In this text, examples abound of that special quality.

—Jack Higgs

INTRODUCTION

ETSU has a long history of producing winners—perhaps not winning teams on the field of play each year, but winners in life. So many of the people involved with the program have gone on to have a positive influence on countless lives through coaching or teaching, establishing successful businesses, or serving in local government. This book was written to honor the men and women who sacrificed their time, and sometimes their bodies, to provide a football game and all its trappings for the fans of ETSU.

The genesis of the book began when the two authors were discussing photographs for a pictorial history of ETSU, and Jerry Robertson exclaimed, "This is what the football team needs!" Chip Kessler had written a history of the basketball team previously, and Berney Burleson had compiled statistics and some anecdotes for the football team covering 1920 to 1970, but it was never published. With the loss of the team after the 2003 season due to financial considerations and the university's current review of the feasibility of bringing back the team, it seemed like the right time to shed light on the program's long, proud history.

The goal was to honor as many of the players as possible by including them in the photographs, which was only possible in this book's format by using team photographs as the backbone of the book. Unfortunately, the Archives of Appalachia had very few of the team photographs available, and the ETSU Photo Lab had images from 1977 on. Therefore, it was a challenge to find sources for these photographs. Other than the two sources previously mentioned, the best reference for what was available was the school's annuals. Looking through the annuals and the archives, it was discovered that no team photographs appeared to have been made from 1929 to 1932 or in 2002.

Going through the school's annuals year by year, the growth and evolution of East Tennessee State from a normal school to a university was well documented. Also documented was the growth of the team from only about 15 young men, many of whom had never played football yet who were called on to play both offense and defense, to a team of nearly 60 well-conditioned athletes playing very specialized positions. For this reason, the annuals were used significantly in compiling the history and reflecting the tone of the times when the team won and the team lost.

The ETSU annual was first published in 1919 as the *Old Hickory*; then it became the *Chalk Line* in 1930, when the format was significantly reduced due to the shortage of dollars and materials during the Depression. In 1937, two years after the sports teams adopted the nickname "Buccaneers" after the name was put to a student body vote, the annual took the name as well. The final year of publication of the yearbook was 1998 when declining participation by the students to have their photographs made led to cancellation of the yearbook. From that point on, the ETSU media guides were used as the primary source of information.

Added to this backbone of information were the anecdotes and first-hand accounts of those who played, coached, cheered, or worked the sidelines over the years. These important accounts were too numerous and detailed to include in this format, and it is hoped that one day someone will assemble these stories and this currently untold history into another volume with many of the nearly 1,000 photographs collected for this book. If anyone reading has images or stories to share, the Buc Football and Friends Foundation would very much like to add them to their growing archive. They can be reached via the Web at www.bucfootball.com/history.html. Your contributions will be vital to preserving the history of Buccaneer football. Go Bucs!

1

Blue and Gold Beginnings

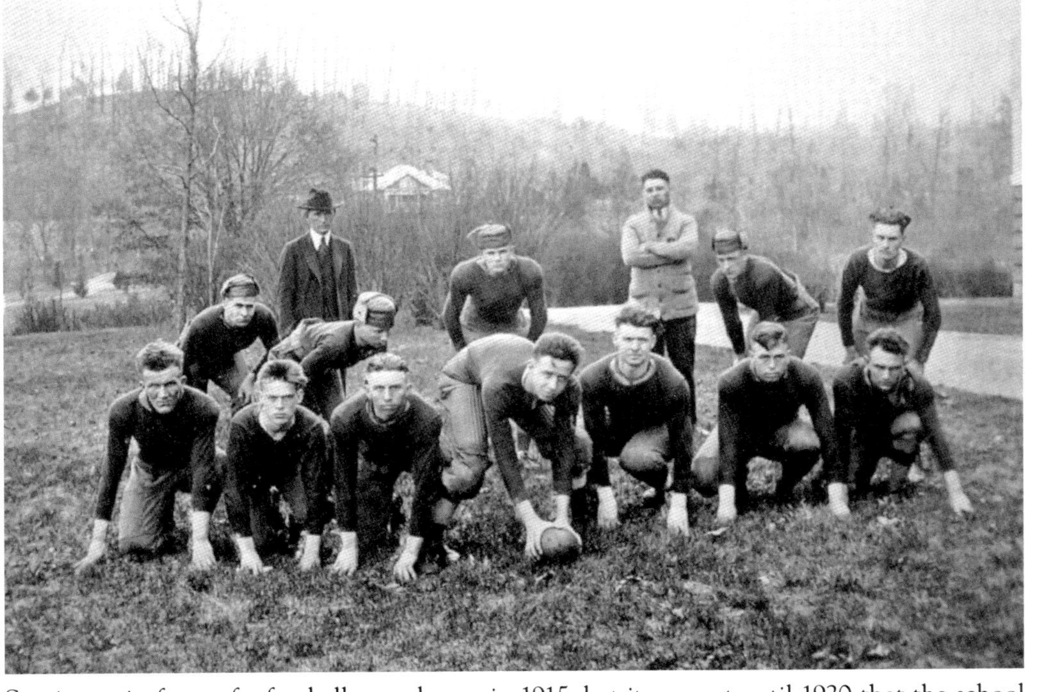

Sentiment in favor of a football team began in 1915, but it was not until 1920 that the school could raise the funds for equipment and find enough able-bodied men to play. The inaugural edition of the football team finished the season 3-4 in 1920 and initiated their long-standing rivalry with Milligan College. Overall the skill of players in the upper east Tennessee region was at a novice level since the game was only informally played in the area until around the time of World War I, when most of the area high schools formed football teams. (Photograph courtesy Buc Football and Friends Foundation.)

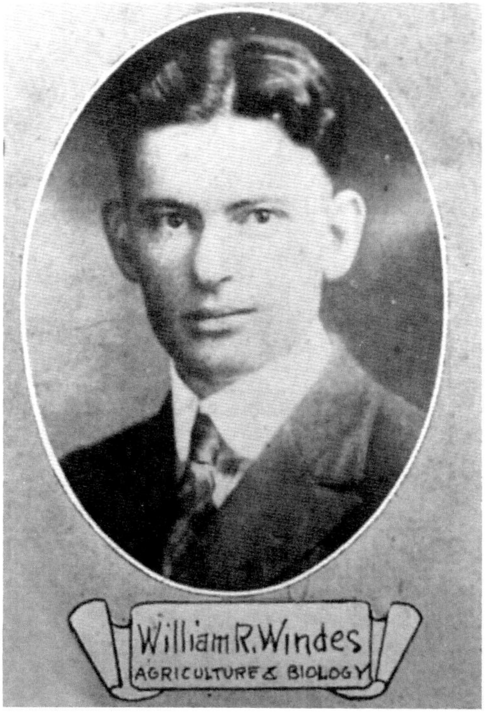

Prof. William R. Windes, a 1917 UT graduate who taught agriculture and biology, was tapped to coach a 1920 team that consisted of 11 first-string players and 4 substitutes. They lost their first game against Johnson City High School and won their last game against Greeneville High. In between, they defeated Washington College and Johnson City High and lost games to Milligan College, Tennessee High School, and Carson-Newman. (Photograph courtesy Buc Football and Friends Foundation.)

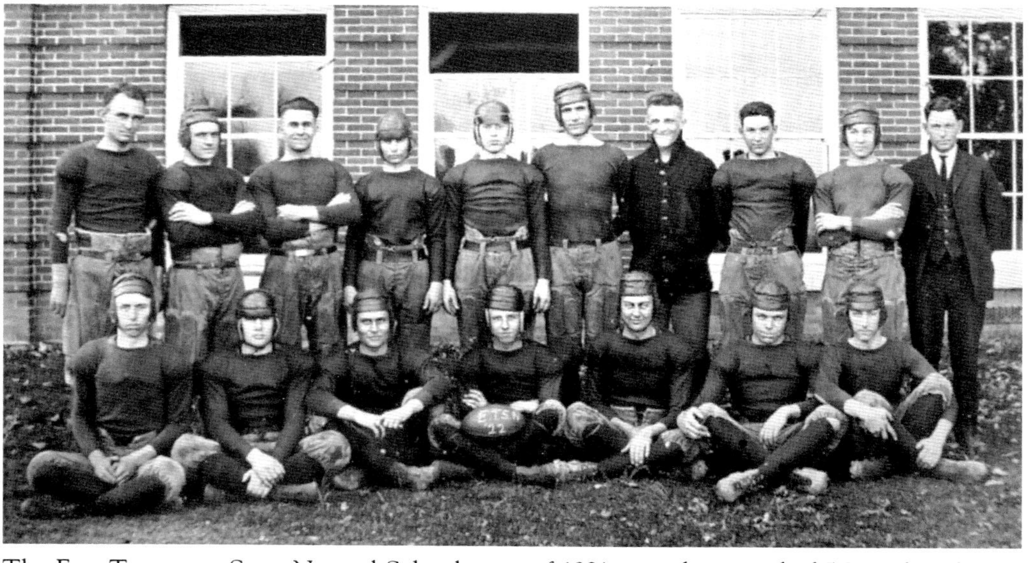

The East Tennessee State Normal School team of 1921 posted a record of 5-3, with only one game against strictly high school–level competition. They also played the Johnson City All-Stars, a team composed of a combination of high school and former college players. Coach Windes stepped down as coach after the season and finished with a career record of 8-7-0. During his tenure, the school joined the Appalachian Intercollegiate Conference and the East Tennessee Athletic League. (Photograph courtesy Buc Football and Friends Foundation.)

English professor Willis Beeler "Bull" Bible assisted head coach W. K. Windes during the 1920 season, making him and fellow teacher/coach A. V. McFee the first assistant football coaches. He later oversaw the activity fund, the primary source of financial aid that provided jobs for deserving athletes, and served on the Athletic Committee until his retirement in 1961. His brother, Dana X. Bible, was elected to the College Football Hall of Fame as a coach. (Photograph courtesy Buc Football and Friends Foundation.)

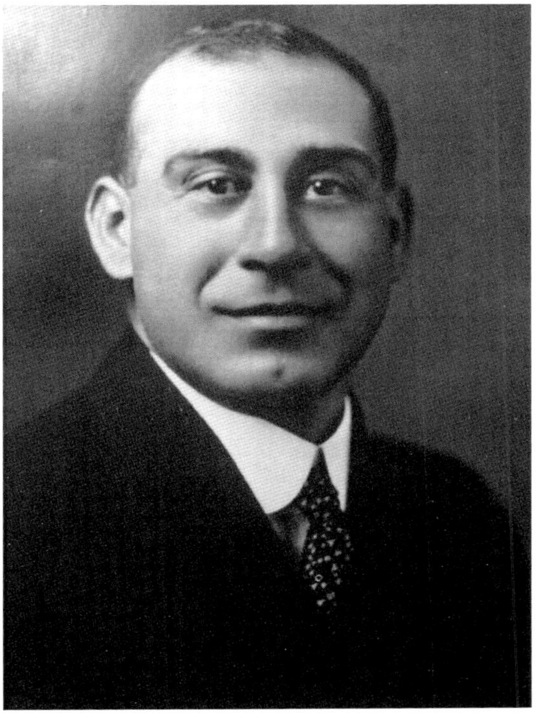

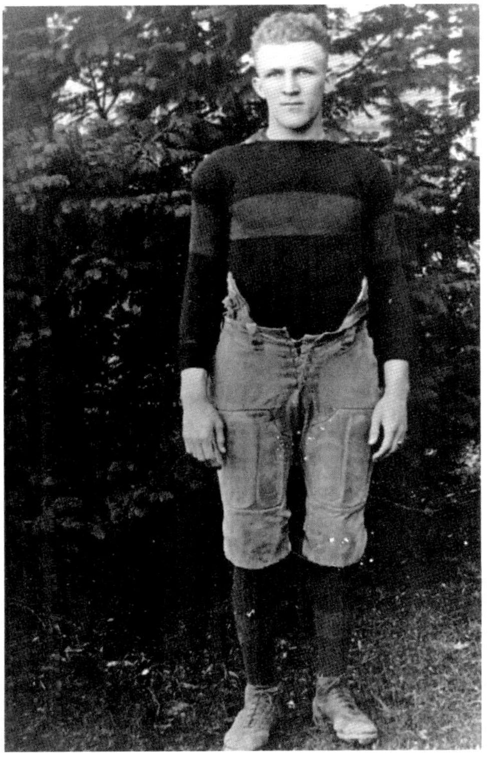

Kermit Quillen, elected to the 1920s All-Decade team as a left halfback, was a member of the first football team, playing from 1920 to 1923, and he played basketball and baseball. He helped the "Normalites," "Wolves," or "Huskies" as they were sometimes called during that time to a 3-0 upset of Milligan College in 1922. He was inducted into the ETSU Athletics Hall of Fame in 1977. (Photograph courtesy Buc Football and Friends Foundation.)

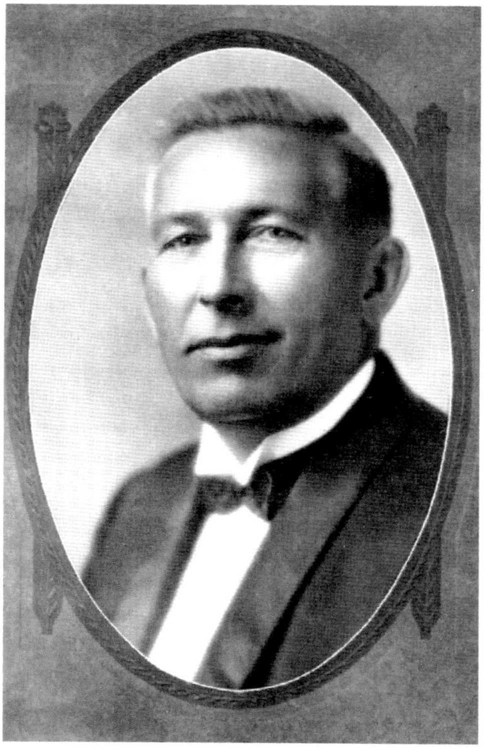

Prof. A. Vernon McFee served as an assistant coach during all of W. R. Windes's term as coach and for at least one year, 1922, under J. K. Luck. He was also credited by Berney Burleson for serving as the team's trainer, a first. McFee was a graduate of Cincinnati's College of Music and taught public school music at ETSNS from 1920 to 1927. (Photograph courtesy Buc Football and Friends Foundation.)

In 1922, the Normals sported half a team that had never played football before and split their record at four and four. The highlight of the year was the Thanksgiving Day showdown with cross-county rival Milligan. Special streetcars transported much of the estimated crowd of 3,000 fans to Wilder Park. After defeating Milligan 3-0 on a second field goal attempt by Ancil Barron, the team went to the Hotel Windsor to celebrate with a big banquet. (Photograph courtesy Buc Football and Friends Foundation.)

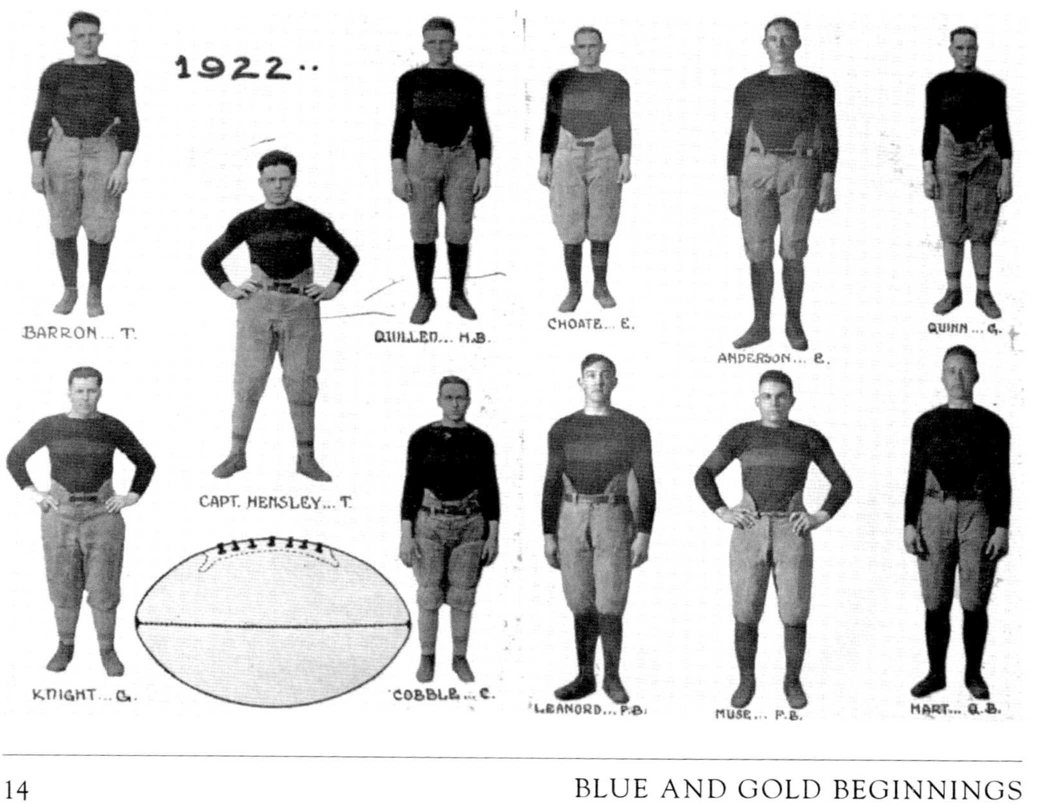

Coach James Karl "JK" Luck coached from 1922 to 1924. He compiled an 11-14 record over three seasons. Luck, a graduate of the University of Tennessee, coached football and basketball and taught agriculture during his tenure. (Photograph courtesy Buc Football and Friends Foundation.)

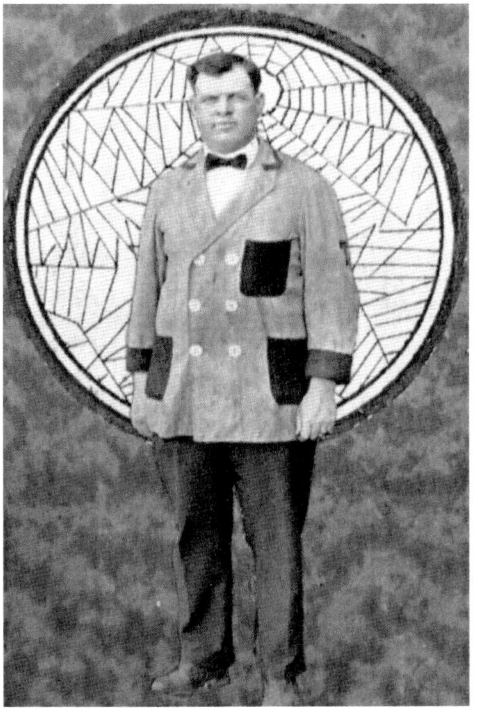

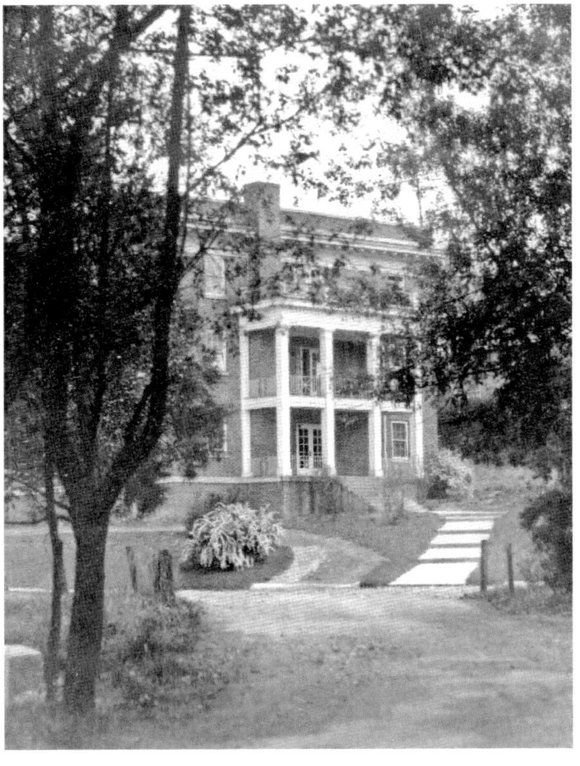

The men's dormitory, later named Ritter Hall, housed all 35 to 40 male students enrolled in school, including the athletes, during the 1920s. The first matron, Judson McFee, watched over the students and enforced the rules from 1923 to 1928. (Photograph courtesy Buc Football and Friends Foundation.)

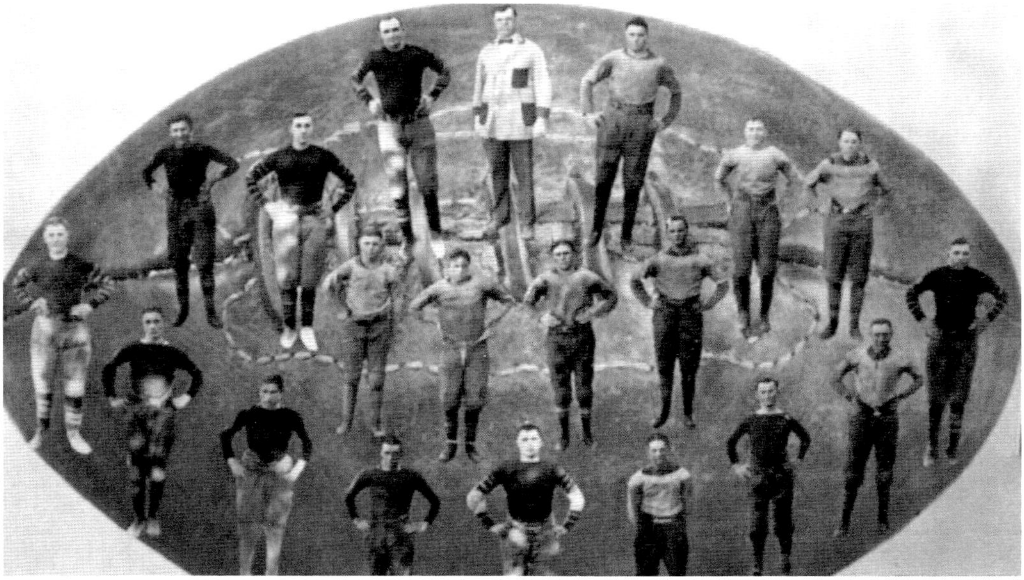

The fourth year of football at the Normal may have been one of its worst. The 1923 team suffered six defeats to two wins, with five losses by a margin of 38 points or greater. The most lopsided was a 108-0 pounding at the hands of King College. This year marked the first time the team played UT (a 7-47 defeat) even though it was the freshman team. (Photograph courtesy Buc Football and Friends Foundation.)

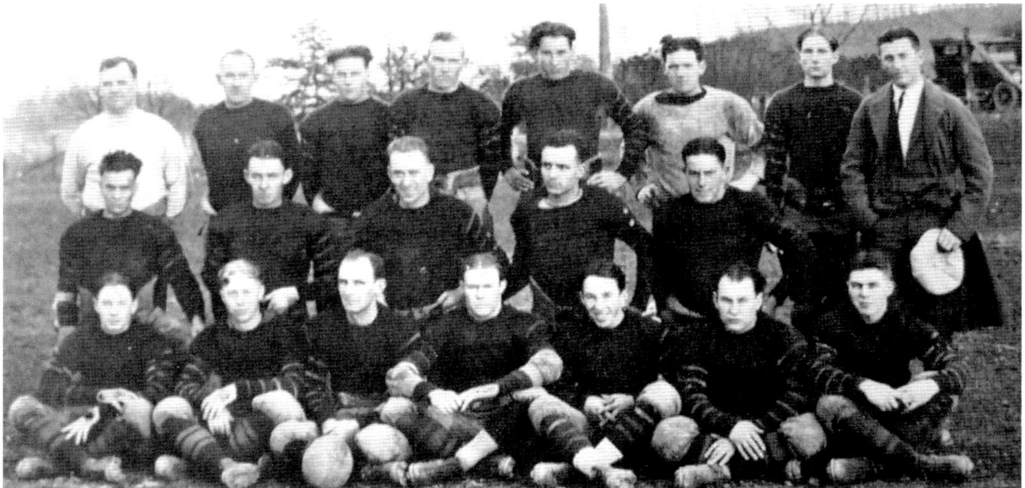

Though the 1924 "Normalites" went 3-4, they could boast of playing with 18 new jerseys, trousers, pairs of socks, and "the very best shoes, helmets and shoulder guards." That year also marked the end of an era for the school and team. Coach Luck would leave, the team would never play UT (freshmen or otherwise) again, and the school would leave their "normal" period when the school became East Tennessee State Teacher's College (ETSTC). (Photograph courtesy Buc Football and Friends Foundation.)

In 1925, John Siler Robinson took over the reins of the ETSTC's male sports squads as well as the agriculture class. Coach "Robbie," a World War I veteran and a graduate of the University of Tennessee, led the team for five years and compiled a record of 13 wins, 21 losses, and 2 ties. He was so beloved by the student population that the 1929 yearbook was dedicated to him. (Photograph courtesy Buc Football and Friends Foundation.)

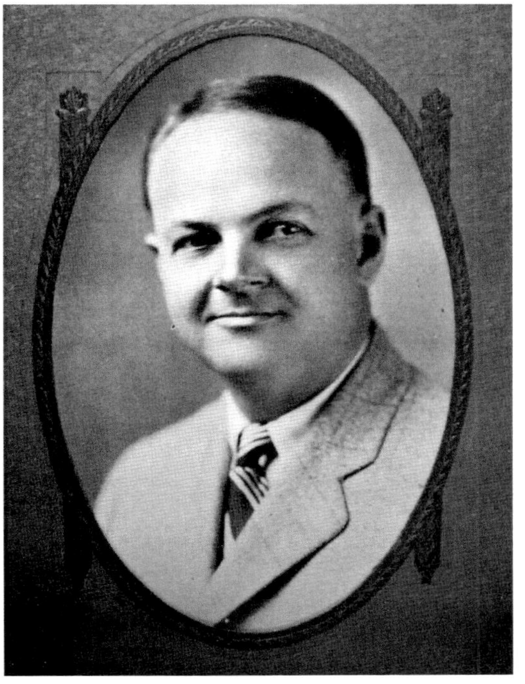

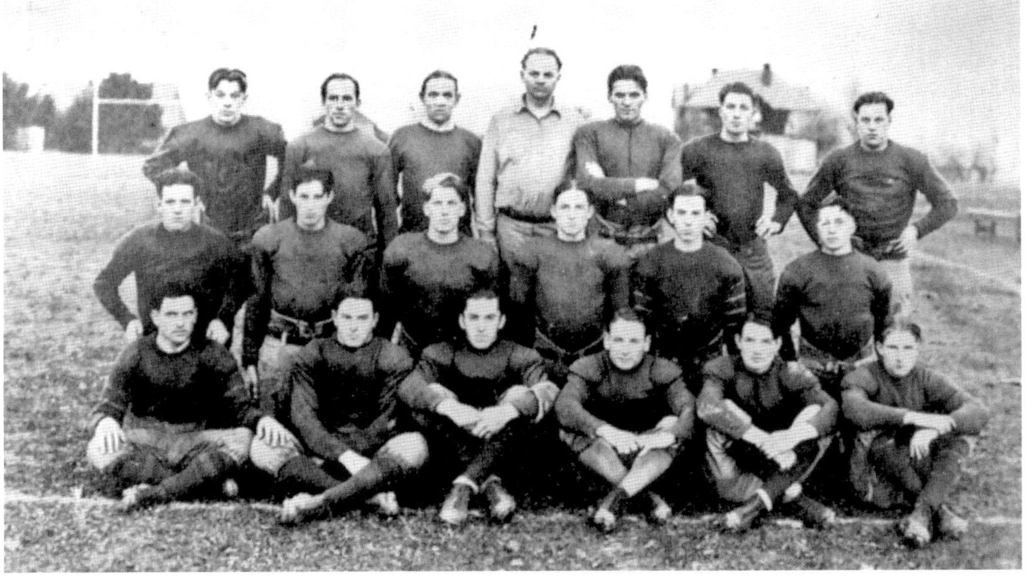

The year 1925 was the first time the team was officially referred to by the nickname "Teachers." The squad finished 3-4 entirely against college-level competition—the first time this had occurred. The increased level of competition and the fact that 19 of the 38 "boys" registered at the school went out for practice (the most ever), led to the statement in the *Old Hickory* yearbook that this was "one of the most successful seasons in its history." (Photograph courtesy Buc Football and Friends Foundation.)

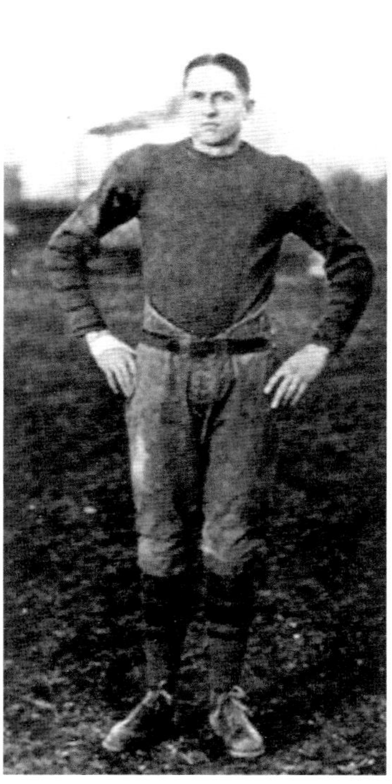

James I. "Jim" Mooney, a three-sport star for the Teachers, played halfback. However, he was best known for his feats on a baseball diamond. After starring for State, he played for the New York Giants and St. Louis Cardinals, pitching in the fourth game of the 1934 World Series with the Cardinals. Mooney returned to State as baseball coach in 1939, retiring in 1966 after 23 seasons. He was inducted into the school's hall of fame in 1977. (Photograph courtesy Buc Football and Friends Foundation.)

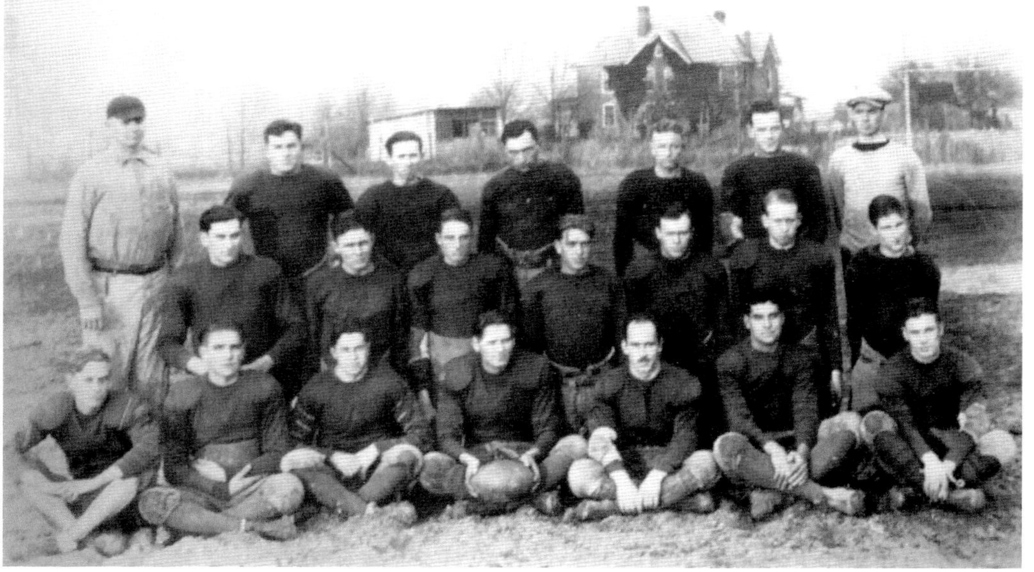

The 1926 edition of the Teachers' team finished the season with two wins, three losses, and a scoreless tie with Mars Hill. Coach Robinson gained an assistant coach, William "Willie" Flinn Rogers, who would teach history and government at State from 1925 to 1968. This team only lost one letterman, but their fortune the following year remained unchanged. (Photograph courtesy Buc Football and Friends Foundation.)

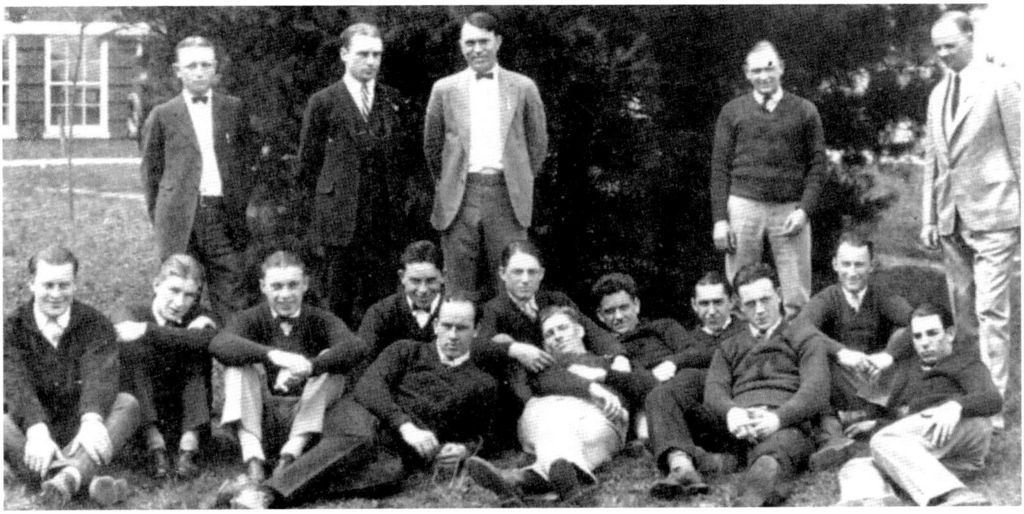

This gathering of the inaugural men's "T" Club took place in the spring of 1926. This letterman's club was founded on the following four principles: promote college spirit in the student body with larger participation in intercollegiate sports, foster loyalty to every activity of the teachers college, promote clean sportsmanship, and discourage the wearing of all other letters on the campus. The club's sponsor for much of its history was usually the head coach of the football team. (Photograph courtesy Buc Football and Friends Foundation.)

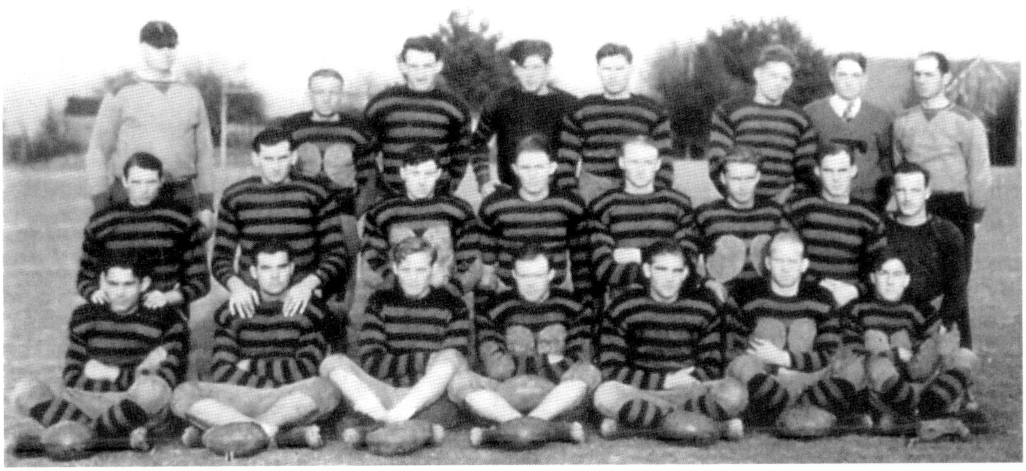

In 1927, the team won their last two games against Hiwassee and Bluefield but lost their first five games. They were blanked in all but one of those five when they scored six points against Concord. The *Old Hickory* indicated that Coach Robbie was handed a similar task in previous years, which was to develop a team out of mostly "green material." The two-game winning streak at the end of the year seems to prove this point. (Photograph courtesy Buc Football and Friends Foundation.)

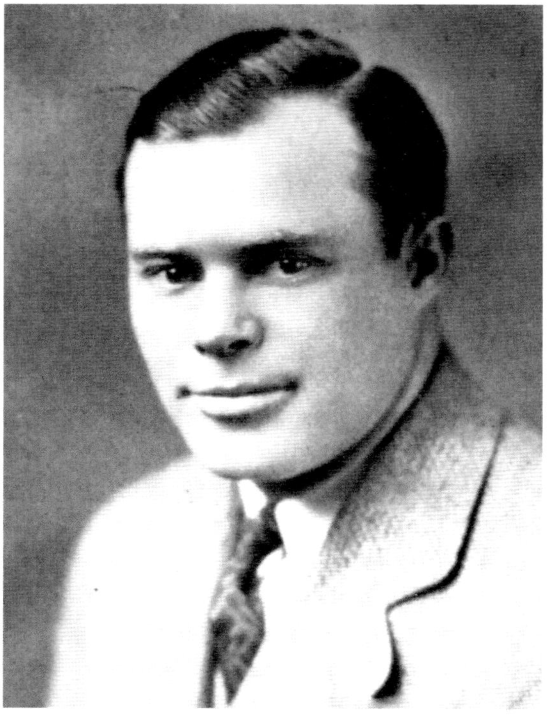

Jack "Casey" Painter, the Teachers' star fullback, played from 1923 to 1927 and served as captain of the team during his senior year. He was said to be a vicious runner who was impossible for any two men to bring down. He was elected to the ETSU Athletic Hall of Fame in 1981. (Photograph courtesy Buc Football and Friends Foundation.)

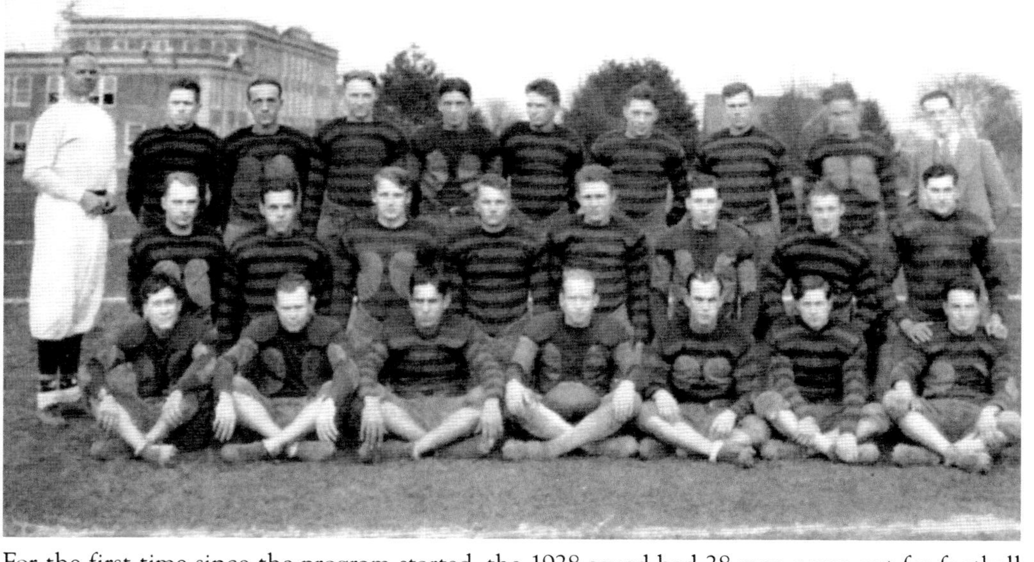

For the first time since the program started, the 1928 squad had 28 men come out for football with 10 of them returning lettermen. As a result, the team had its first winning record since 1921, when they played a portion of the schedule against high school competition. The 1928 season also marked the first time East Tennessee State Teachers College played Appalachian Training School of Boone (which would become Appalachian State University), one of their key rivals. (Photograph courtesy Buc Football and Friends Foundation.)

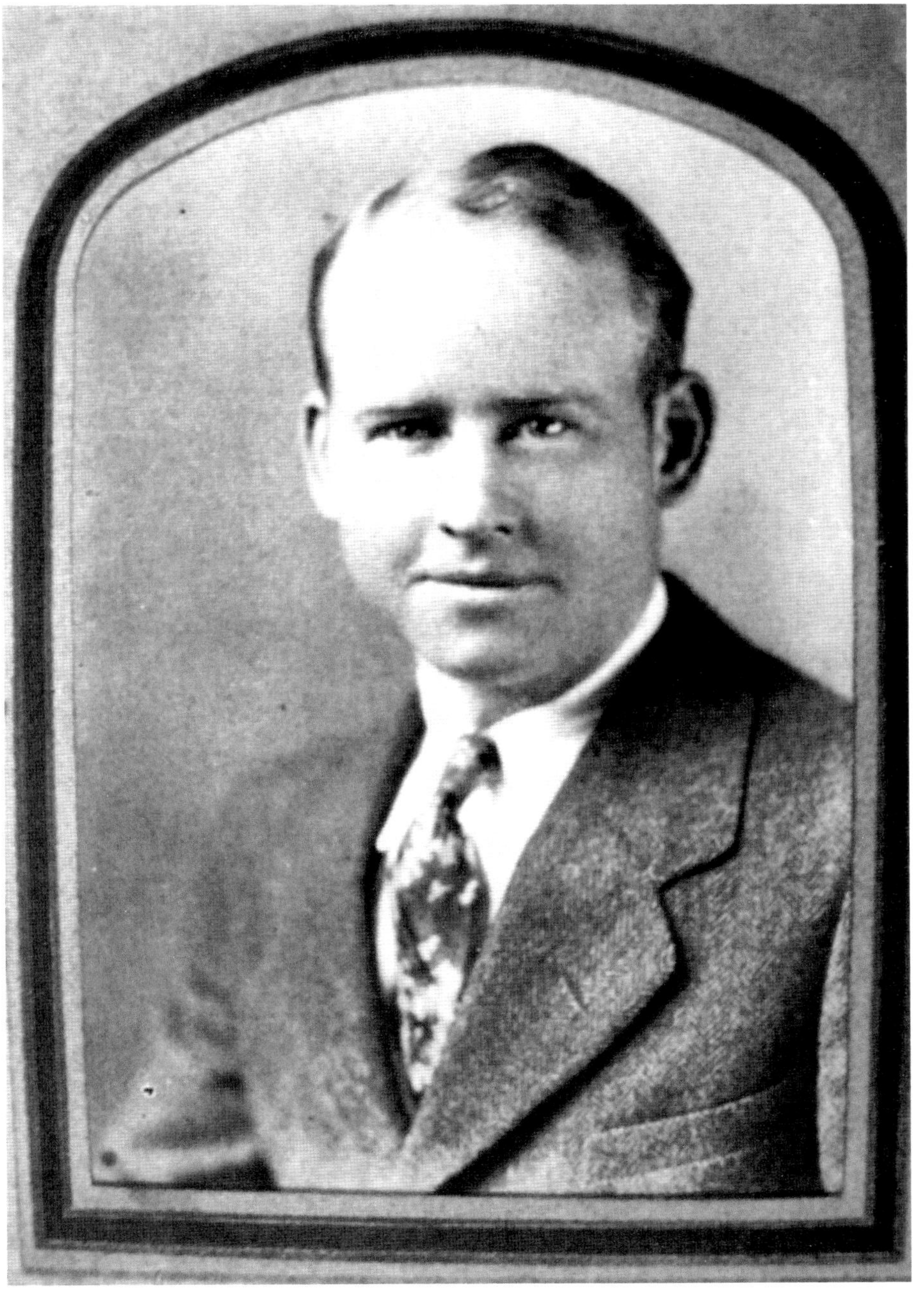

Edward "Buzz" Kennedy, captain of the 1928 team, played football and baseball from 1926 to 1929. He was a "passing half," known as quarterback today, and his passing was said to bring fear to the opposition. He also "booted extra points." After graduation he coached at Savannah and Cocke County High School. He was an active alumnus who "never missed a Buccaneer game or function," was named Outstanding Alumnus in 1972, and was elected to the inaugural class (1975) of the Pirate Club Hall of Fame. (Photograph courtesy Buc Football and Friends Foundation.)

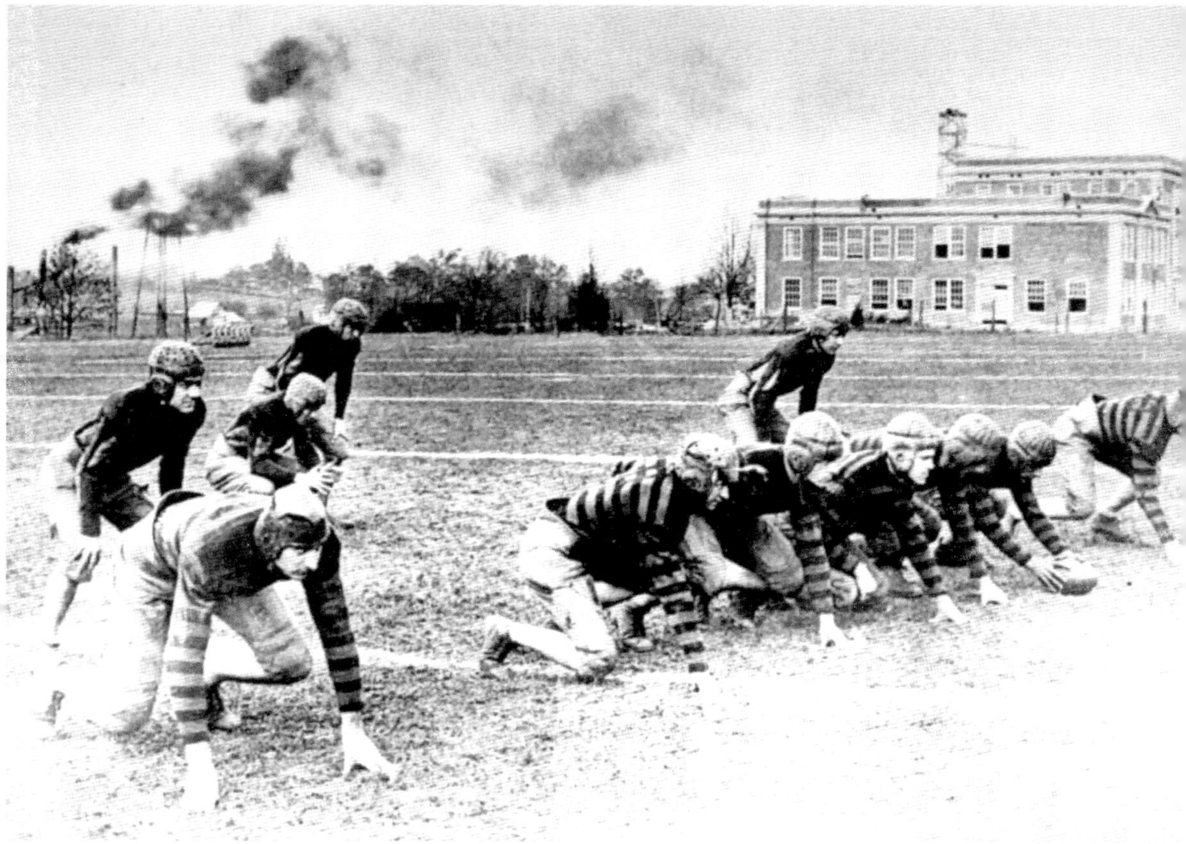

The first athletic field was said to be hard and uneven. Early in his presidency, Dr. Sherrod had the field leveled and graded with teams of mules, shifted the baseball diamond closer to the gymnasium, and had a grandstand constructed for the viewing public's comfort. This field was parallel with Walnut Street and was situated between the original gymnasium (now Mathes Hall) and the grounds of what would shortly become the training school. In this photograph of the 1928 team lined up on the field, the training school building is visible from the vicinity of the current science building. Pictured from left to right are (first row) DeVault Galloway, Hugh Yoakum, Rue Dalton, McNeal Dew, Jess Humphreys, Arthur Isbill, and Clarence Bralley; (second row) Paul Nicely, Jack Painter, Ed Kennedy, and Paul Gourly. (Photograph courtesy Buc Football and Friends Foundation.)

2

Birth of the Buccaneers

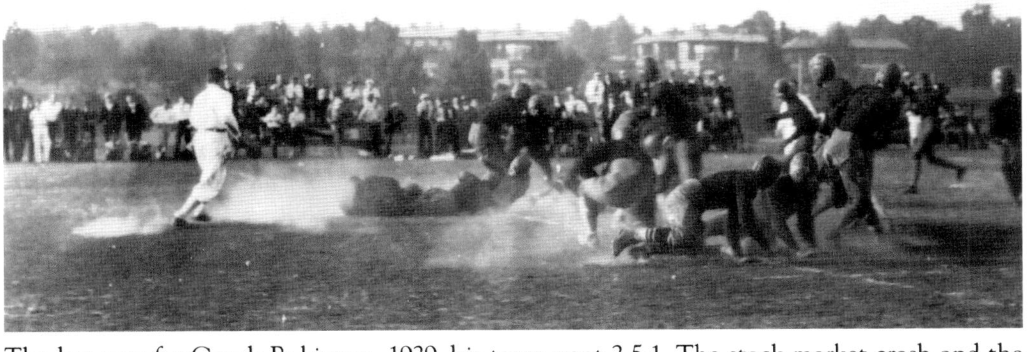

The last year for Coach Robinson, 1929, his team went 2-5-1. The stock market crash and the beginning of the Great Depression signaled tough times for the college and all of its programs. Everything from the size of the school annual to salaries to funding for the sports programs would decrease significantly over the next several years and would not rebound until after the start of World War II. In this undated photograph, buildings on the grounds of the Soldiers Home (now the Veterans Administration Hospital) are visible in the background. (Photograph courtesy of the Archives of Appalachia.)

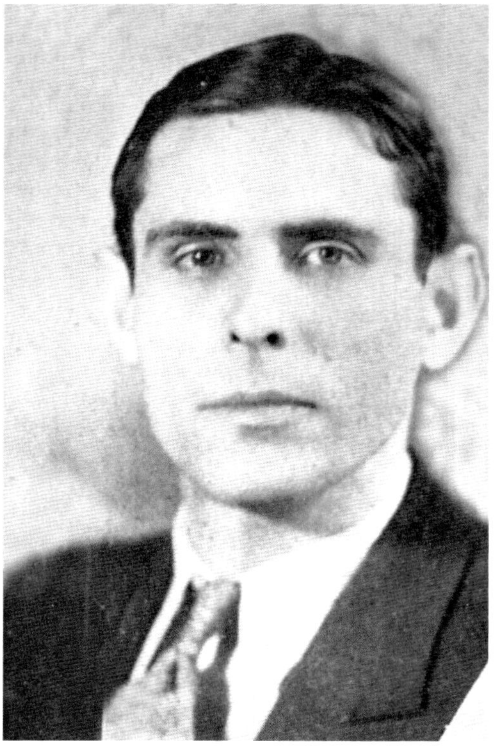

Arthur R. "Cap" Isbill, captain of the 1929 squad, played center from 1927 to 1930 and earned All-Conference laurels his junior and senior years. He also played baseball and basketball while in school. He had a very successful high school coaching career first at Unicoi County and then Lee Edwards in Asheville, North Carolina. His former players, citing the profound impact he had their lives, nominated him for the ETSU Hall of Fame, in which he was inducted in 1978. (Photograph courtesy Buc Football and Friends Foundation.)

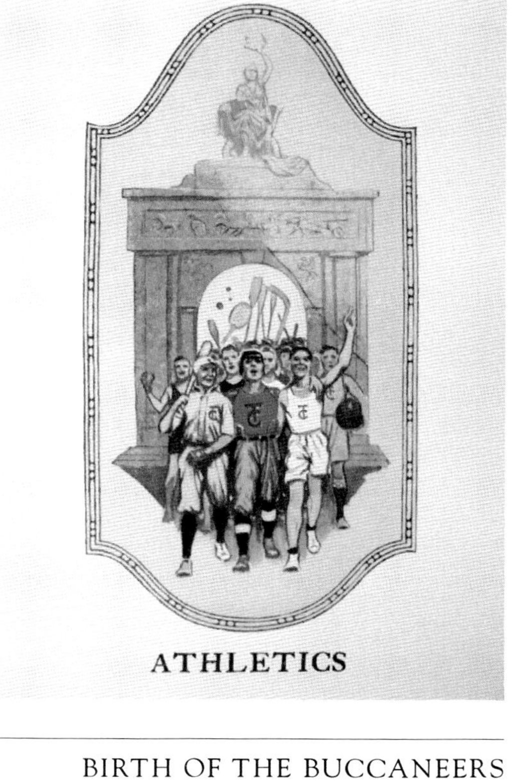

During the Depression, the team gained a new coach, J. S. Batey, and a new name for the school, State Teachers College, Johnson City (STCJC). However, the 1930 team responded like the economy with a downward trend, losing all seven games, failing to score in six of the contests. It's no wonder that the *Chalk Line* yearbook stated that Coach Batey "chooses not to talk" concerning the forthcoming season. (Photograph courtesy Buc Football and Friends Foundation.)

Jackson Smith Batey Jr., a graduate of Middle Tennessee State Normal School and the University of Tennessee (B.S. and M.S.) coached football and basketball for two years and baseball for six years and taught physical education and agriculture from 1930 to 1935 at STCJC. His record for the two years he coached football was 1-10-2. According to Berney Burleson, his record reflected a lack of faculty and financial support. (Photograph courtesy Buc Football and Friends Foundation.)

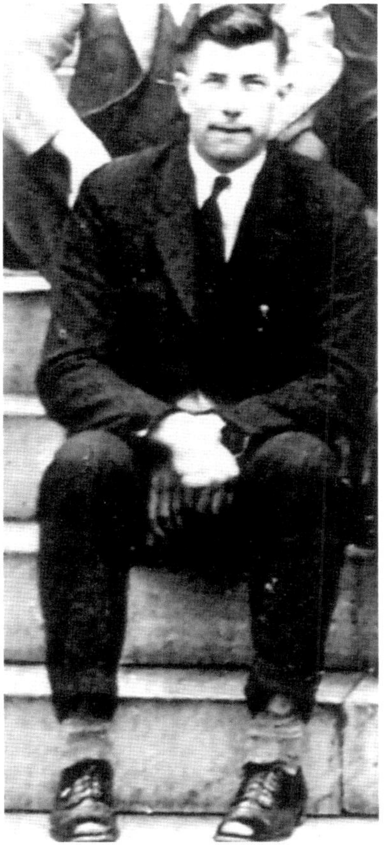

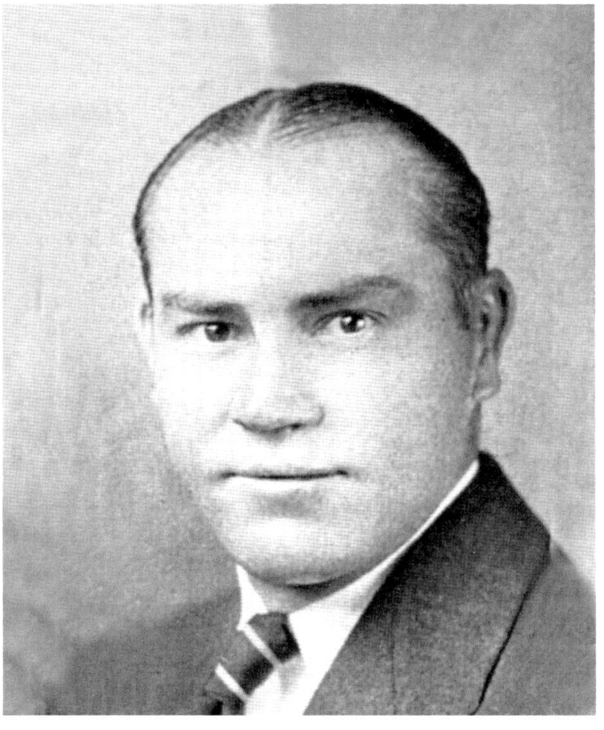

The fortunes of the 1931 team were somewhat better than the previous year in that they only lost three games, but they only managed to win one, 18-0 against Mars Hill College. Alex Kennedy (pictured), team captain, surprised the guests at the football banquet held in Parish Hall at St. John's Episcopal Church with his "powers of oratory," noted the *Chalk Line*. Pres. Charles Sherrod also spoke, pointing out a recent article that set forth 80 percent of the football players in America carried for life some injury received while playing football. (Photograph courtesy Buc Football and Friends Foundation.)

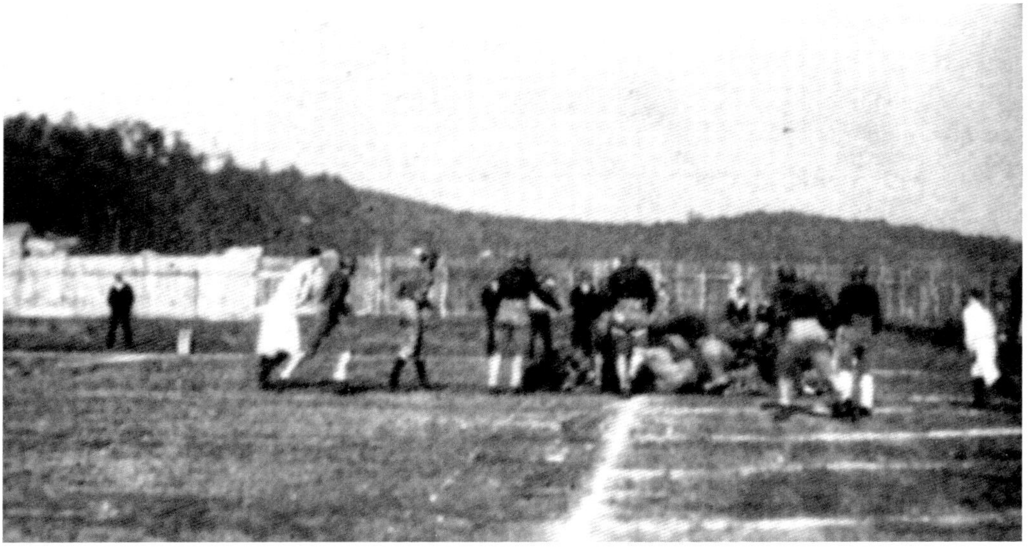

For the first time since 1928, the Teachers squad did not post a losing record, finishing a respectable 3-3-1 in 1932. The season's highlight was their first game against Western Carolina, a 26-0 victory. This 1932 team was also the first of 11 teams to be coached by J. G. McMurray, ushering in a golden age of football for the school with only two losing seasons and being recognized by the national media in 1936. (Photograph courtesy Buc Football and Friends Foundation.)

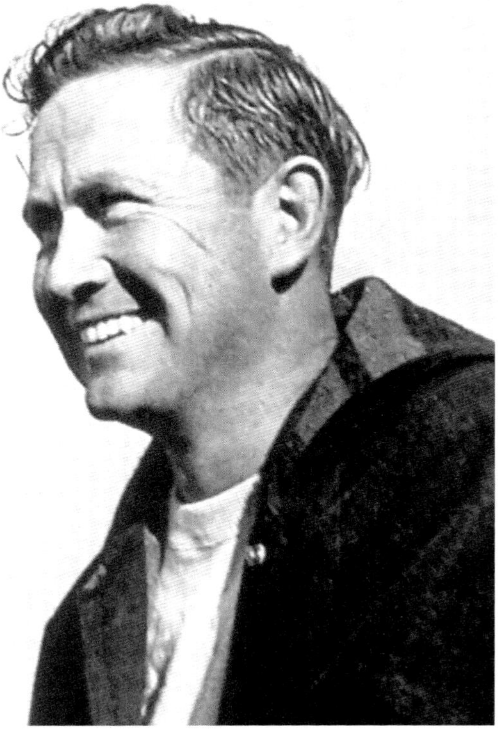

Dr. Gene McMurray took over most of the coaching duties, including football, basketball, tennis, track, and baseball, winning Smoky Mountain conference championships in each sport but track. He also served as the first director of athletics. In 1947, he left for Ole Miss to serve as chairman of the Department of Health, Physical Education, and Recreation until 1967. He served as a professor until his death in 1971. During his tenure at State, he finished with 51 wins, 32 losses, and 5 ties, which left him second all-time in wins and first all-time with a .608 winning percentage. A graduate of Maryville College and Columbia University, he was one of the few coaches in the South to hold a doctorate. Prior to coaching at East Tennessee State College, he coached at Erwin and Rockwood High Schools and then spent three years at Milligan College. (Photograph courtesy Buc Football and Friends Foundation.)

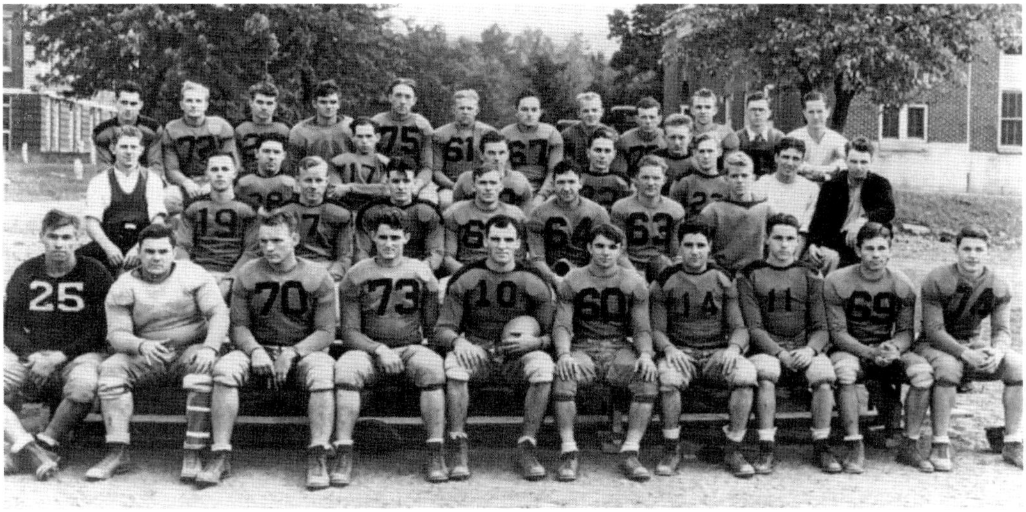

The 1933 teachers college "Professors" racked up six wins to only one loss with two ties, by far the best record of any team to that point in time and against the "hardest schedule ever attempted by the school." The captain of the team was Dean Chase Bailey (first row with the football) who was elected to the ETSU Athletics Hall of Fame's inaugural class in 1975. He lettered four times to go with the eight other letters he earned in basketball and baseball. (Photograph courtesy Buc Football and Friends Foundation.)

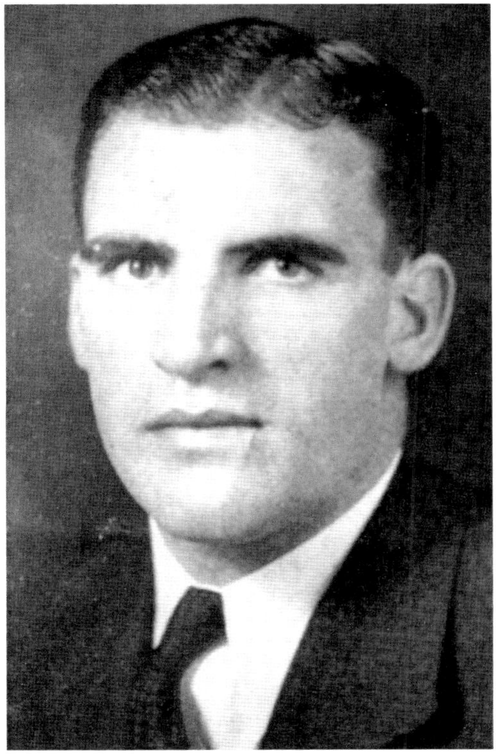

Dean Chase Bailey, an All-Conference quarterback, had a record-setting career while at State. He held the record for most touchdowns in one season and was third in career touchdowns and fifth in points scored over a career. He went on to coach basketball and baseball at Lincoln Memorial University, where his teams won 10 Smoky Mountain and Volunteer State Athletic Conference (VSAC) championships. (Photograph courtesy Buc Football and Friends Foundation.)

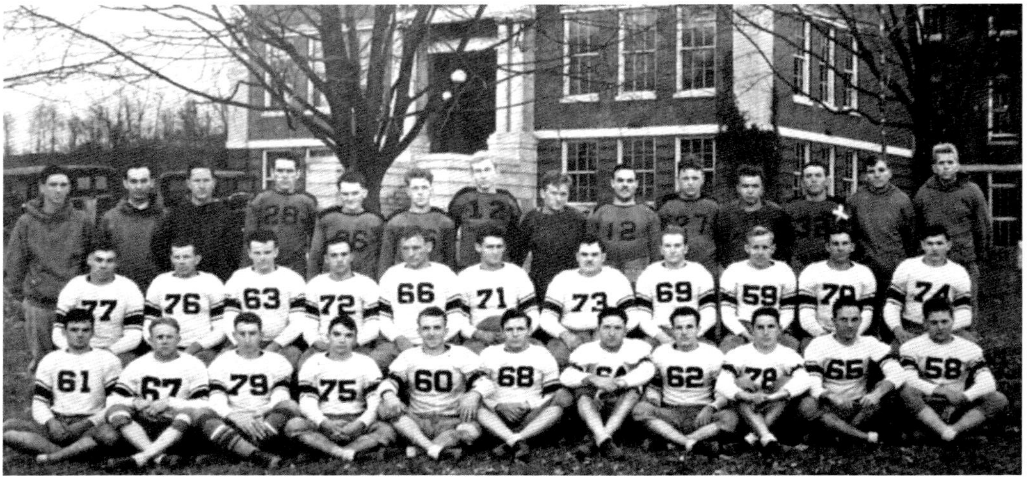

A total of 40 men, 13 of whom had lettered the previous year, responded to the call for football membership in 1934. Despite a 3-3-2 record, they finished third in the conference. One of the season's memorable moments was the Thanksgiving afternoon game with Milligan College before a record-setting crowd at the new Roosevelt Stadium. Alas, the Bucs lost 0-14. Seniors Pryor Hunt (team captain) and Lynn Massengill were considered the "best players to ever play their respective positions at T.C.," according to Berney Burleson. (Photograph courtesy Buc Football and Friends Foundation.)

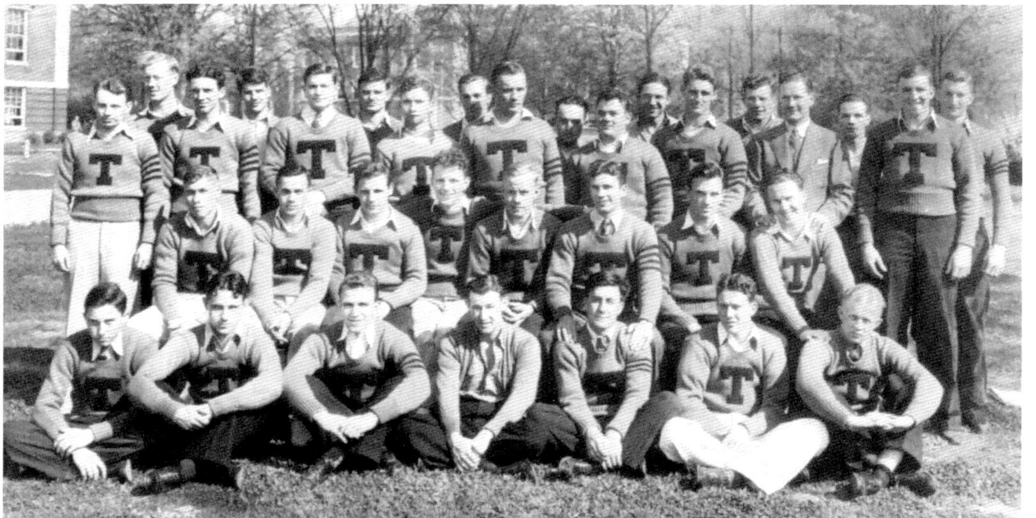

With the expanding enrollment of male students at State and their increased involvement in the school's athletics programs came an increased membership in the school's letterman society. As seen in this photograph of the 1935 T Club, the male membership nearly doubled from its founding in 1926. Included in the photograph (first row, second from left) is McBerney "Berney" Burleson, who played football in the early 1930s, worked at State, and served in later years as the team's unofficial historian. (Photograph courtesy of Jan Burleson.)

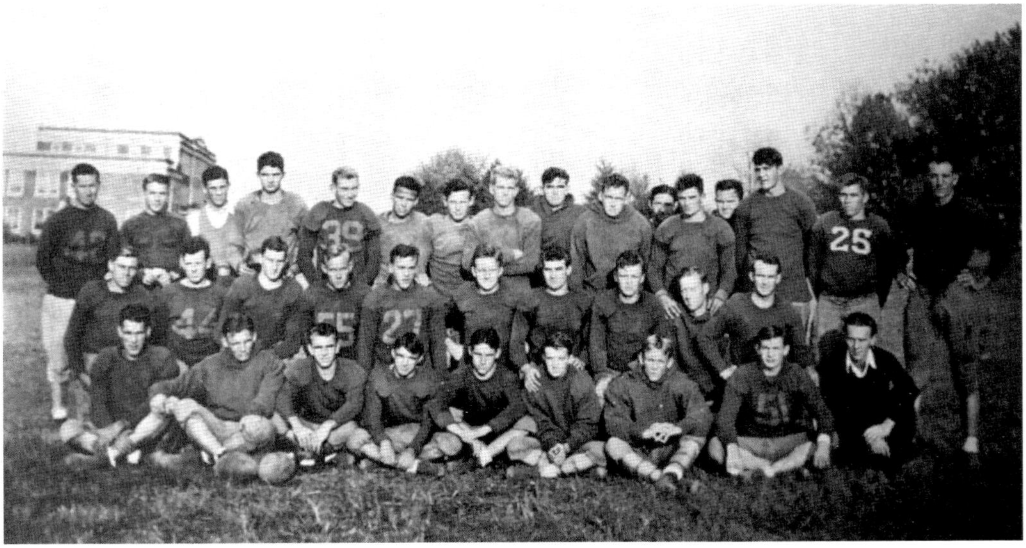

In 1935, the football team was called the Buccaneers for the first time. Coach McMurray is credited with coming up with the new name, which stuck despite objections by Prof. Bull Bible, who claimed that pirates had unsavory reputations. The team had a very successful season, finishing second in the Smoky Mountain conference with a 5-3 ledger. (Photograph courtesy Buc Football and Friends Foundation.)

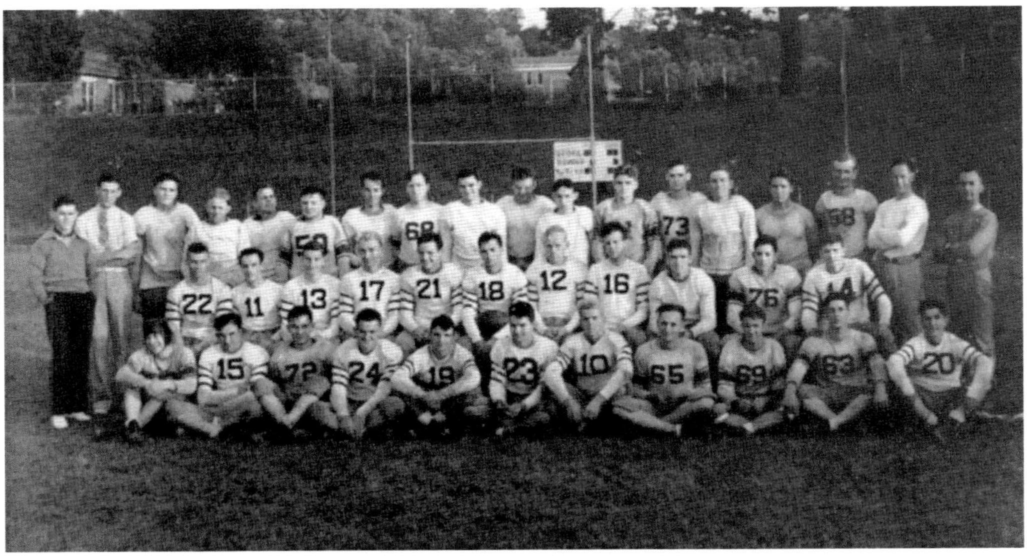

National recognition came to the Bucs in 1936 for starting the season unbeaten, unscored-on, and untied, making them the last team in America to be defeated that season. Equally impressive was the fact that the blue and gold registered victories against Carson Newman, Mars Hill, and Western Carolina by mere 2-0 margins. Unfortunately, the team lost the last two games of the season, the final one against archrival Milligan College, 6-7. (Photograph courtesy Buc Football and Friends Foundation.)

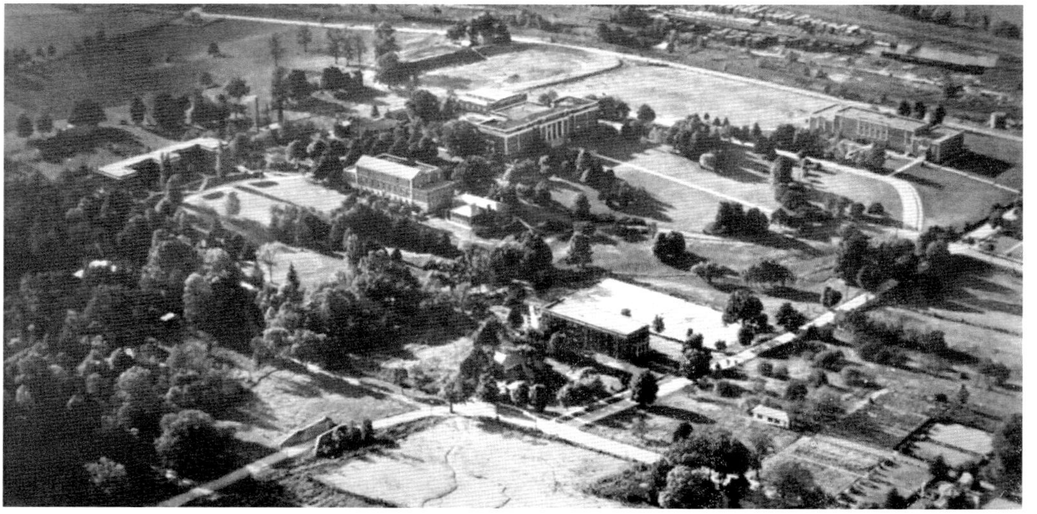

The new stadium built by the CCC in 1935–1936 was rotated roughly to the Mini-Dome's existing location, which is perpendicular to Walnut Street and located behind the old gym. The gym, which originally contained a 50-by-70-foot court and facilities for both men and women, was one of the original buildings on the campus in 1911. It was renovated in 1955, converted to classroom use, and eventually renamed Mathes Hall. It currently houses the music department. (Photograph courtesy Buc Football and Friends Foundation.)

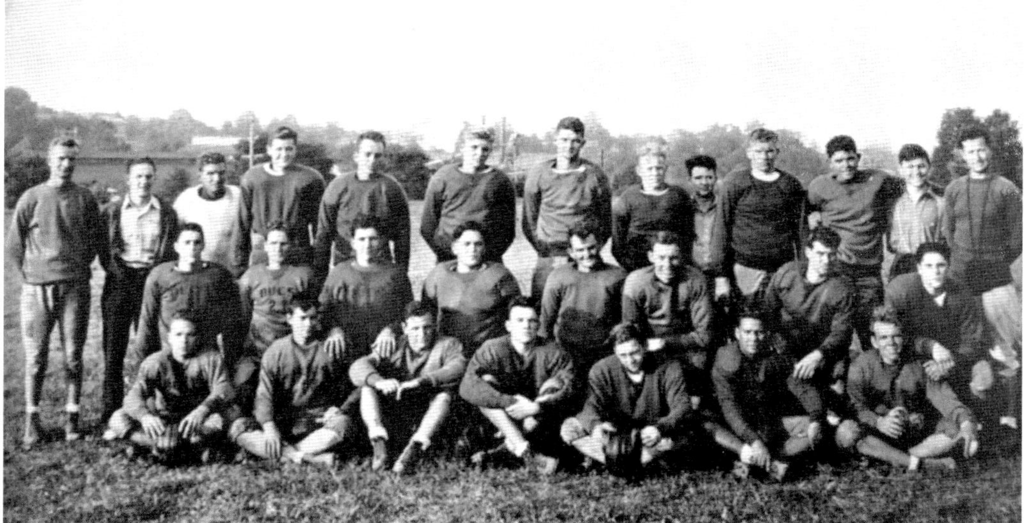

The 1937 Buc team finished the season 4-5, their first losing season in six years. Walter Clark, who played on the line and doubled as a back (first row, third from left), was elected team captain. He and lineman Ed "Bull" Congdon won the distinction of making all-conference four consecutive years during the 1930s. Another interesting note is that R. Buxton (third row, fifth from right) was the first to be officially listed as a trainer as opposed to an assistant coach. (Photograph courtesy Buc Football and Friends Foundation.)

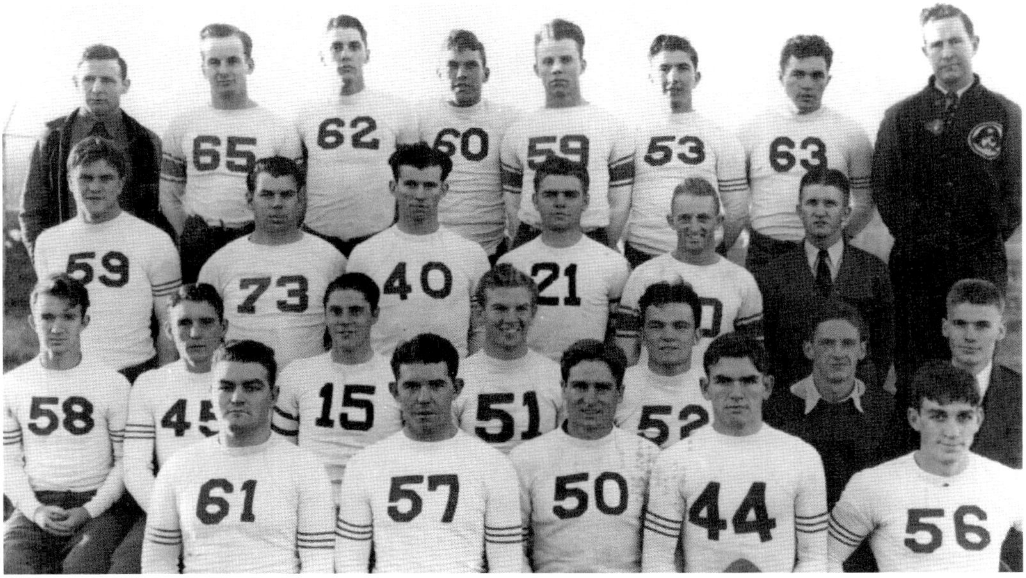

Contrary to previous yearbook advertisements, the 1938 edition of the Buccaneers was arguably the most successful team in the program's history until then. They went 6-2 and were crowned Smoky Mountain Athletic Conference (SMAC) champions for the first time since they joined the conference in 1929. Coach McMurray was assisted by Walter Clark, the Bucs football captain from the previous year. (Photograph courtesy Buc Football and Friends Foundation.)

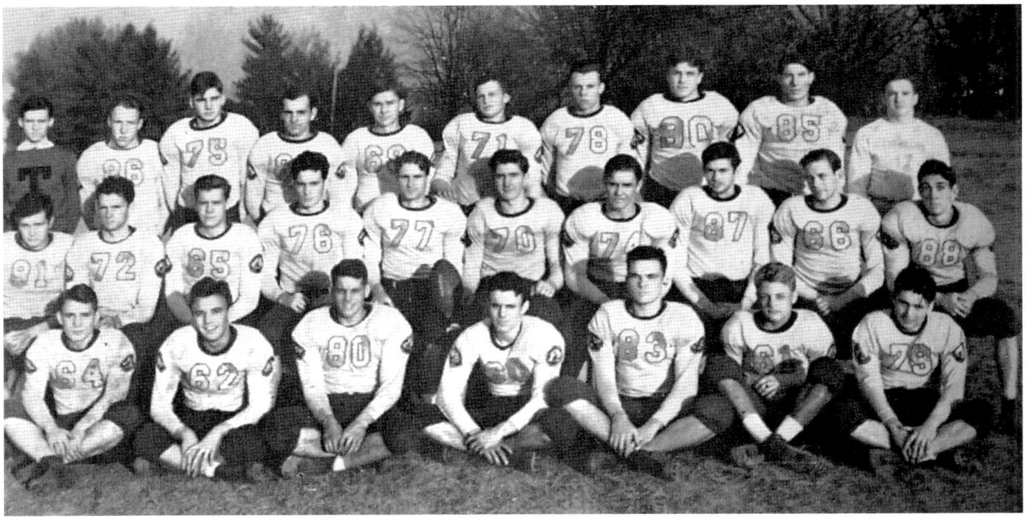

Handicapped and riddled with frequent injuries, the 1939 "Pirates" finished the year 5-3, breaking even in conference play with victories over Maryville, Tusculum, and Cumberland. Their three losses were to King, Carson Newman, and Milligan. The King game is notable because the 7-19 State loss was counted as a win by the SMAC commissioner. King was considered to have forfeited because of their 14 ineligible players who participated in the game. (Photograph courtesy Buc Football and Friends Foundation.)

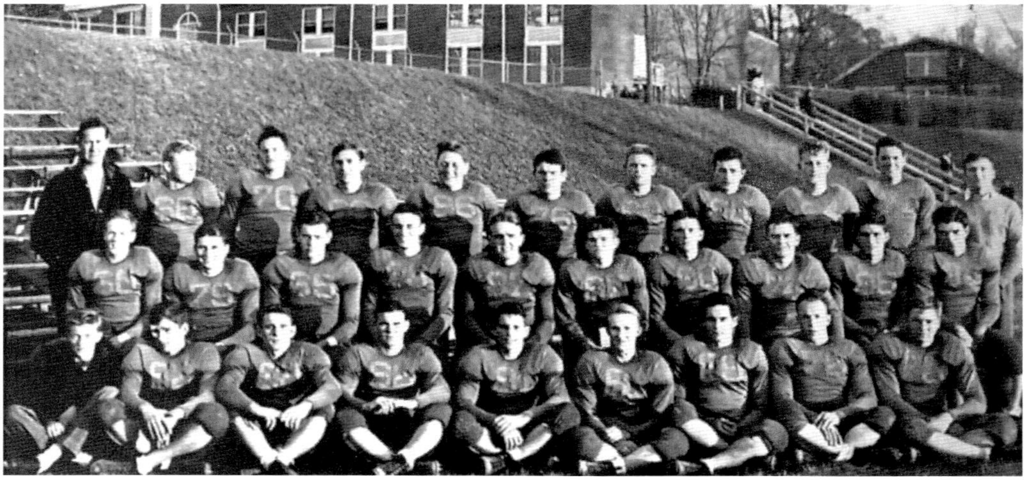

McMurray's "Corsairs" broke even in 1940 with a 4-4 record. Coach McMurray went the entire year with two team managers and no assistant coach. Bud Carpenter and Frank Parsely were named cocaptains for the year. The team played Carson Newman twice, both losses, and split a pair of games with Emory and Henry in Virginia. (Photograph courtesy Buc Football and Friends Foundation.)

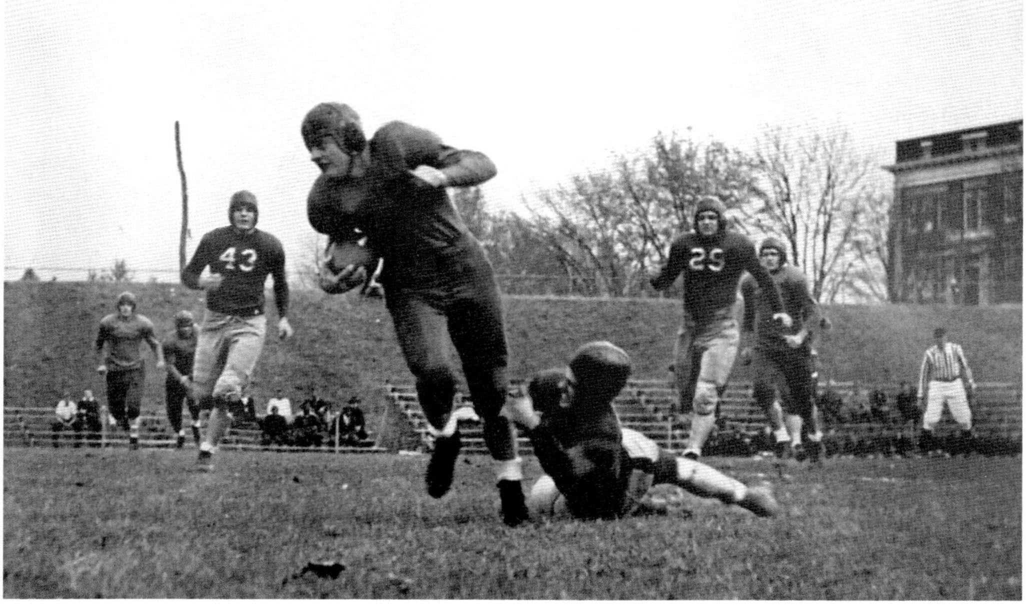

This 1940 photograph shows a Buccaneer runner as he breaks away from an opposing (possibly Milligan) defender. Annual controversy surfaced each year as members of the SMAC would make accusations against member schools for playing ineligible players. Such a controversy in 1936 resulted in a Buccaneer forfeit against Carson Newman, whom they defeated 2-0. In many cases, roving players would go from school to school claiming freshman status. Policing at the time was difficult. (Photograph courtesy Buc Football and Friends Foundation.)

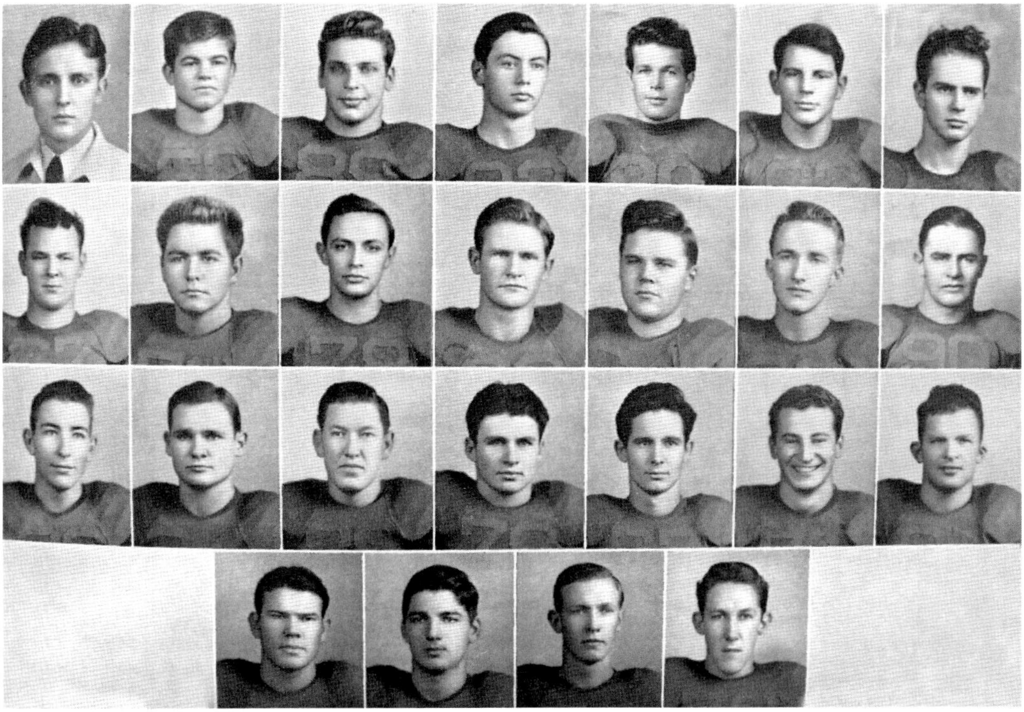

This 1941 squad would be the last football team until after the end of World War II. With a war raging in Europe and the bombing of Pearl Harbor just around the corner, the 1941 squad finished the season at 2-5. Jim Mooney, the head baseball coach, stepped in to assist with the football and basketball coaching duties. Buck Hunt and Bill Mitchell served as cocaptains of the team. (Photograph courtesy Buc Football and Friends Foundation.)

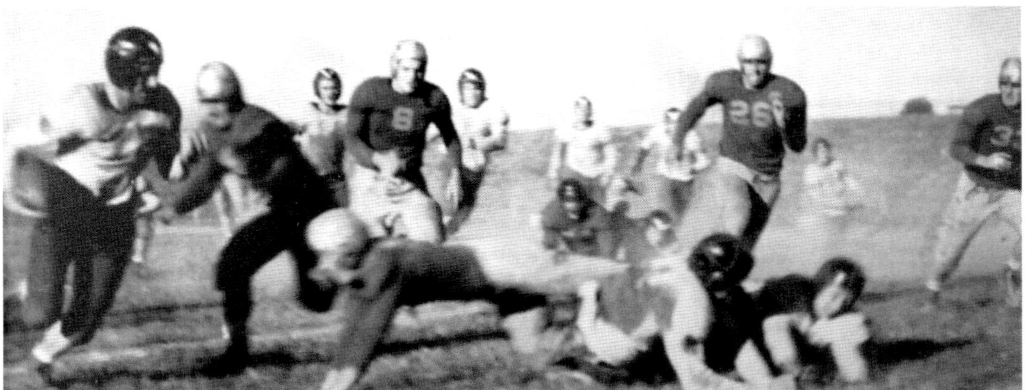

State's defense pursues the opposing runner doggedly in this 1941 photograph taken at a home game. The Bucs would resume play with most of their other rivals at the war's end but would not play archrival Milligan again until 1948. Perhaps their last prewar meeting, a 0-26 pounding at the hands of the Buffaloes, had something to do with this. (Photograph courtesy Buc Football and Friends Foundation.)

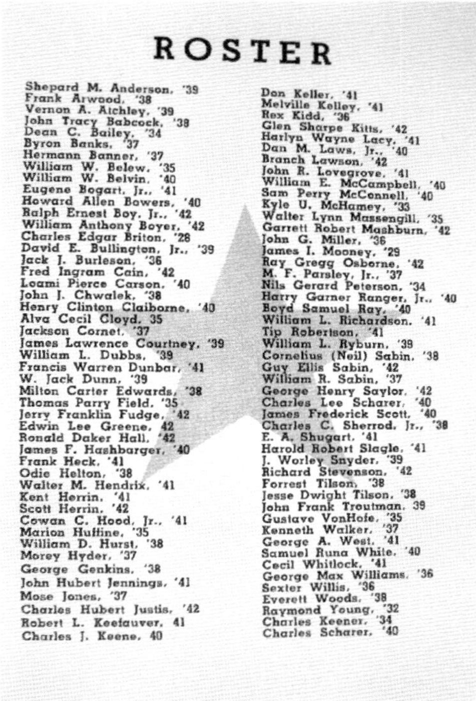

ROSTER

Shepard M. Anderson, '39
Frank Arwood, '38
Vernon A. Atchley, '39
John Tracy Babcock, '38
Dean C. Bailey, '34
Byron Banks, '37
Hermann Banner, '37
William W. Belew, '35
William W. Belvin, '40
Eugene Bogart, Jr., '41
Howard Allen Bowers, '40
Ralph Ernest Boy, Jr., '42
William Anthony Boyer, '42
Charles Edgar Briton, '28
David E. Bullington, Jr., '39
Jack J. Burleson, '36
Fred Ingram Cain, '42
Loami Pierce Carson, '40
John J. Chwalek, '38
Henry Clinton Claiborne, '40
Alva Cecil Cloyd, 35
Jackson Cornet, '37
James Lawrence Courtney, '39
William L. Dubbs, '39
Francis Warren Dunbar, '41
W. Jack Dunn, '39
Milton Carter Edwards, '38
Thomas Parry Field, '35
Jerry Franklin Fudge, '42
Edwin Lee Greene, 42
Ronald Daker Hall, '42
James F. Hashbarger, '40
Frank Heck, '41
Odie Helton, '38
Walter M. Hendrix, '41
Kent Herrin, '41
Scott Herrin, '42
Cowan C. Hood, Jr., '41
Marion Huffine, '35
William D. Hurst, '38
Morey Hyder, '37
George Genkins, '38
John Hubert Jennings, '41
Mose Jones, '37
Charles Hubert Justis, '42
Robert L. Keefauver, 41
Charles J. Keene, 40
Don Keller, '41
Melville Kelley, '41
Rex Kidd, '36
Glen Sharpe Kitts, '42
Harlyn Wayne Lacy, '41
Dan M. Laws, Jr., '40
Branch Lawson, '42
John R. Lovegrove, '41
William E. McCampbell, '40
Sam Perry McConnell, '40
Kyle U. McHamey, '33
Walter Lynn Massengill, '35
Garrett Robert Mashburn, '42
John G. Miller, '36
James I. Mooney, '29
Ray Gregg Osborne, '42
M. F. Parsley, Jr., '37
Nils Gerard Peterson, '34
Harry Garner Ranger, Jr., '40
Boyd Samuel Ray, '40
William L. Richardson, '41
Tip Robertson, '41
William L. Ryburn, '39
Cornelius (Neil) Sabin, '38
Guy Ellis Sabin, '42
William R. Sabin, '37
George Henry Saylor, '42
Charles Lee Scharer, '40
James Frederick Scott, '40
Charles C. Sherrod, Jr., '38
E. A. Shugart, '41
Harold Robert Slagle, '41
J. Worley Snyder, '39
Richard Stevenson, '42
Forrest Tilson, '38
Jesse Dwight Tilson, '38
John Frank Troutman, 39
Gustave VonHofe, '35
Kenneth Walker, '37
George A. West, '41
Samuel Runa White, '40
Cecil Whitlock, '41
George Max Williams, '36
Sexter Willis, '36
Everett Woods, '38
Raymond Young, '32
Charles Keener, '34
Charles Scharer, '40

Many of State's past and present students and staff, including Coach Mooney, volunteered for the war effort. Some, like Lynn Massengill, did not return. Massengill, who was also a member of the inaugural Hall of Fame class, was killed in a plane crash in 1947 while in the Air Force. Pictured is the yearbook dedication from 1943. (Photograph courtesy Buc Football and Friends Foundation.)

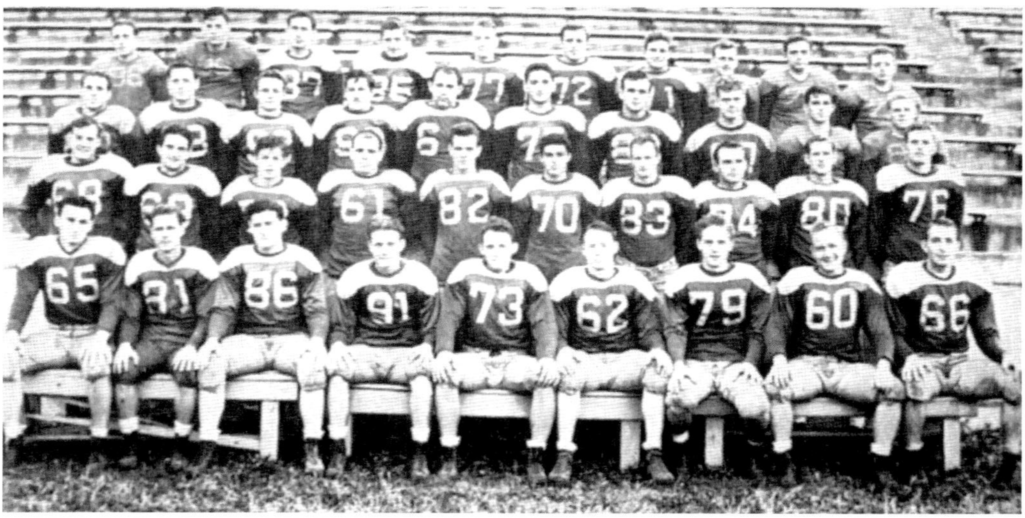

Coach McMurray finished his tenure at State with a 7-1 record in 1946. This win total had never before been achieved by any of the school's football teams and would not be equaled for 16 more years. Returning veterans came back to a poorly funded and ill-equipped team that would be dubbed "The Barefoot Boys" because half of the 70 members trying out for the team had no shoes. It was only three days prior to the first game with Brevard that enough shoes had been repaired, borrowed, and purchased to outfit the 40 remaining players. (Photograph courtesy Buc Football and Friends Foundation.)

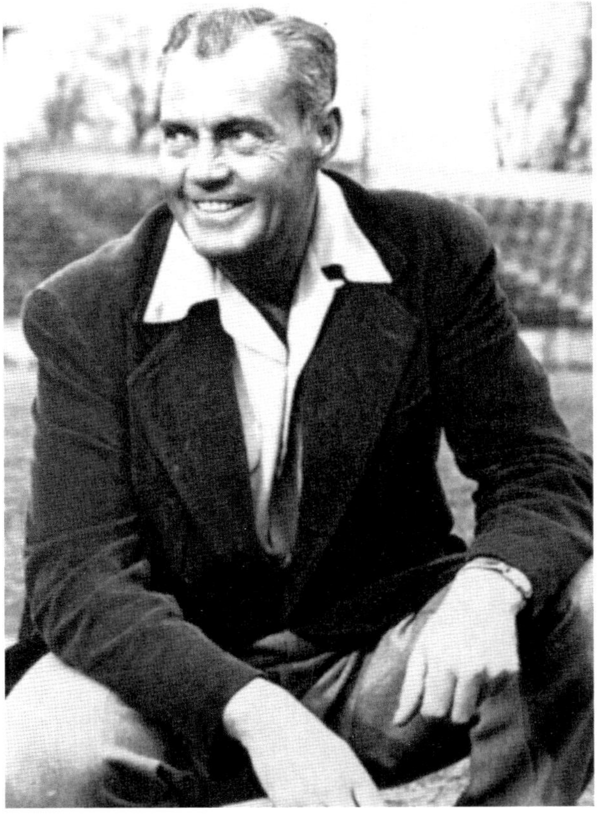

Coach Loyd T. "Preacher" Roberts had big shoes to fill and a tough task to tackle upon taking over as head coach of the Bucs in 1947. Coach McMurray pulled the football program back into postwar existence, but Coach Roberts needed to continue this work by incorporating returning veterans into the mix of new recruits. In addition to this challenge, he also coached the basketball, track, and tennis teams and served as the school's second director of athletics (1947–1953). For the five years he coached football, he compiled a 23-20-2 record and a .533 winning percentage, which still ranks third all-time. He resigned his duties as head football coach because of bleeding ulcers that prompted his physician's warning to "quit coaching and smoking if he did not want to drop dead." (Photograph courtesy Buc Football and Friends Foundation.)

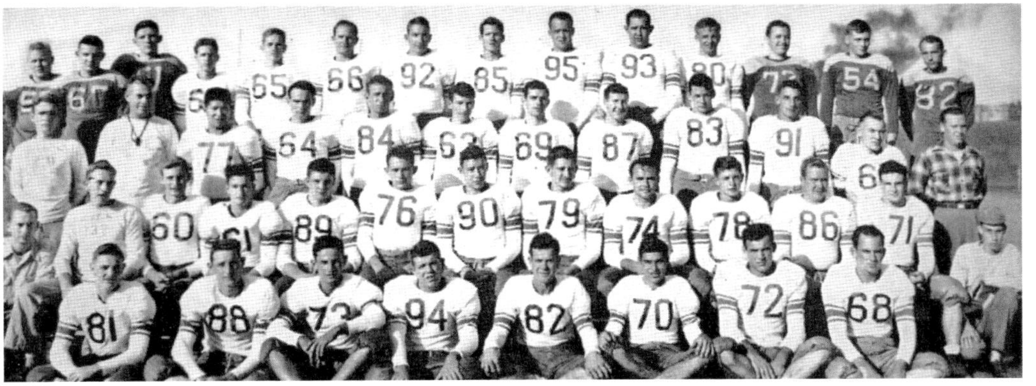

Coach Roberts's first team, cocaptained by Clyde Holsclaw and Joe Green, completed the 1947 schedule with a 5-4 ledger. His only assistant coach was A. W. "Bud" Carpenter, a former Buccaneer player and cocaptain of the 1940 team. Funding and equipping the team was still a difficult issue with the total team budget including salaries at only $6,400. (Photograph courtesy Buc Football and Friends Foundation.)

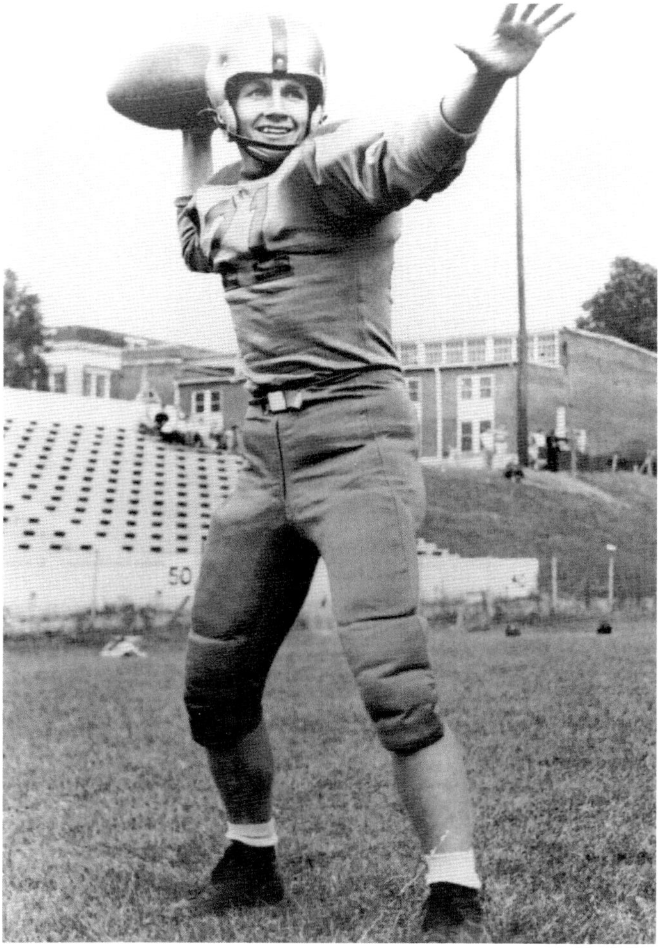

Jack Vest was an outstanding quarterback who figured prominently in the teams of 1946–1949. He also lettered in baseball and basketball, in which he was a prolific scorer. After graduation in 1950, he coached in St. Paul, Virginia, and Winston-Salem, North Carolina. He left coaching for the business world but also turned to officiating where he refereed games in the SC, ACC, AFL, and NFL. He was posthumously inducted into the ETSU Hall of Fame in 1977. (Photograph courtesy Buc Football and Friends Foundation.)

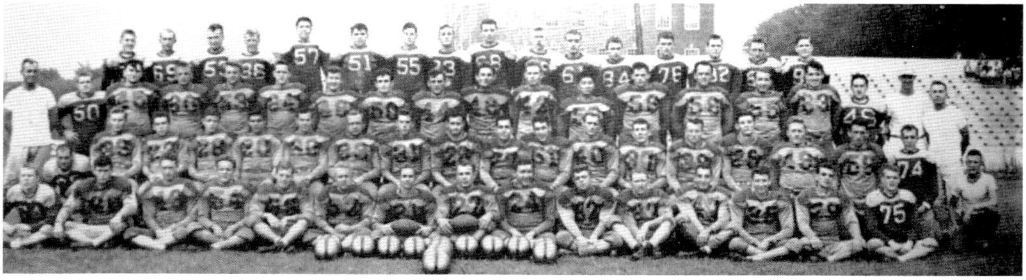

The 1948 team improved to 6-2-1. After getting an increased budget of $8,050, Coach Roberts made perhaps his greatest contribution to the Buccaneer sports program when he hired two new coaches: J. Madison Brooks as line coach, assistant director of athletics, and head basketball coach and Julian Doss Crocker as backfield coach and track mentor. (Photograph courtesy Buc Football and Friends Foundation.)

Roberts's (center) tenure as a high school coach in Homer, Louisiana, in the 1930s provided the contact with Coach Brooks (left), who took a coaching job in Homer in 1945. Brooks would later gain legendary status in his position as basketball coach for bringing the Buc basketball program into the national limelight with appearances in the NAIA Basketball Tournament. Jack Green (right), brother to player Joe Green, served as trainer and assistant coach in the early 1950s. (Photograph courtesy of Loyd T. Roberts II.)

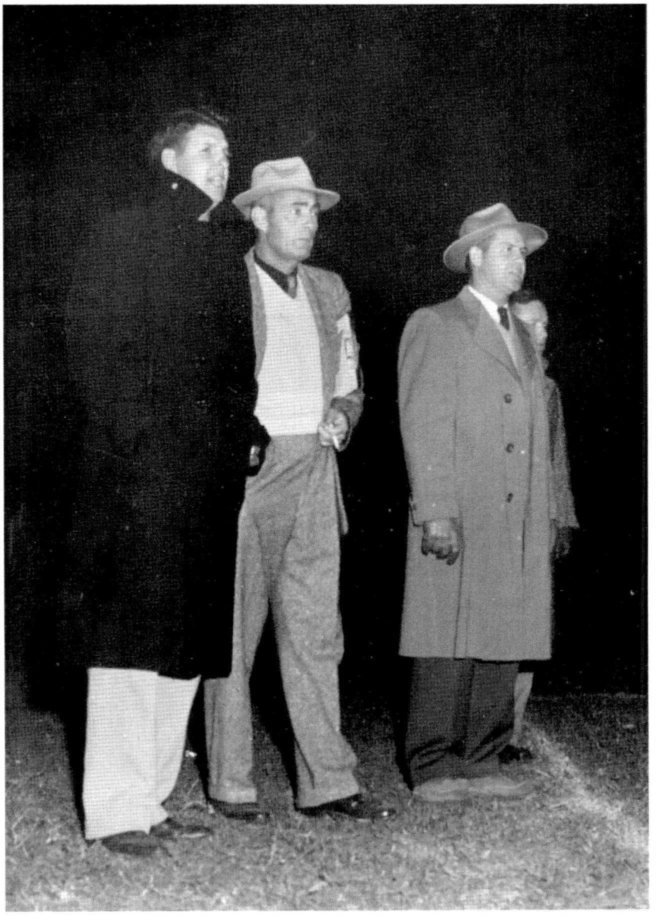

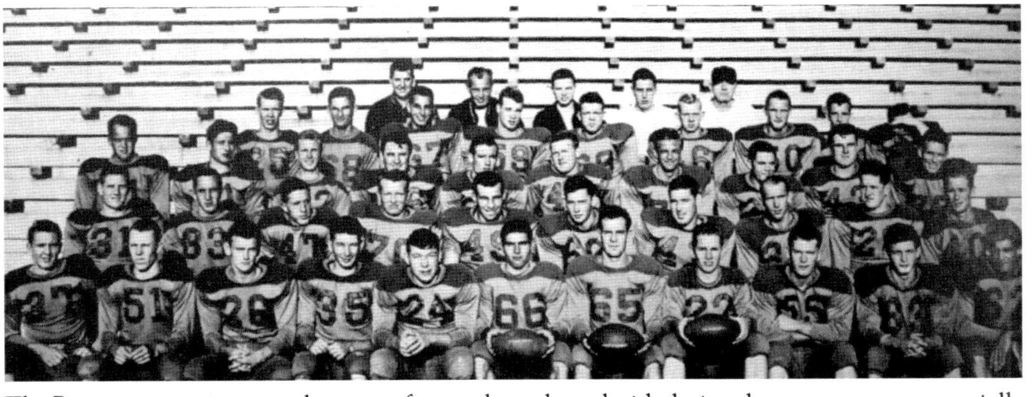

The Buccaneer passing game became a force to be reckoned with during the postwar years, especially with the emergence of quarterback Jack Vest in the late 1940s. For 1949, this translated into another winning season and a 5-4 record. Bob Tranbarger served his second term (the first was in 1946) as cocaptain of the team, and he was the first gridiron player to be named to an All-American (Paul B. Williams) team. (Photograph courtesy Buc Football and Friends Foundation.)

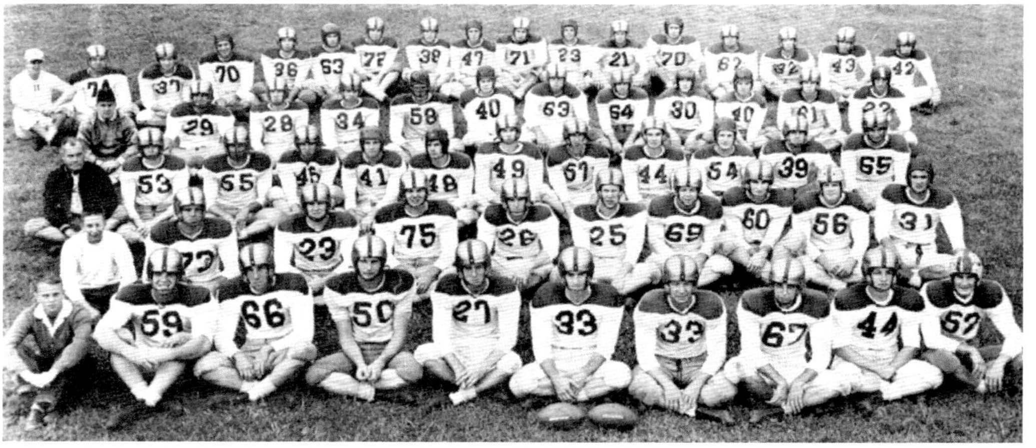

While the Buccaneers had their first losing season (3-5-1) under Coach Roberts and the first since 1941, the 1950 squad did manage to beat local rival Tusculum College and tie Milligan College. One bright spot was the transfer of Hal Morrison from UT, providing Buc passers a primary, record-setting target for the next three years. The same year also marked the first that athletes received scholarships after going on strike the previous year. (Photograph courtesy Buc Football and Friends Foundation.)

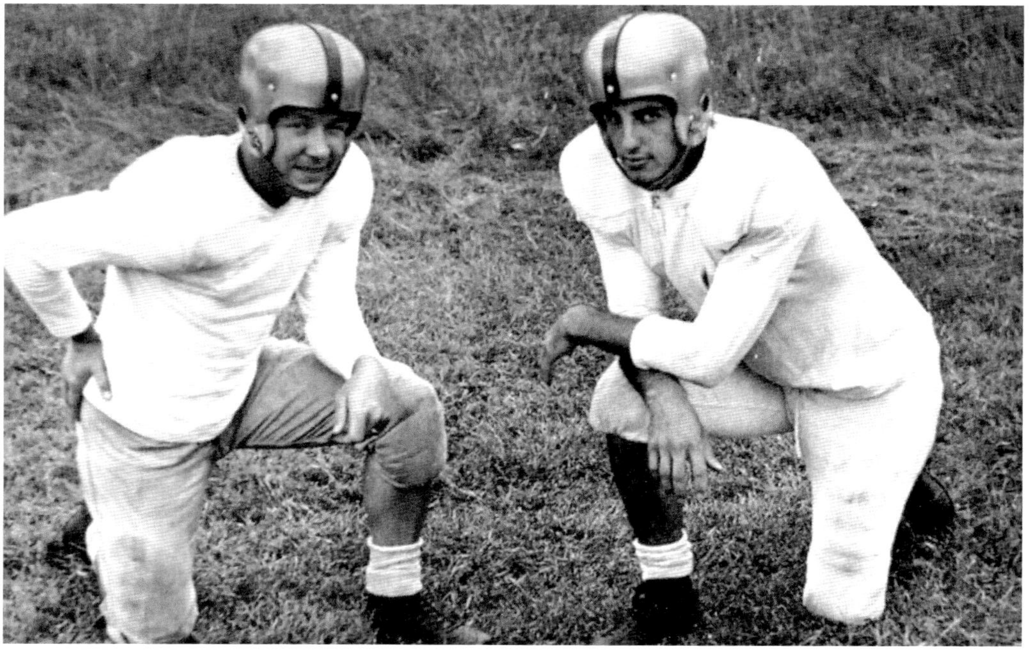

Seniors Mack Sutherland (left), the team's center, and Bob "Snake" Evans (right), also a center, were selected cocaptains in 1950. Evans would go on to coach high school sports at Science Hill High in Johnson City. Coaching high school sports throughout upper east Tennessee and the Southeast and touching the lives of countless students in this capacity was typical of many a Buc player. (Photograph courtesy Buc Football and Friends Foundation.)

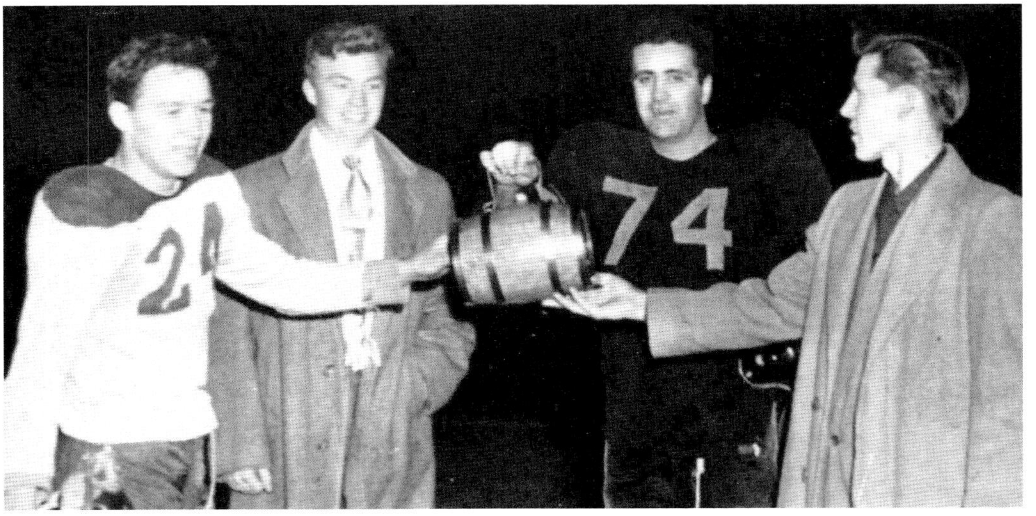

The 1950 classic between Milligan and State ended in a 6-6 deadlock, but the game was thrill-packed from start to finish with the ball changing hands 15 times on turnovers. Ben Howze, State's quarterback, had a spectacular defensive performance, intercepting five Milligan passes. Milligan opened the second half with a score, but State roared back nine plays later with a Howze-to-Morrison touchdown pass. Pictured are team representatives admiring the prize of the contest—a keg! (Photograph courtesy Buc Football and Friends Foundation.)

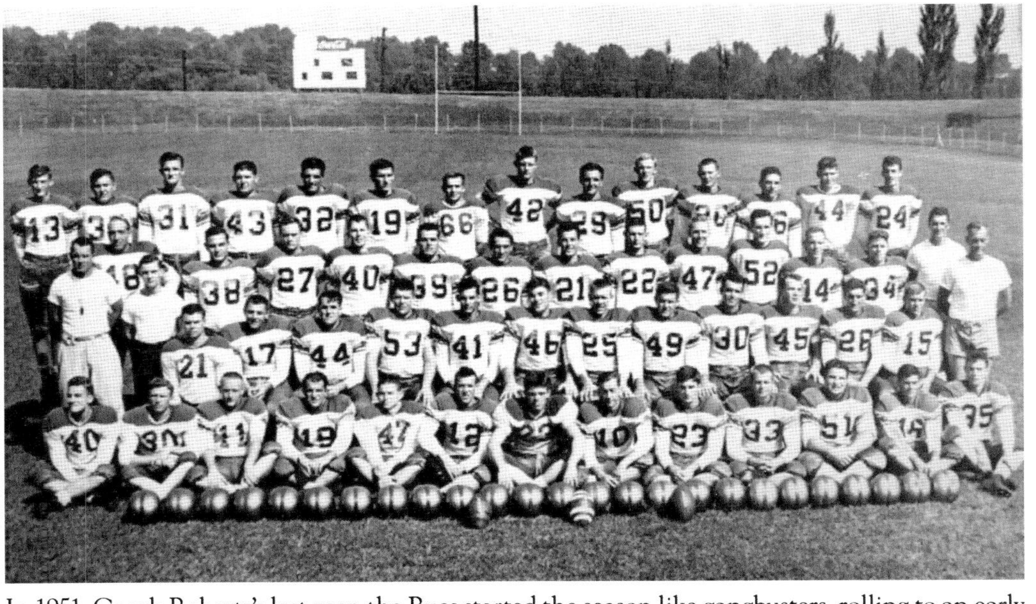

In 1951, Coach Roberts's last year, the Bucs started the season like gangbusters, rolling to an early 4-1 record with defeats of Austin Peay (the first of many times these teams would play), Carson Newman (33-2), Hiwassee, and Mars Hill. The second half of the season was the polar opposite at 0-4 for a composite record of 4-5. The team was led by senior cocaptains Kenneth "Birdlegs" Bryan and Gene "Shadow" Hall. (Photograph courtesy Buc Football and Friends Foundation.)

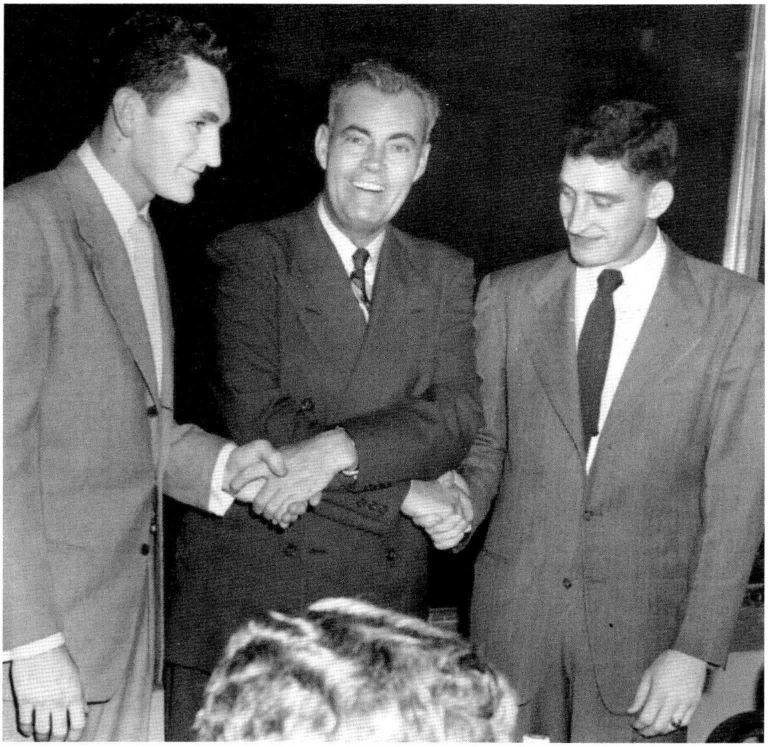

Hal Morrison (left) and Cecil Maddux (right) are congratulated by Coach Roberts (center) after being elected captains of the 1952 football team. The banquet, at the Roan Restaurant, was held annually at the end of each season and would typically be the venue for selection and announcement of the captain(s) for the coming year. (Photograph courtesy of Loyd T. Roberts II.)

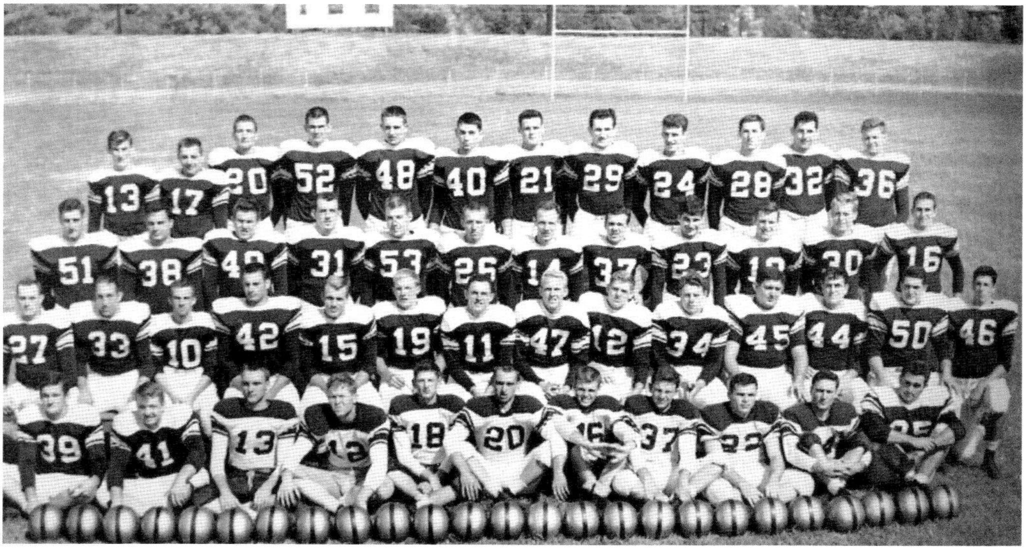

Star Wood started his ETSU Hall of Fame (elected 1980) coaching career in 1952 with a team that posted a 5-2-2 record. Two significant games were played this season. The first was a 27-27 tie with the Appalachian State Mountaineers where the Bucs came back from a 14-point deficit, and the second was their first Burley Bowl appearance, a 34-16 throttling of the Emory and Henry Wasps. (Photograph courtesy Buc Football and Friends Foundation.)

Starling "Star" Jackson Wood, a 1937 graduate of Milligan College, served as head coach for 1952–1953 and again from 1955 to 1965. He was the first head coach to specialize in football and not serve as coach in another sport, though he did serve as the third athletic director from 1953 to 1963. In his distinguished career at ETSU, he won more games (63) than any other coach, including three Burley Bowl victories in 1952, 1953, and 1955. (Photograph courtesy Buc Football and Friends Foundation.)

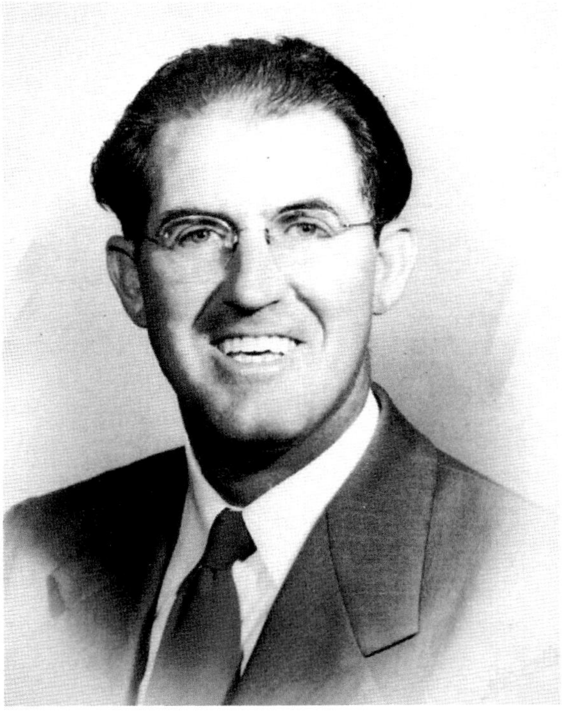

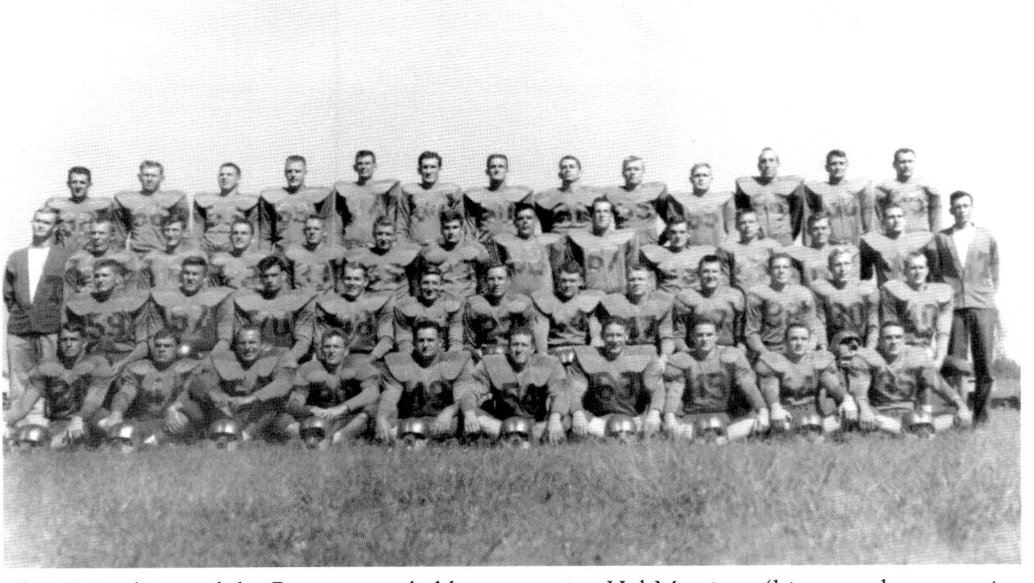

The 1953 edition of the Buccaneers, led by cocaptains Hal Morrison (his second consecutive year as captain) and Bob Porter, finished the year 5-4 with an invite to the ninth-annual Burley Bowl. They played the Wasps again with a similar outcome—a 48-12 thrashing that resulted in accusations of State running up the score and the president of Emory ending the rivalry, which started in 1923. (Photograph courtesy of Hal Morrison.)

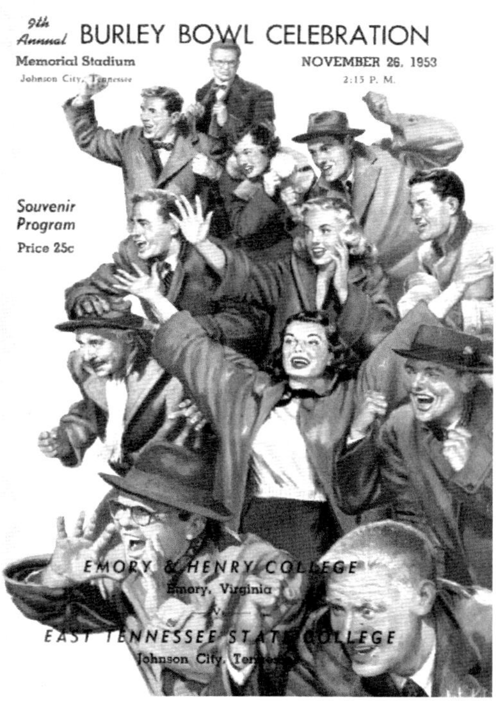

The Burley Bowl, played from 1945 to 1956, was the climax of the Burley Bowl Festival, which featured a parade through downtown Johnson City and a football game between a local college and a successful out-of-state opponent on Thanksgiving Day. The festival opened the tobacco market season in Greater Johnson City. The 1952 and 1953 games were engineered and put on the schedule by Preacher Roberts in 1951. (Photograph courtesy of Tim Jones.)

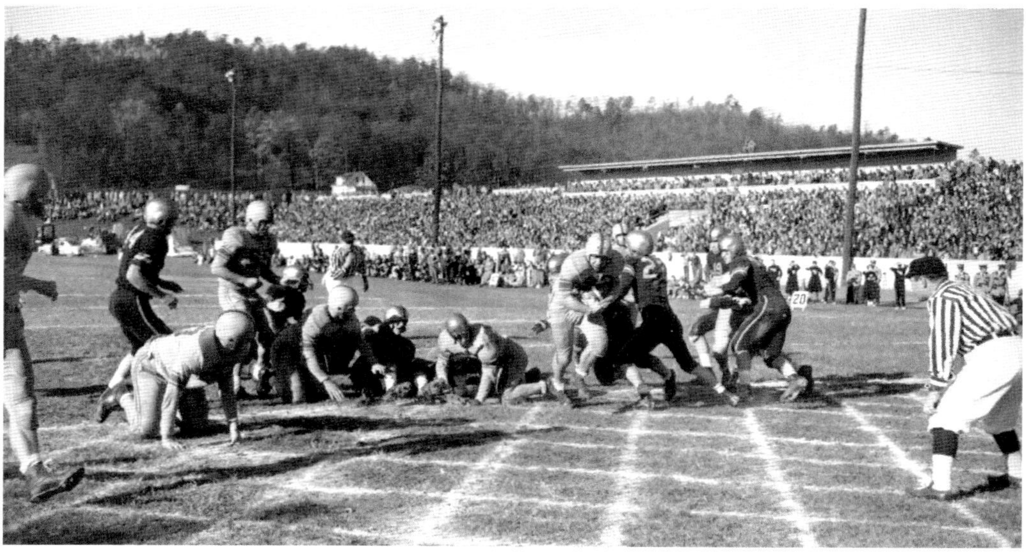

The 1953 Burley Bowl is considered one of the great games in ETSU history by Berney Burleson. The game was played before 5,000 ice-cold fans at Memorial Stadium against Emory and Henry. This was the last game as a Buc for Hal Morrison, who increased his scoring total to 87 on the year by catching a touchdown pass from Pete Wilson and kicking six extra points. The heralded battle between the Buc offense and the Wasp defense turned out more lopsided than even the staunchest Buc fan could have predicted. (Photograph courtesy Buc Football and Friends Foundation.)

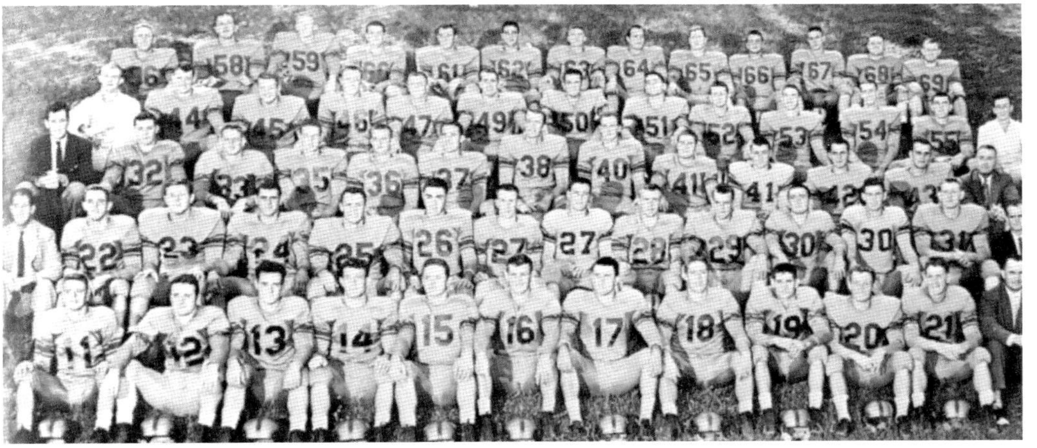

Under new coach Hal Littleford, the Bucs produced their third season in a row of five wins in 1954 with four losses and a tie. Hal Morrison began his long and distinguished coaching career as a graduate assistant coaching the freshman team and assisting with the ends. Coach Crocker returned to help with the line, and Coach Wood worked with the ends. The team played in their third consecutive Burley Bowl but was defeated 27-13 by the Appalachian State College Mountaineers. (Photograph courtesy Buc Football and Friends Foundation.)

When Star Wood assumed his role as athletic director, head coaching duties were turned over to assistant coach Hal Littleford, who was being groomed as a potential head coach. He served only one year in this capacity (1954) then resigned for financial reasons. He realized after getting a $100 increase in pay for winning the VSAC title that coaching would not provide an adequate income. He went on to run a very successful insurance business and served as mayor of Johnson City from 1967 to 1969. (Photograph courtesy Buc Football and Friends Foundation.)

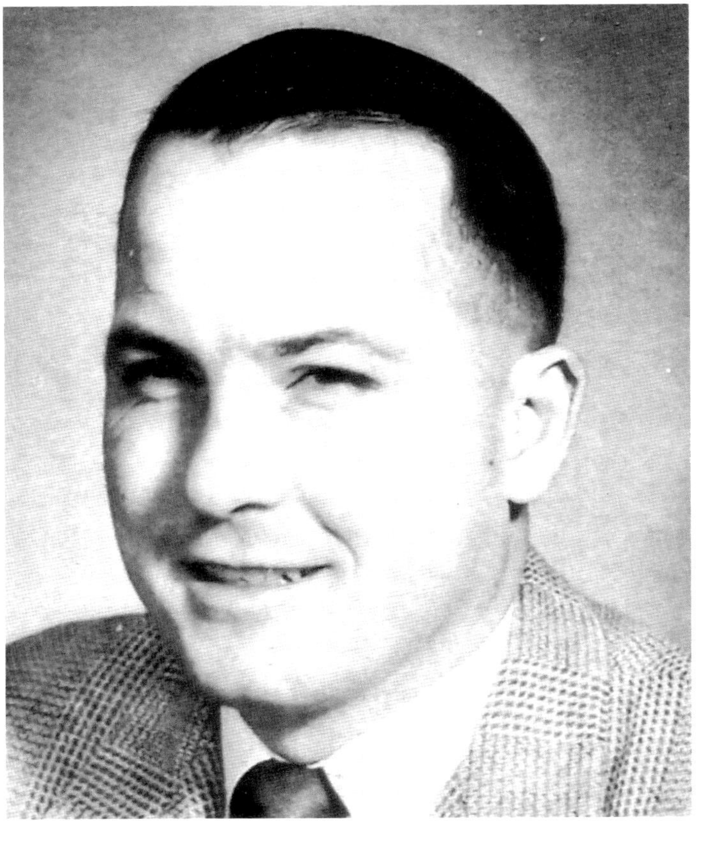

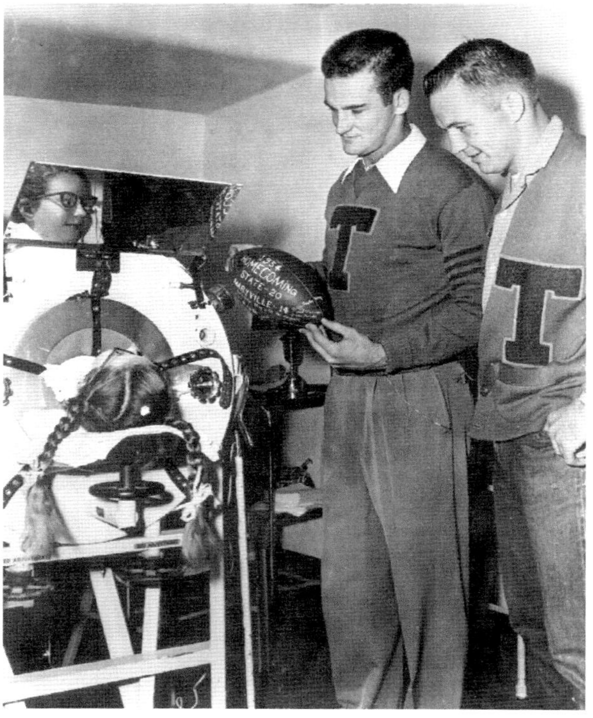

Buccaneer cocaptains Jack Boone (center) and Buddy Saulsbury present the 1954 homecoming game ball to coach Madison Brook's daughter, Sally, who had contracted polio earlier in the year. (Photograph courtesy Buc Football and Friends Foundation.)

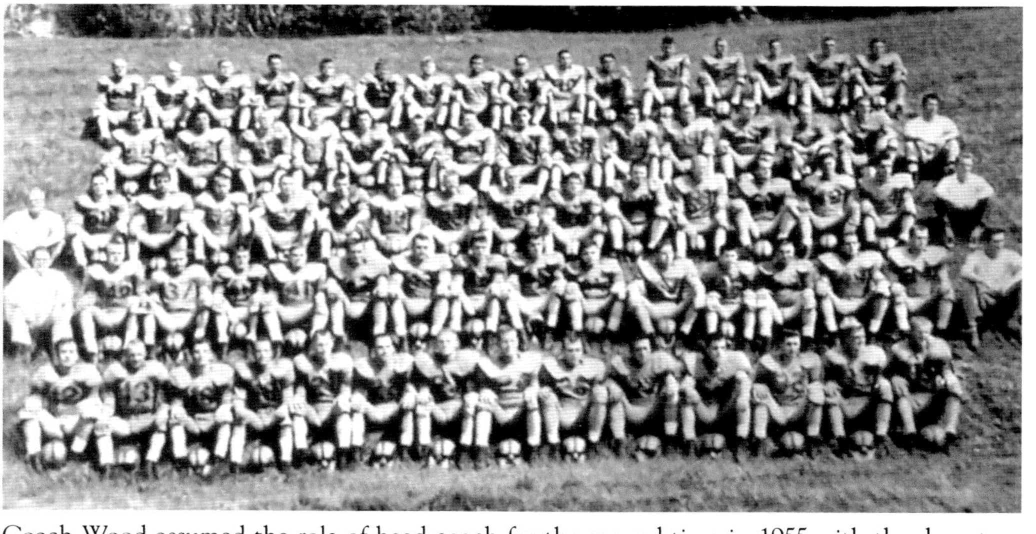

Coach Wood assumed the role of head coach for the second time in 1955 with the departure of Coach Littleford. The team responded with a one-game improvement in their performance, matching their last six-win season in 1948. State gained a measure of revenge against Appalachian State, defeating them 7-0 in the 11th-annual playing of the Burley Bowl and finishing the season 6-3-1. Coach Calvin "Shorty" Frey from Tennessee Polytechnic Institute (TPI) joined the team as an assistant coach as did Pete "The Arm" Wilson, who threw to Hal Morrison in his record-setting 1953 season. (Photograph courtesy Buc Football and Friends Foundation.)

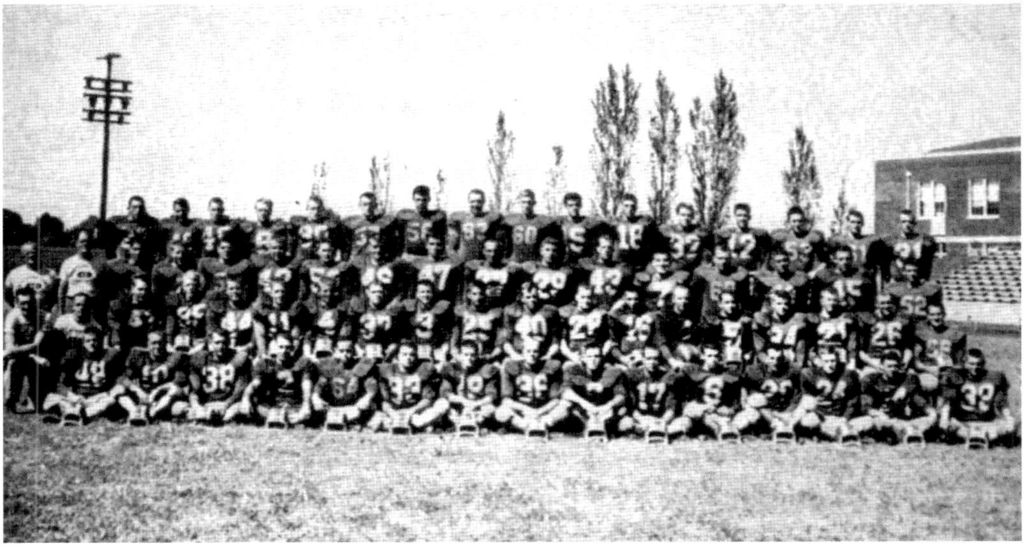

The 1956 Buccaneers, then at 4-4, were invited to play a powerful Memphis State Tigers team in the 12th-annual (and final) Burley Bowl. At the half, the score was even, but the Tigers turned it on in the second half, handing the Bucs a 20-point defeat, 32-12. The Burley Bowl years had come to an end with ETSC having a final bowl record of 3-2, the most wins of any team in the series. (Photograph courtesy Buc Football and Friends Foundation.)

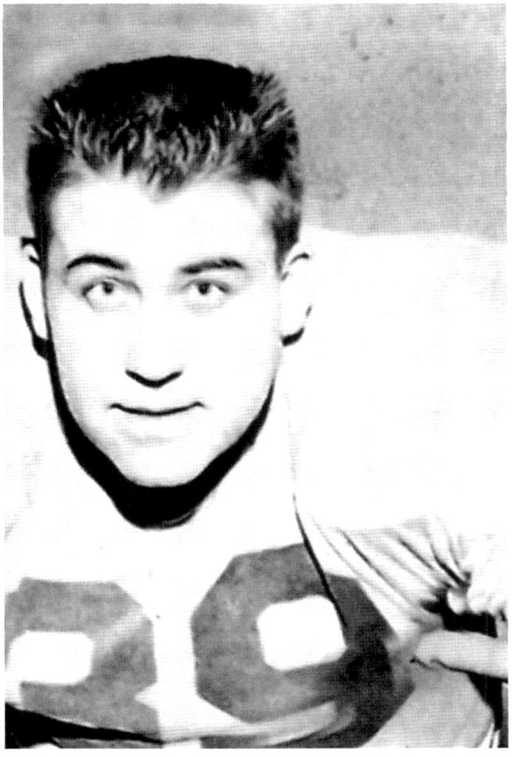

The addition of David Egley Walker as a Buccaneer lineman in 1956 was a significant event in the history of the school. Walker later served as an assistant football coach from 1963 to 1965, and he serves as director of track and field in 2007. His winning ways in track brought national recognition to the university through the recruiting of the "Irish Brigade" and coaching them to a second-place finish at the 1972 NCAA Cross-Country championships. (Photograph courtesy Buc Football and Friends Foundation.)

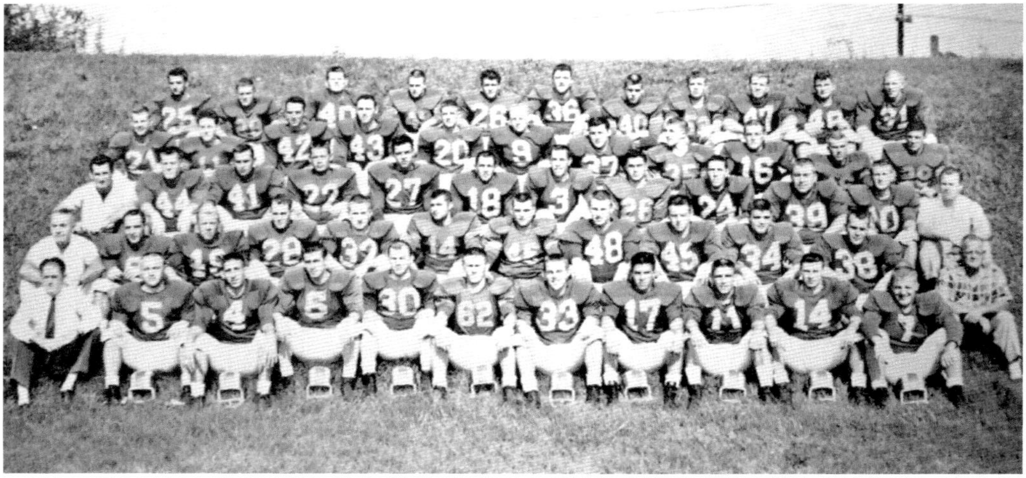

In their last season prior to joining the Ohio Valley Conference (OVC), an 11-game schedule and injuries to key skill players (such as Bernard "Piggy" Nolan) took its toll. The Bucs lost four of their last five games, ending 1957 at 5-6. During the early 1950s, ETSC held joint membership in both the Smoky Mountain Athletic Conference and the VSAC but left the SMAC in 1952. Leaving the VSAC for the better-known and better-organized OVC would lead to bigger and better things for the Buccaneers. (Photograph courtesy Buc Football and Friends Foundation.)

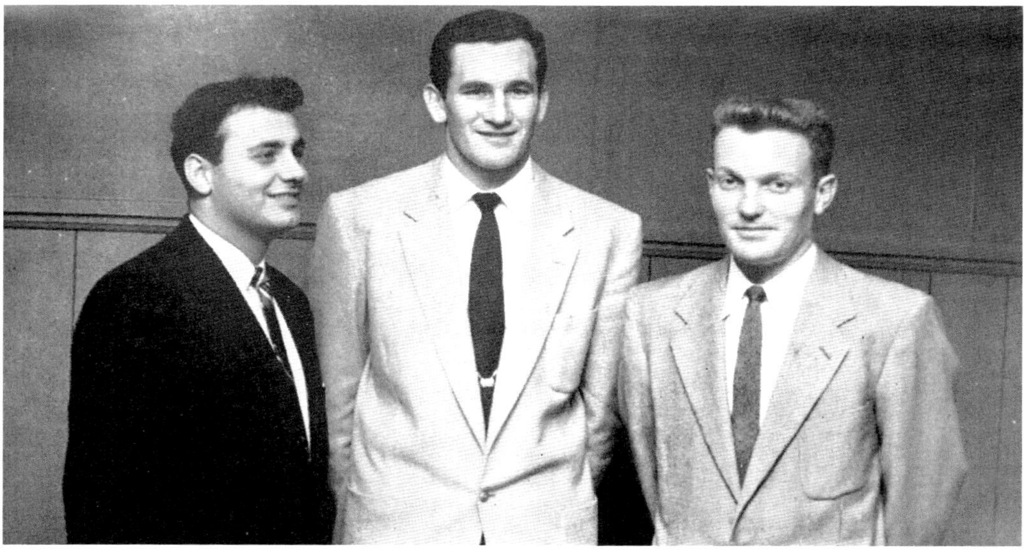

Pictured from left to right are assistant coaches Jimmy Demo, Hal Morrison, and Pete Wilson. Wilson, a native of Athens, Tennessee, transferred to State from junior college. In 1954, he finished his two-year career as quarterback with All-VSAC honors and numerous passing records, including best completion percentage (.630) for a season, which still stands. After graduation, he served as a graduate assistant coach at State for a year, then as a coach at Science Hill, and again as an assistant coach at State from 1962 to 1965. He was elected to the ETSU Hall of Fame in 1984. (Photograph courtesy Buc Football and Friends Foundation.)

3

OVC Bound

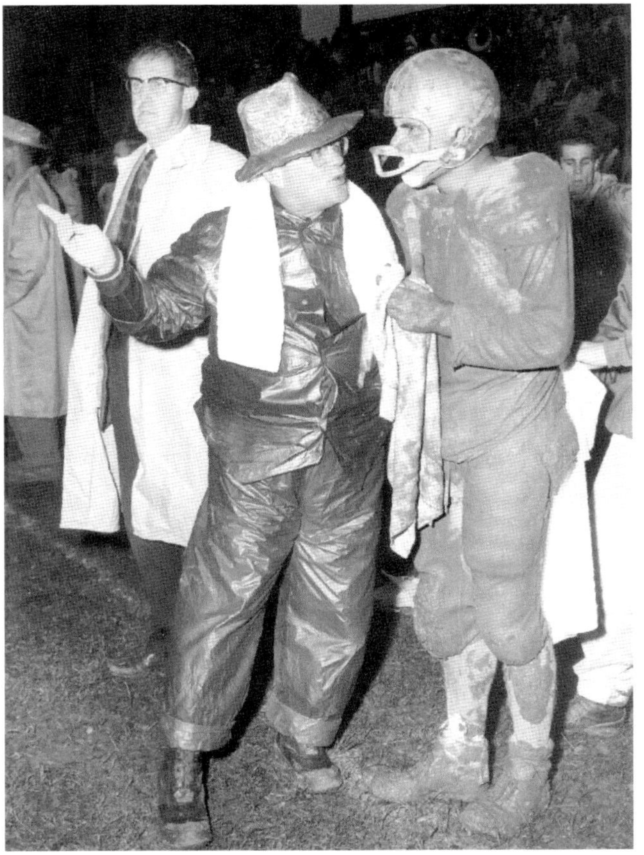

Head coach Star Wood looks on as coach Shorty Frey confers with a muddy Mickey Banyas. Banyas garnered second team Little All-American honors as a standout linebacker and center on the offensive side. He was elected to the ETSU Athletics Hall of Fame in 1983. This photograph originally appeared in the 1958 *Buccaneer*, the ETSC annual. (Photograph courtesy of Tim Jones.)

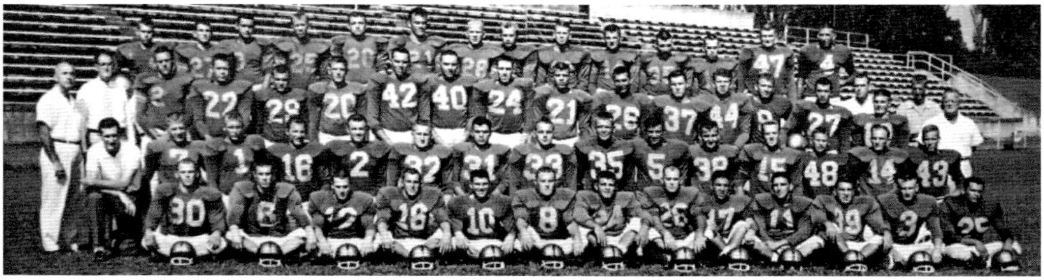

Cocaptains linebacker Mickey Banyas (34) and defensive end George Litton (28) led the 1958 Pirate team to a 5-4 mark, which was good for a second-place finish in their first year in the OVC. Middle Tennessee State College (MTSC) and Tennessee Tech College (TTC) were cochampions at 5-1. Both Banyas and Litton earned All-OVC honors, and this team still holds the ETSU record for fewest yards allowed in a season. After graduating, Litton coached nationally ranked teams at Lees-McRae College and Gardner-Webb University. (Photograph courtesy Buc Football and Friends Foundation.)

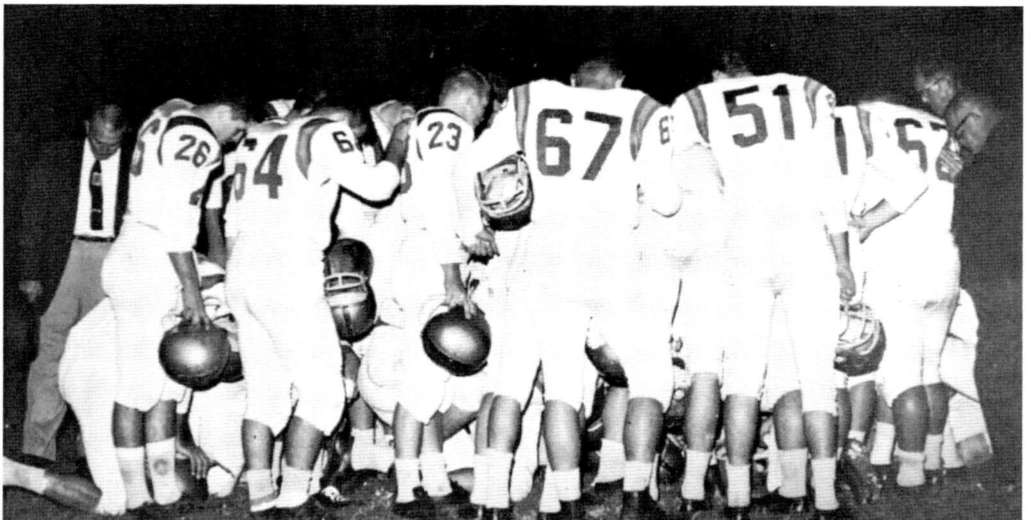

For the second year in a row, ETSC finished as runner-up to cochampions MTSC and TTC. The Bucs lost both games to the cochampions for two OVC losses on the season and a 6-3 record in 1959. Their lone non-conference loss was to Jacksonville State, 13-0. Guard Darman Place, cocaptain with fellow senior Jim Crigger, earned All-OVC honors and honorable mention for Little All-American. (Photograph courtesy Buc Football and Friends Foundation.)

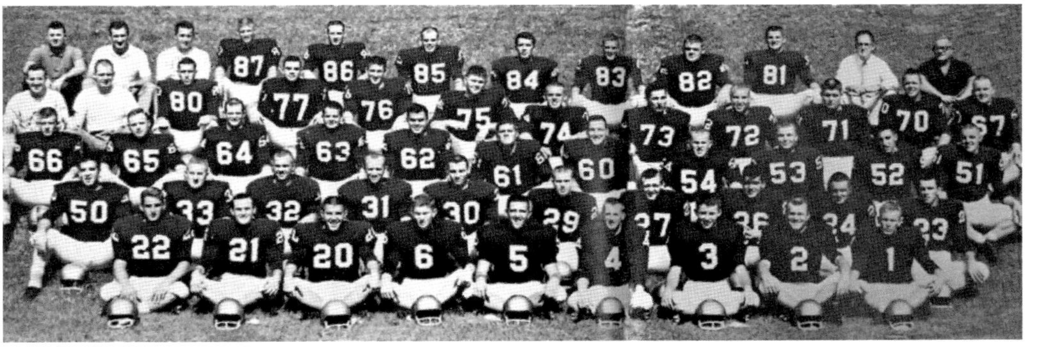

Rebuilding from heavy losses on the line and in the backfield, the Buc footballers fell to 3-4-2 in 1960. As the team matured and gained experience over the course of the year, play improved and the team won two of their last three games. Despite limited team success, halfback Ronnie Quillen (20), left end Bill Hughes (83), and right tackle Jack Stokes (70) were honorable mentions for the Little All-American Team, while Quillen and Hughes were named to the All-Conference Team. (Photograph courtesy Buc Football and Friends Foundation.)

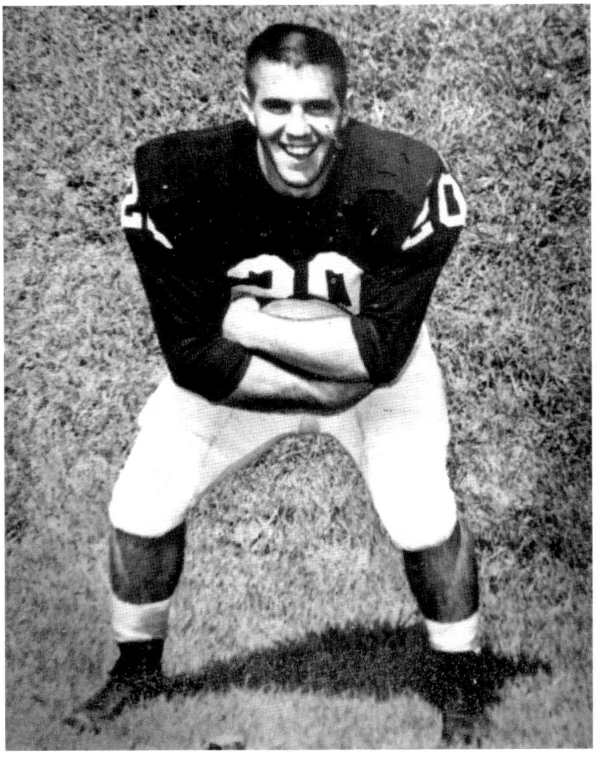

Star halfback Ron Quillen, who led the OVC in rushing in 1960, was one of 33 players named to the Williamson All-American squad in addition to his Little All-American honors. He went on to play in the Canadian Football League. He was elected to the ETSU Sports Hall of Fame in 1983. (Photograph courtesy of L. T. Helton.)

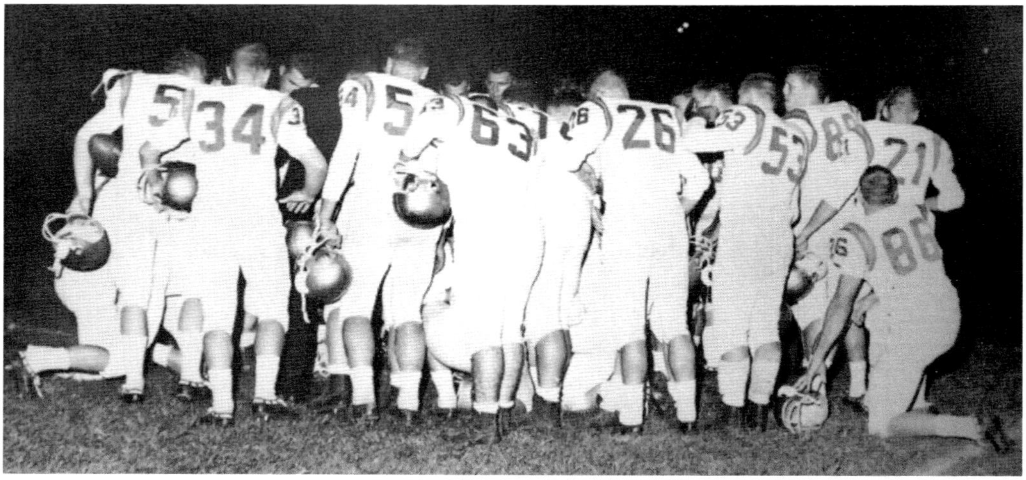

Much like the previous year, the 1961 edition of the football team only had three wins but lost seven games. And like 1960, the poor performance was attributed to a general lack of experience and depth. However, it was another sterling year for individual Buccaneer performers. Freshman halfback Phil Morgan emerged as the OVC's leading rusher with 708 yards on 105 carries, and sophomore Jimmy "Wink" Baker led the league in both passing (859 yards) and total offense (1,265 yards). (Photograph courtesy Buc Football and Friends Foundation.)

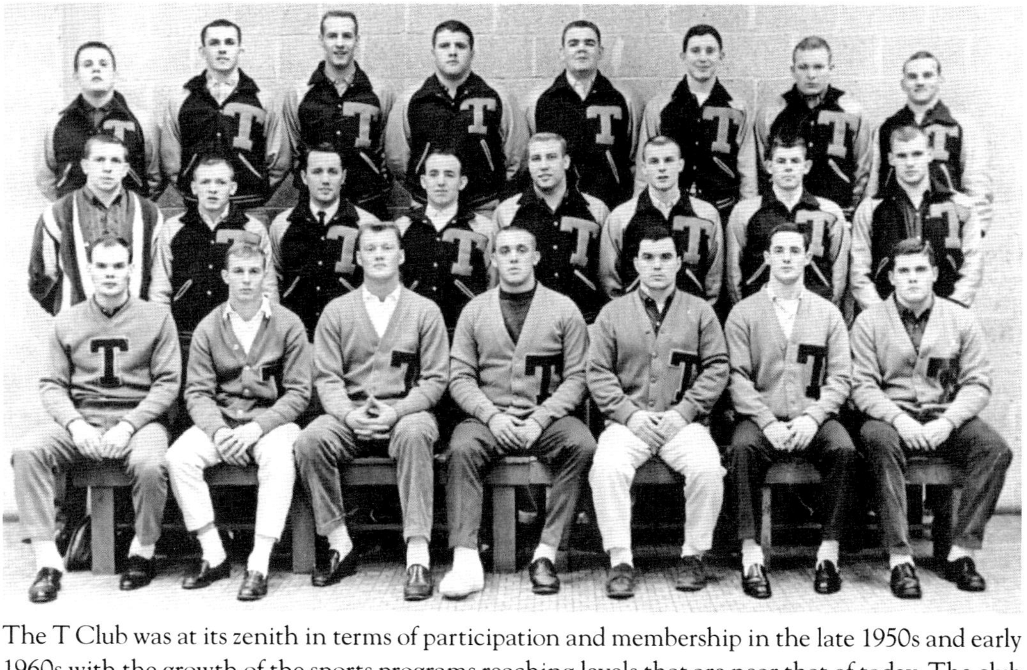

The T Club was at its zenith in terms of participation and membership in the late 1950s and early 1960s with the growth of the sports programs reaching levels that are near that of today. The club during this time was still responsible for fostering loyalty and promoting spirit but had also evolved into a service organization that became known for its annual sale of mums as a fund-raiser. The 1961 T Club is pictured above. (Photograph courtesy Buc Football and Friends Foundation.)

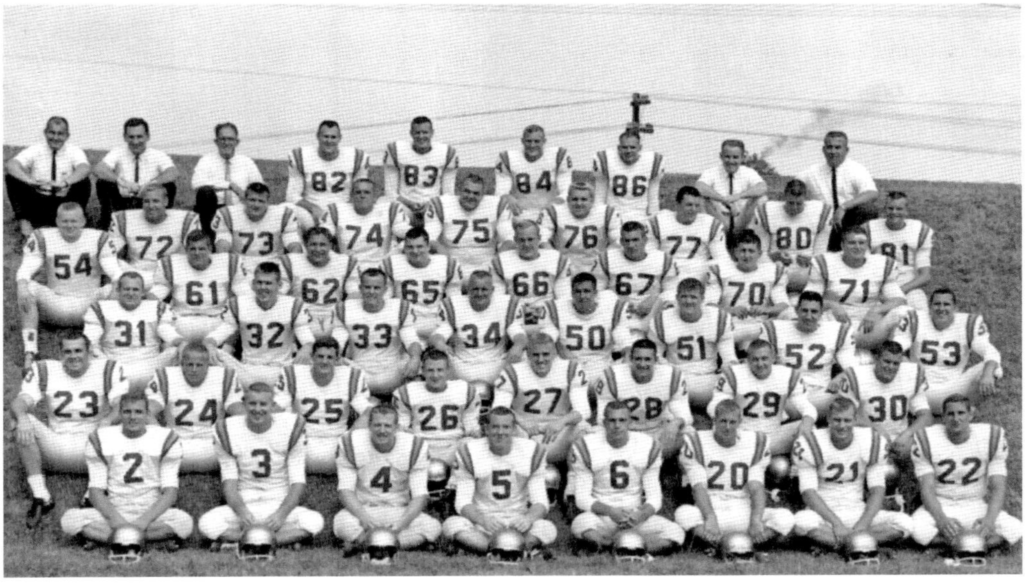

In 1962, the Buccaneers finally put it all together—stellar individual performances with strong team play—to finish the season 7-3 and 5-2 in the OVC, good for a four-way share of first place. For the Bucs, it was the first time at the top since joining the conference. This was the best won-loss record for ETSU since 1946. (Photograph courtesy Buc Football and Friends Foundation.)

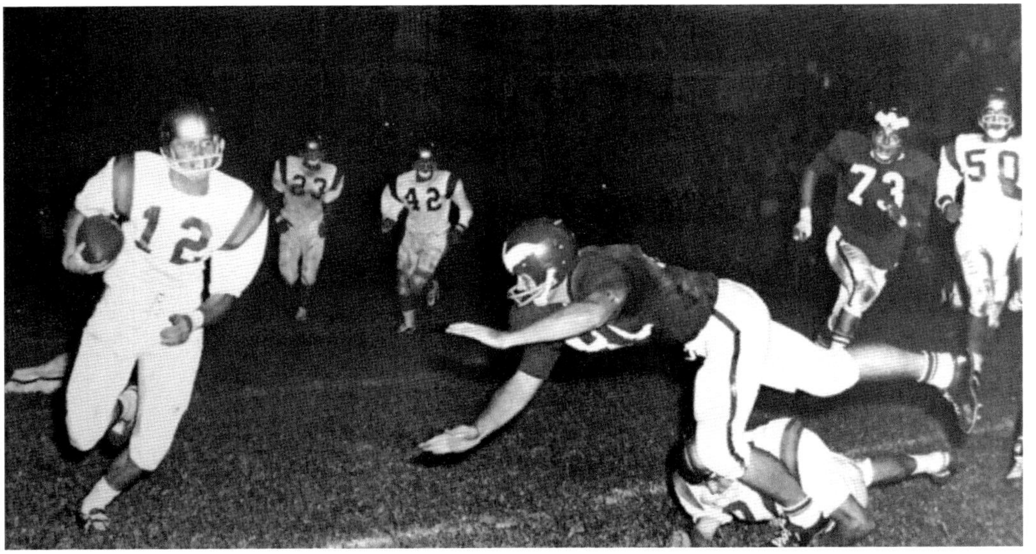

Jimmy "Wink" Baker, on the run versus Western Kentucky, was named Little All-American (second team) and continued to blossom into one of the finest players ever to put on a Buc uniform, placing first in scoring (71 points) and total offense (1,248 yards) in the OVC. Baker, Harry Harmon (first), Phil Morgan (third), Jerry Kirk (first), David Holtsclaw (third), and Pat "The Crowd" Carter (first) were named to the All-OVC team. (Photograph courtesy Buc Football and Friends Foundation.)

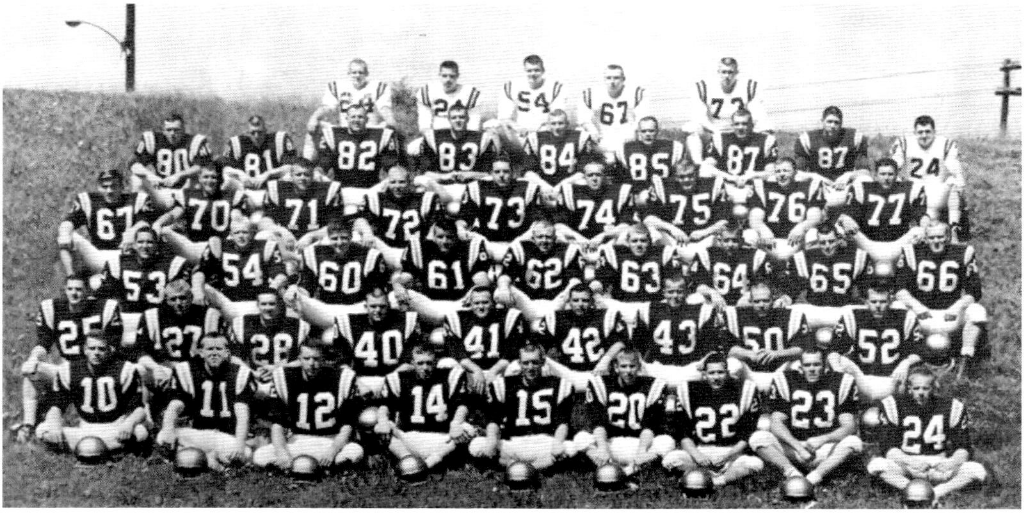

In 1963, another seven-win season against only two losses was not good enough for the Corsair crew to win their conference. A very strong Western Kentucky team went undefeated to win the crown. Jim Baker (12) had another stellar year and was named first team Little All-American and All-OVC. Pat "The Crowd" Carter (75) also repeated All-OVC honors with team captain Wayne King (76) and David Holtsclaw (24), who also were tabbed for the team. (Photograph courtesy Buc Football and Friends Foundation.)

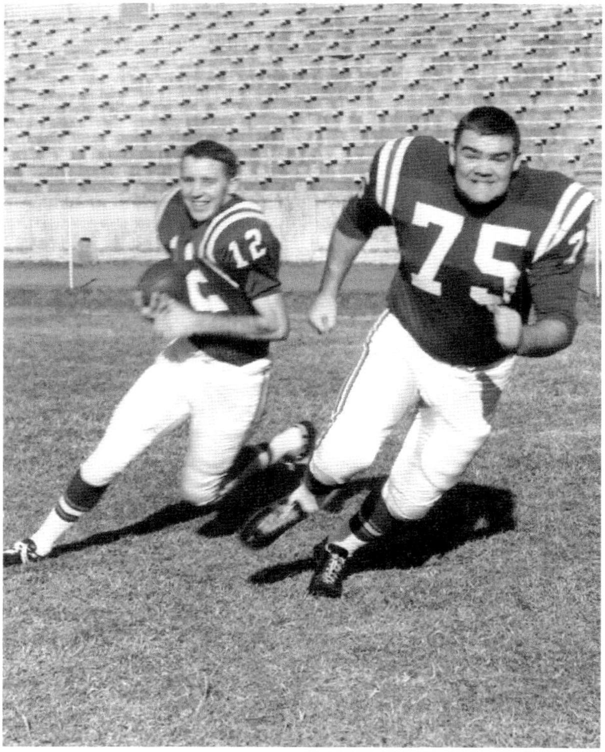

Wink Baker (left) and the Crowd Carter played together from 1960 to 1963, during which time both garnered multiple All-OVC honors. Baker was tabbed for multiple Little All-American accolades from 1961 to 1963, while Carter was recognized on the 1962 team. Both were inducted into the ETSU Athletic Hall of Fame in 1977 and 2000 respectively. With Carter clearing the way, Baker was named OVC Offensive Player of the Year in 1963. (Photograph courtesy Buc Football and Friends Foundation.)

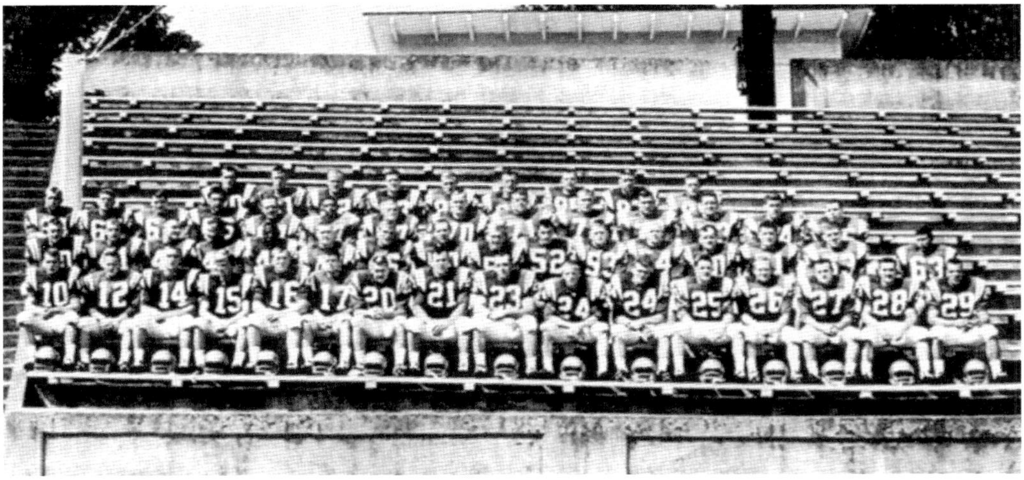

"One step forward and one step back" seemed to be the motto for 1964 as the team would win one and then lose one without sustaining any momentum. There were some memorable games, such as the second half comeback and 26-9 victory against heavily favored Western Kentucky, breaking the Hilltoppers' 14-game win streak. Individually the Bucs would also place eight men—Doug Light, Roy Frazier (future head coach), LeRoy Gray, A. B. Clevenger, Robin Forbes, David Holtsclaw, Jim Anderson, and Pete Hunt—on the All-Conference squads. (Photograph courtesy Buc Football and Friends Foundation.)

In 1964, Johnny Russaw was the first to break the color barrier in football, both as a player and later as an assistant coach (1968) at ETSU. He was a star at Langston, the black high school in Johnson City, prior to desegregation. His coach, Paul Christman, encouraged him to attend ETSU to be a pioneer. During his junior year (1966), he was doused with a hot liquid while entering the stadium at the Citadel in Charleston, South Carolina, a reminder that integrated football in the South during the turbulent 1960s still had a ways to go to acceptance. (Photograph courtesy of Johnny Russaw.)

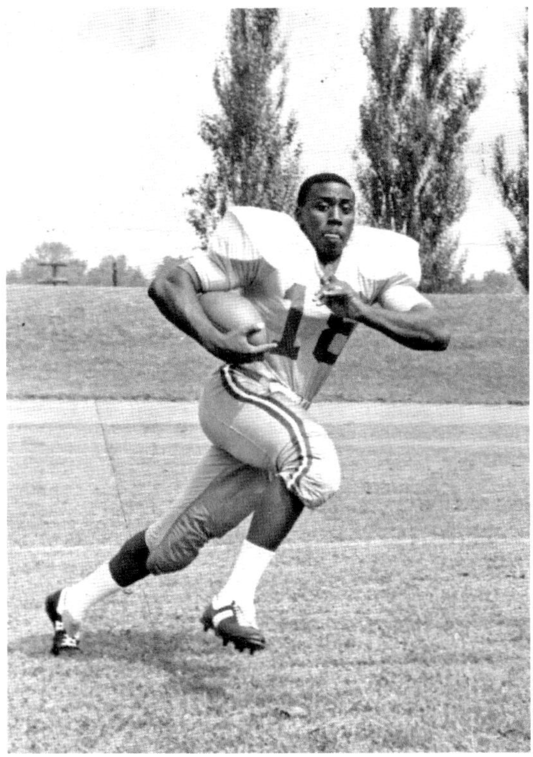

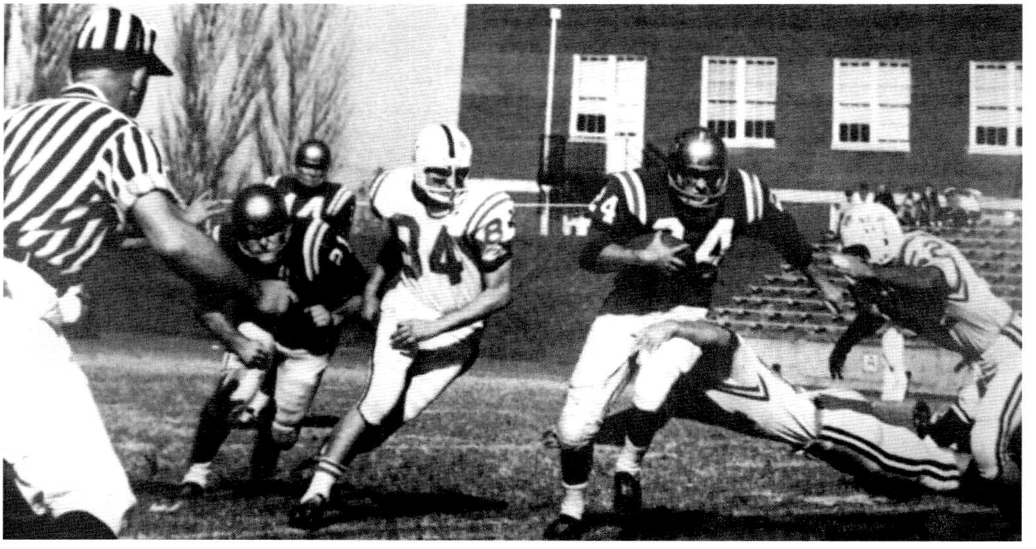

Halfback David Holtsclaw (24), a strong runner, rips through the Middle Tennessee line in the last game of the 1964 season. It was a closely contested game, but the Bucs fell just short to the tune of 9-14. In addition to his All-OVC honors, Holtsclaw was selected to the Little All-American Team. (Photograph courtesy Buc Football and Friends Foundation.)

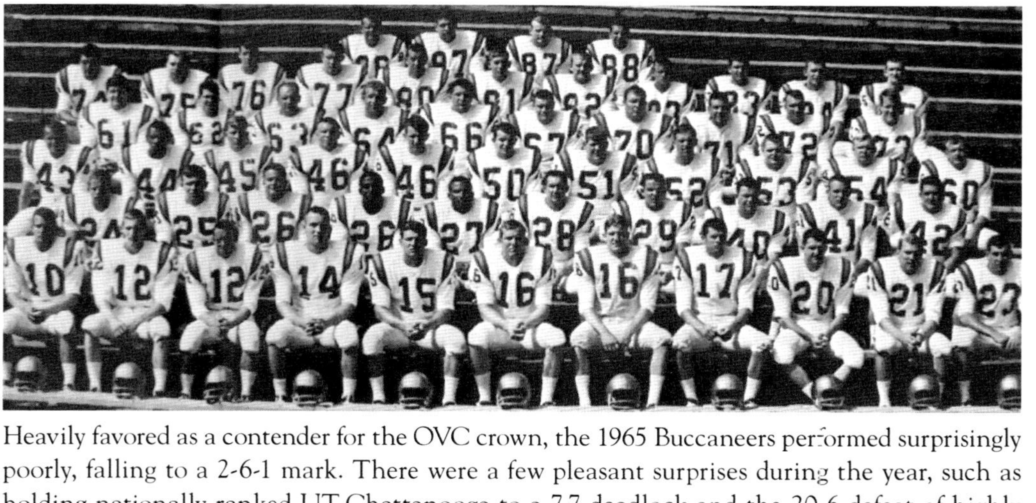

Heavily favored as a contender for the OVC crown, the 1965 Buccaneers performed surprisingly poorly, falling to a 2-6-1 mark. There were a few pleasant surprises during the year, such as holding nationally ranked UT-Chattanooga to a 7-7 deadlock and the 20-6 defeat of highly ranked Wofford. Adding to the season's surprises was the resignation of longtime head coach Star Wood in favor of a position in the English department. (Photograph courtesy Buc Football and Friends Foundation.)

Jerry Robertson, or "Doc" as he was affectionately called by the athletes, played football his freshman year in 1961 and lettered as a student trainer in the early 1960s. He would be hired as State's first full-time trainer in 1965 and became an award-winning, innovative, nationally respected trainer during his almost 40 years working at the university. The new Athletic Medicine Center is named in his honor. (Photograph courtesy Buc Football and Friends Foundation.)

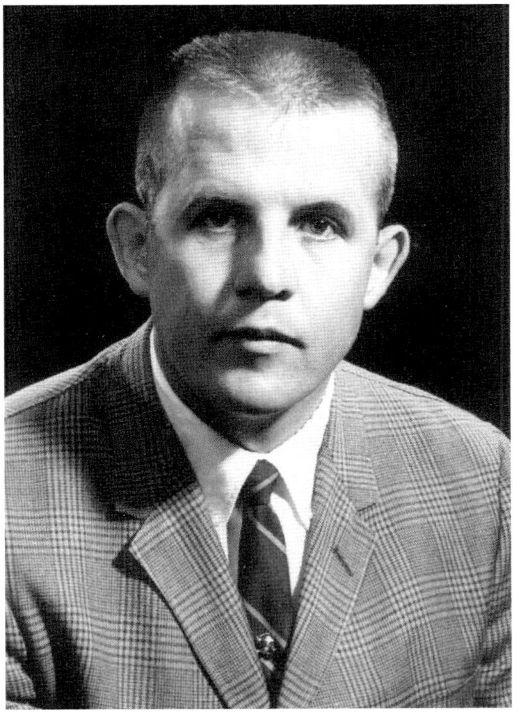

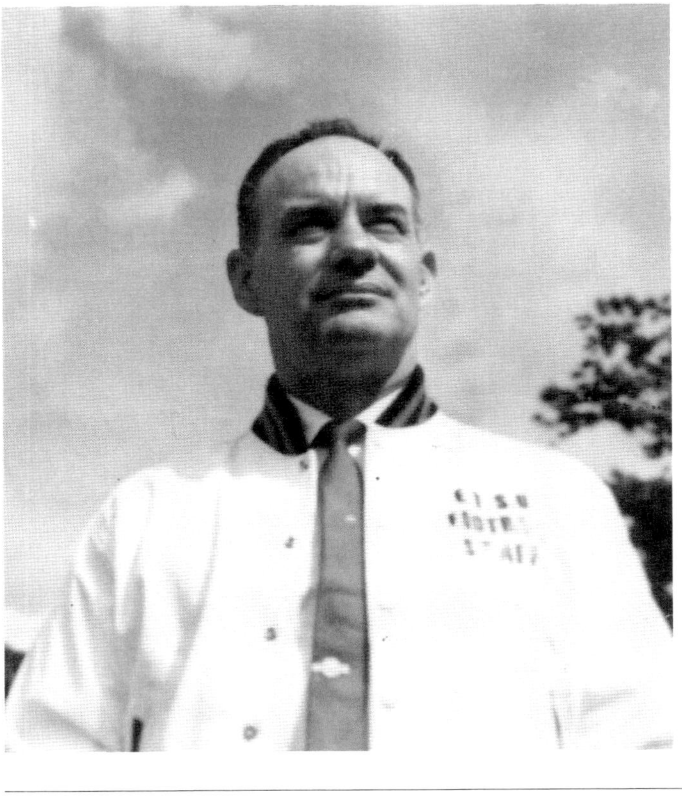

Despite new coach John Robert Bell's thorough preparation and emphasis on recruiting, the 1966 team finished the year 3-6. The Bucs only defeated two OVC foes, Murray and Middle Tennessee State University, which placed them seventh in the conference. The MTSU game was termed "The Upset of the Year" by the United Press International (UPI) because the Bucs' 12-0 defeat knocked the Blue Raiders out of a share of the OVC crown with Morehead State. (Photograph courtesy Buc Football and Friends Foundation.)

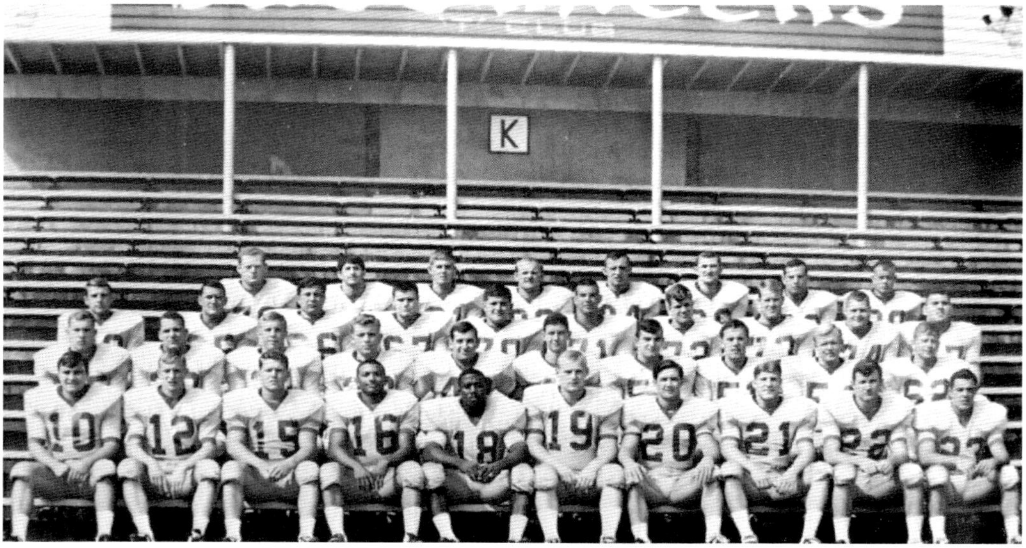

Coach John Robert Bell, a native Tennessean, took over the duties of athletic director and head coach of the football team in 1966. He served as the lead recruiter and assistant coach for the Georgia Tech Yellowjackets under Bobby Dodd prior to his arrival. During his time at Tech, he also worked with James K. Luck Jr. (son of the Bucs' second coach), who also served under Dodd as an assistant and later became the head baseball coach. Bell coached at ETSU for seven seasons, leading the Buccaneers to their greatest season ever and compiling a 31-34-5 record. (Courtesy L. T. Helton.)

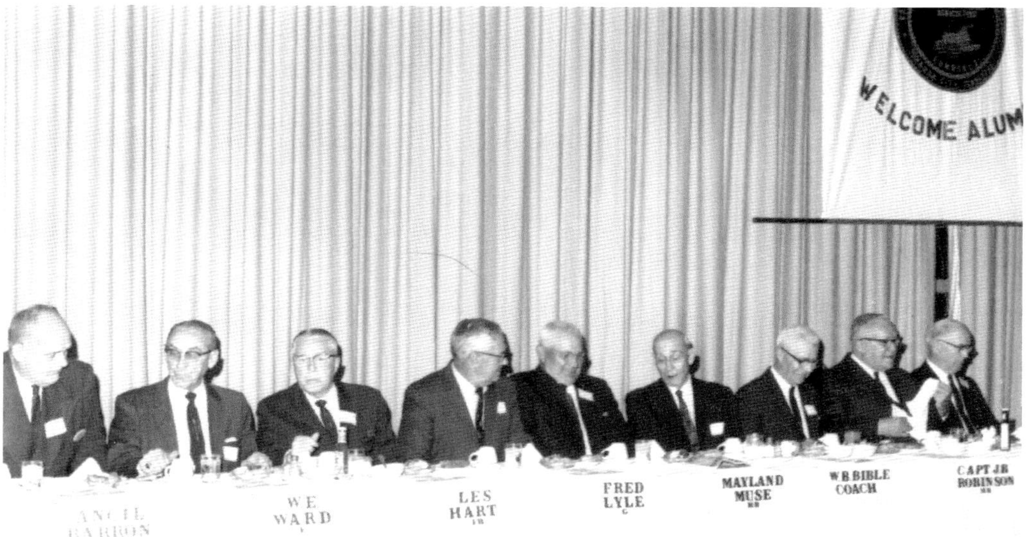

Homecoming activities for 1966 included a reunion of the 1921 football team and recognition of the team during the games festivities. Ancil Barron (far left) still holds the team record for longest punt with a 96-yard kick in 1921 against Washington College. The homecoming game against Wofford College was one of the season's bright spot with a 42-6 pasting of the Terriers. (Photograph courtesy Buc Football and Friends Foundation.)

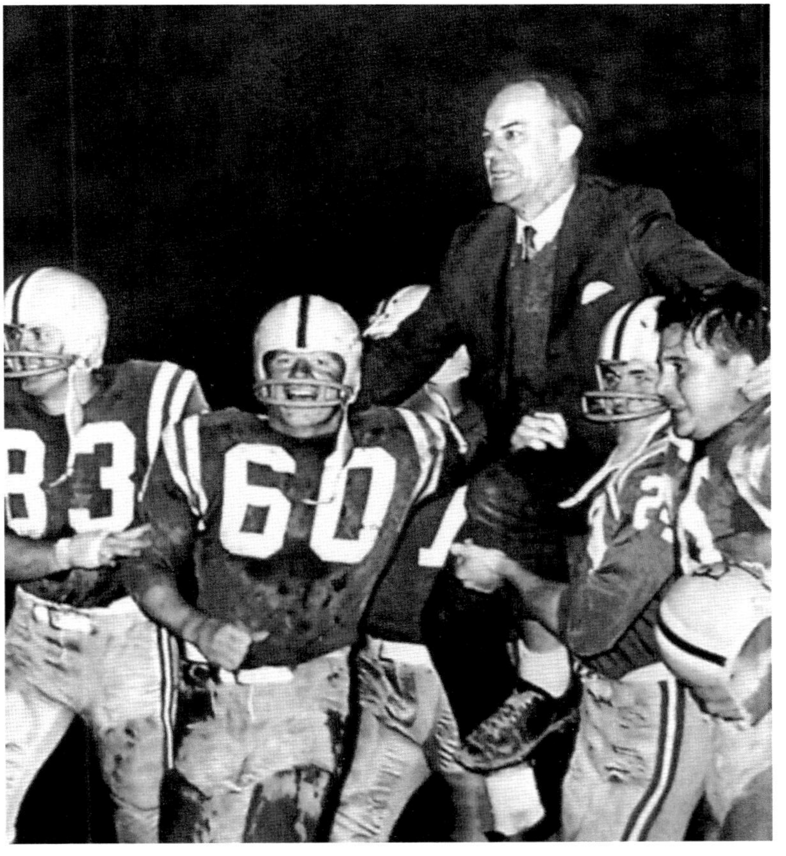

Coach Bell is carried off the home field in victory by a group of jubilant Bucs, including LeRoy Gray (far right), after their defeat of MTSU in the final game of 1966. During the game, the Bucs out-rushed and out-gained the Blue Raiders. Gray was selected to the All-OVC and the Little All-American teams for 1966. (Photograph courtesy Buc Football and Friends Foundation.)

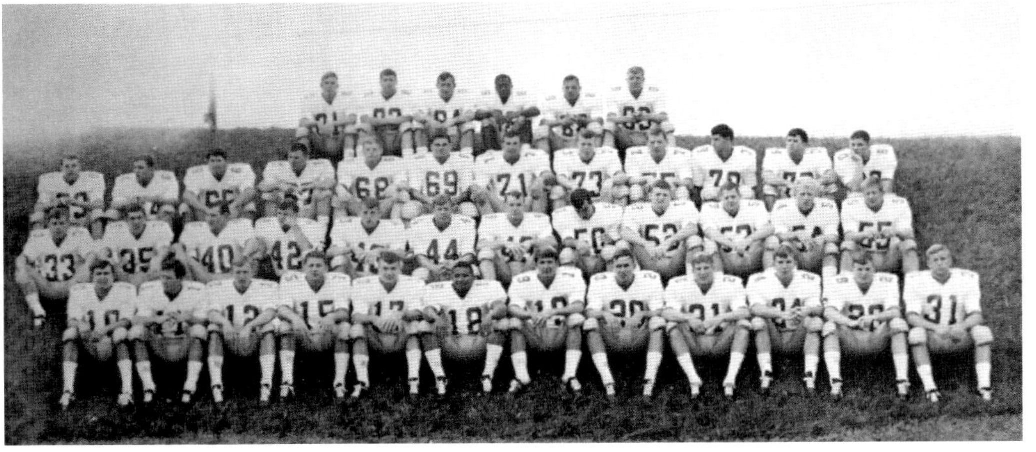

The 1967 "Corsair" offense and "Hardrocks" defense finished the year 3-6-1, tied for fourth in the conference. It was becoming clear that defense would be the backbone of successful teams in the future. Defensive back Ron Overbay (15) was Defensive Player of the Year and was named to the All-Conference Team along with linebacker Doug Linebarger (63). (Photograph courtesy Buc Football and Friends Foundation.)

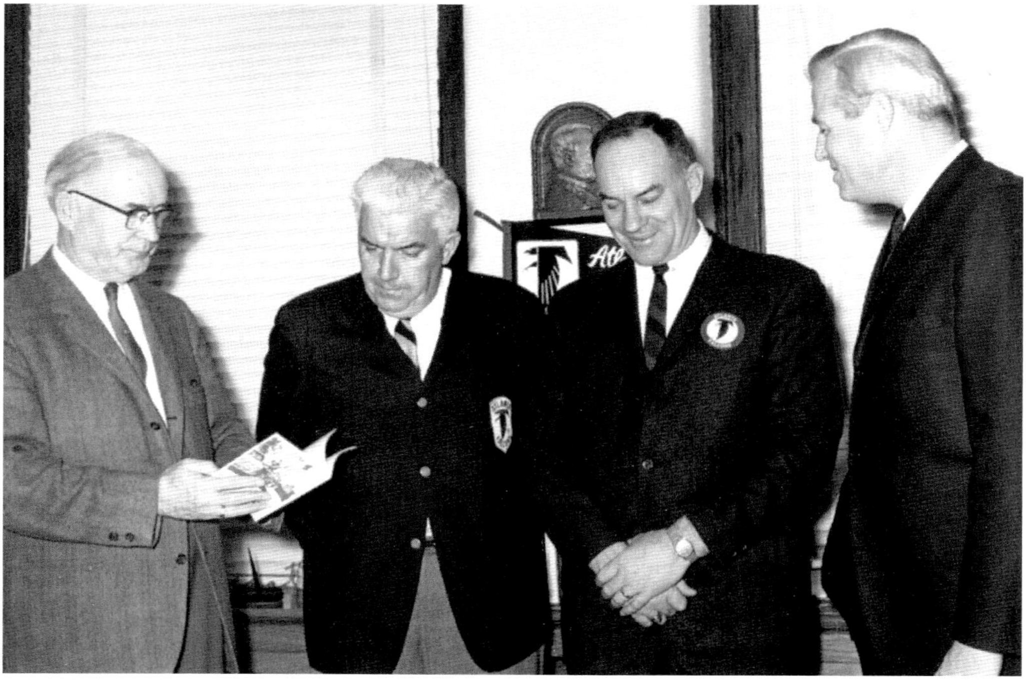

Atlanta Falcons general manger Frank Wall (second from left) is flanked by ETSU president Burgin Dossett (left) and ETSU head coach John Robert Bell (second from right). After spending their first training camp in Black Mountain, North Carolina, the second-year NFL team started training in Johnson City in 1967 and continued their training camp at ETSU through the 1970 season. During their stay, the Bucs and Falcons shared the field by alternating training times. (Photograph courtesy Buc Football and Friends Foundation.)

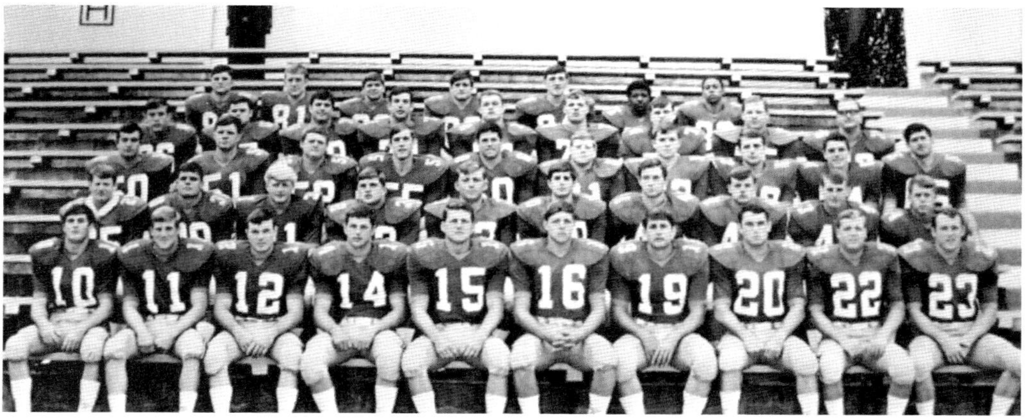

Breaking even in 1968 with a 5-5 record, the "hardrock" Bucs gave a glimpse of things to come by winning their last four games and finishing 4-3 in the OVC for fourth place. Team captain Ron Overbay (15) and Doug Linebarger (63) repeated all of their 1967 honors again in 1968, and center John Walton (50) was also named All-Conference. (Photograph courtesy Buc Football and Friends Foundation.)

Defensive back Ronald L. Overbay played for the Big Blue from 1965 to 1968. During his stellar career, he was named All-OVC and Defensive Player of the Year in 1967 and 1968 and was named to the Little All-American Team in 1968. He set two records while playing, one a team-record 54-yard fumble return for a touchdown and an OVC-record nine interceptions the same year. He was elected to the ETSU Hall of Fame in 1976. (Photograph courtesy Buc Football and Friends Foundation.)

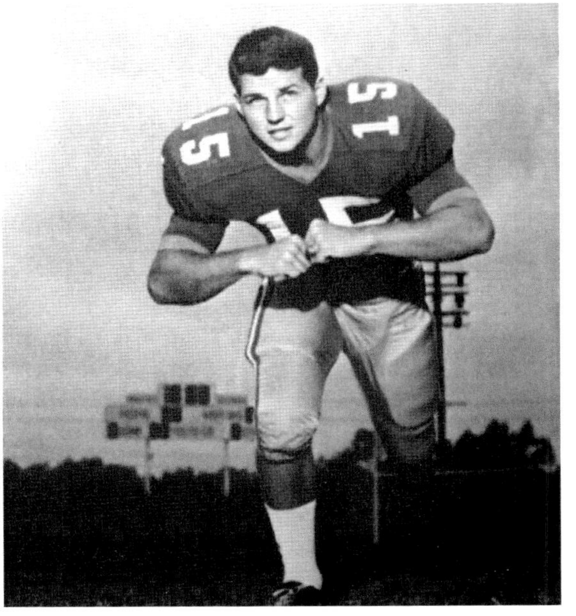

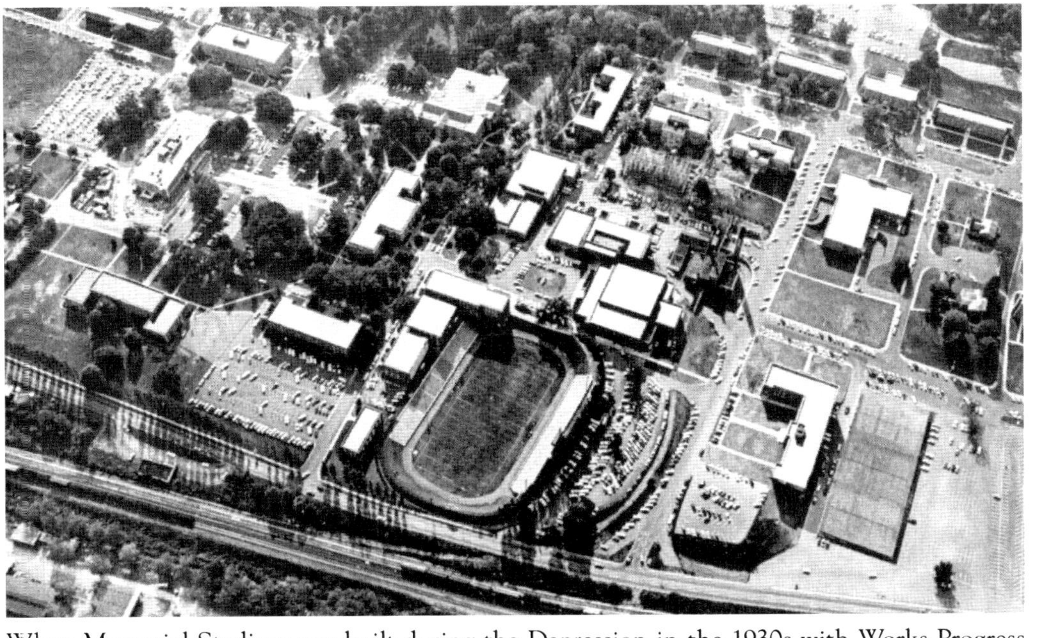

When Memorial Stadium was built during the Depression in the 1930s with Works Progress Administration funds, it seated 1,200 people. Postwar enrollment and new enthusiasm for football encouraged President Sherrod to enlarge the stadium in 1948. For the next 20-plus years, until its demolition in 1973, there were few improvements, unless need necessitated them, such as when the press box was accidentally burned to the ground by some of the coaches' sons. This photograph from around 1968 shows the stadium much as it looked upon its demise. (Photograph courtesy Buc Football and Friends Foundation.)

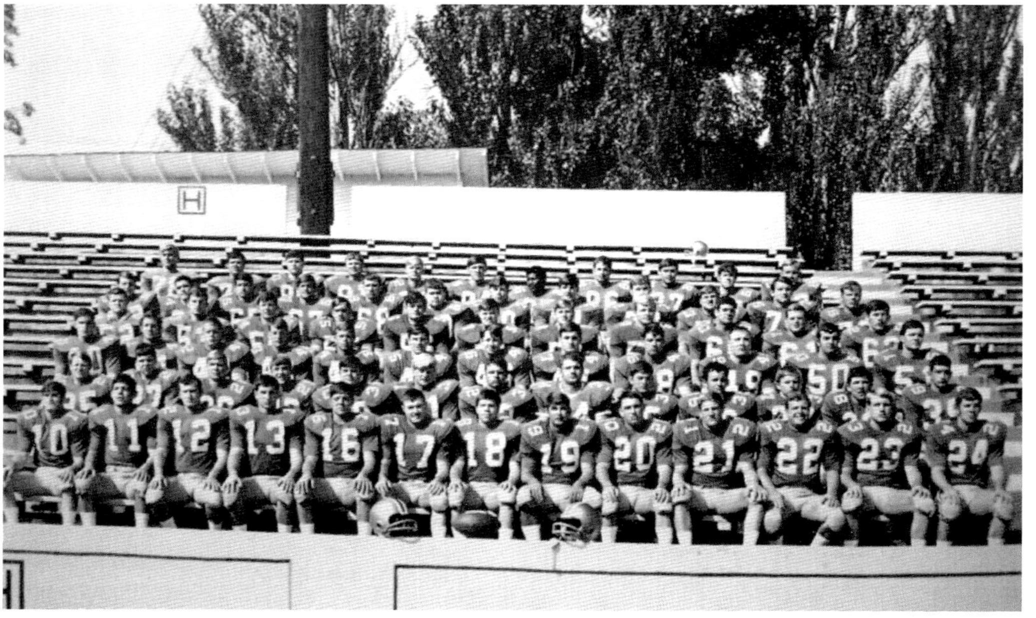

No team before or since the 1969 season has been close to recording 10 wins and no losses. This was the first time since 1962 the Big Blue won the conference title. Five of the "hardrocks" defense—Bill Casey (10), captain Al Guy (43), Doug Linebarger (71), Ron Mendheim (89), and Frank Patterson (79)—were named to the All-OVC team. On the offense, Ronnie Harrold (31) and John Walton (50) were also honored. (Photograph courtesy Buc Football and Friends Foundation.)

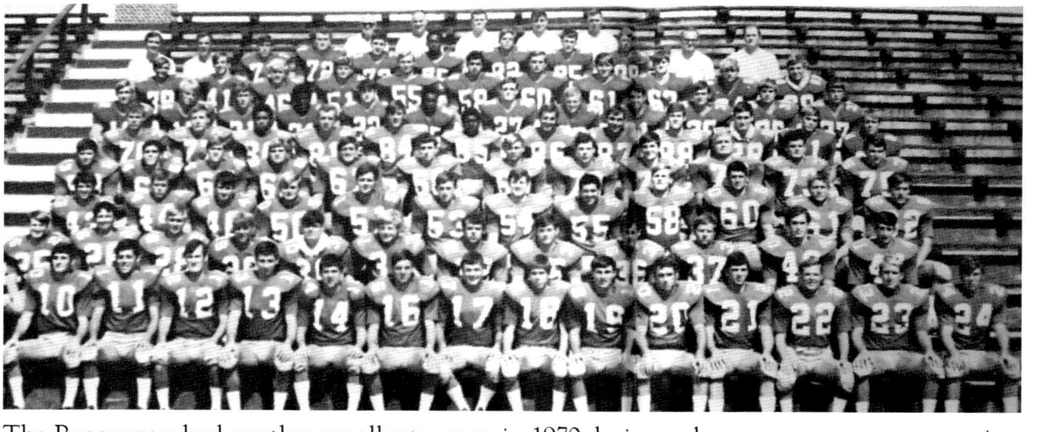

The Buccaneers had another excellent season in 1970, losing only one game versus seven wins, but two ties placed the Bucs third in the OVC with a 4-1-2 record. One of their tie games was with eventual conference champion Western Kentucky (10-10). Individually Larry Graham (16) was named Offense Player of the Year and was one of five Bucs—with defensive back Bill Casey (10), center Greg Chesnutt (64), offensive tackle David Wade (74), and defensive end Willie Bush (85)—named to the All-Conference squad. (Photograph courtesy Buc Football and Friends Foundation.)

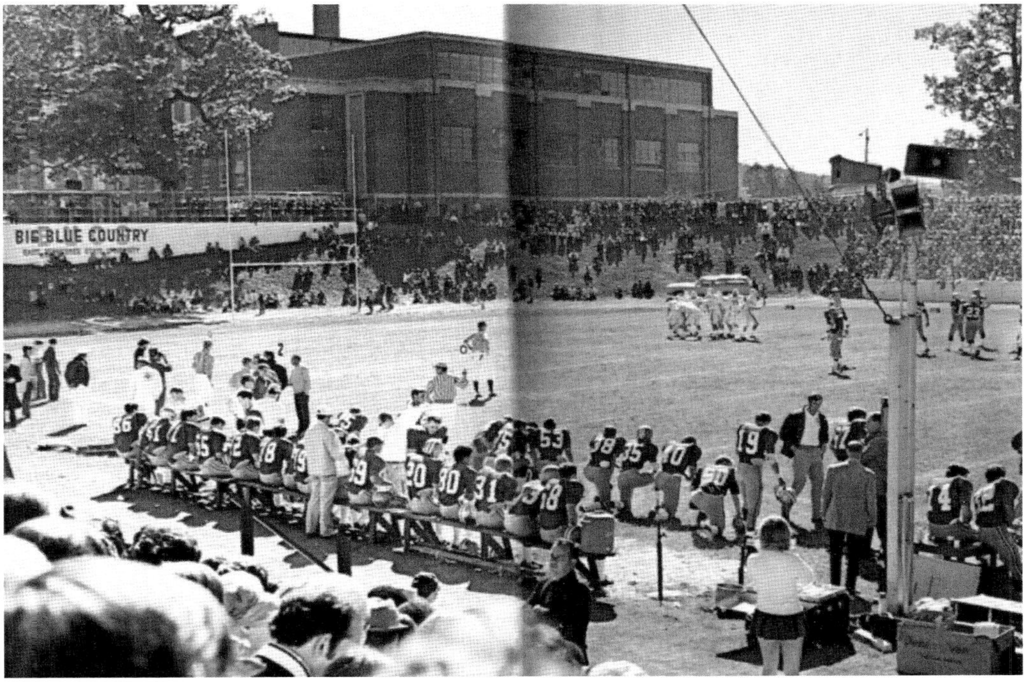

All the elements of Big Blue football in the late 1960s and early 1970s are visible in this c. 1970 photograph: a crowded stadium full of fans with standing room only, cheerleaders, trainers, team managers, coaches, players, and referees. This photograph was so representative of Buc football that it was used in the school yearbook and student recruiting material distributed by the university to prospective students. (Photograph courtesy Buc Football and Friends Foundation.)

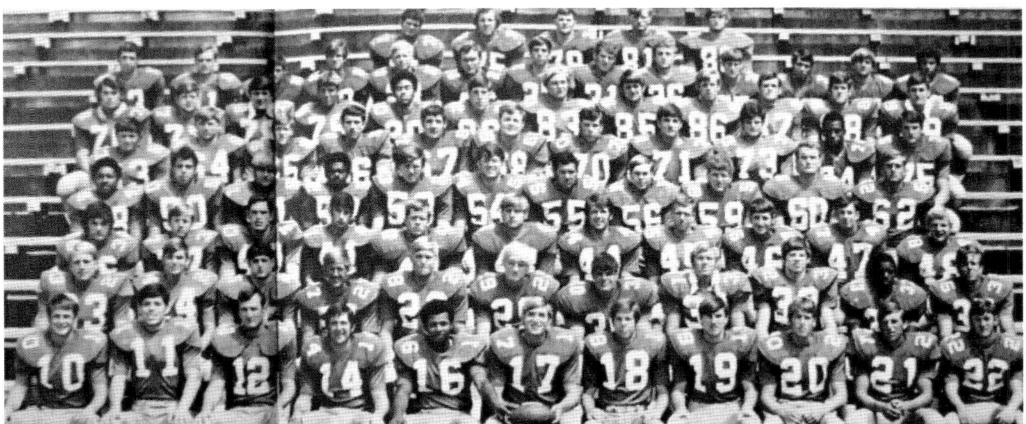

A perfect season in reverse was realized in 1971 as the Buccaneers went winless. Their 0-9-1 record was a mirror image of their final regular-season record in 1969, placing them eighth in the conference. The Bucs only scored 84 points on the season, and their only non-loss was a 6-6 home tie with Murray State. None of the players made conference honors for the year. (Photograph courtesy Buc Football and Friends Foundation.)

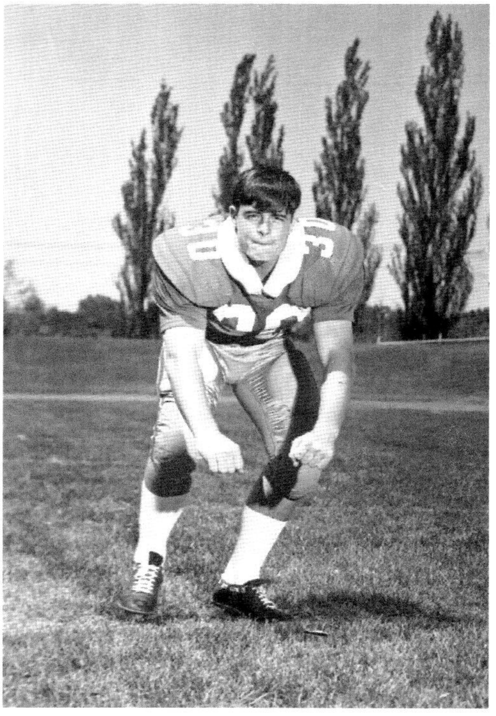

Other than defensive back Bill Casey and linebacker Mike Roberts (pictured), the 1970s were lean years for All-American candidates. Roberts made Little All-American as a linebacker in 1971. Casey was a holdover from the 1969 team, and he followed up his 11-interception season in 1969 with four in 1970 and an All-American nomination. (Photograph courtesy of L. T. Helton.)

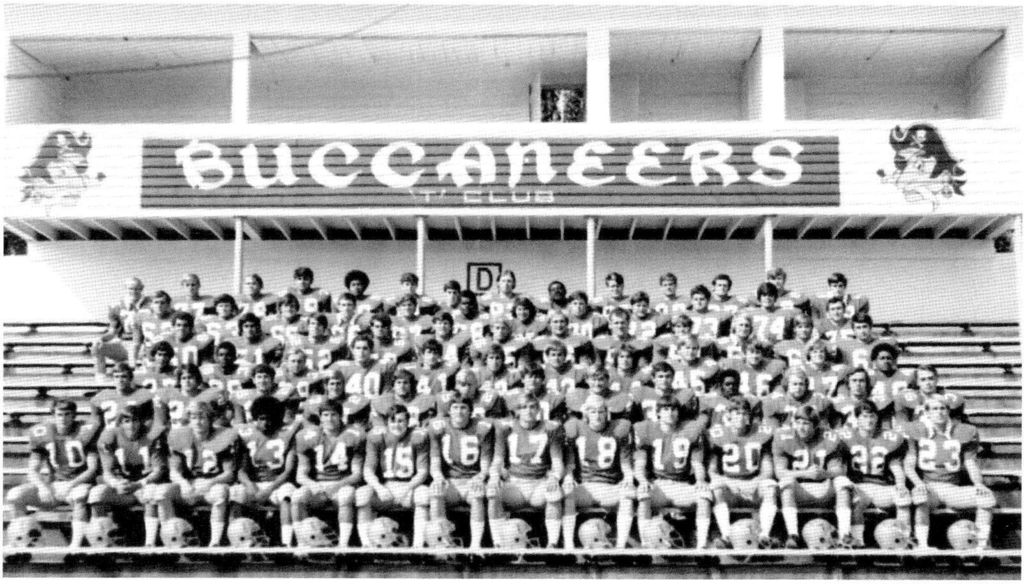

Coach Bell's last season leading the team ended much like his first with three wins (only two in conference) and a seventh-place OVC finish in 1972. This was also the last year of play in Memorial Stadium, also known as "Big Blue Country," the Bucs' home since 1936. In its place, construction of the domed stadium championed by Coach Bell and Solon Gentry was begun. (Photograph courtesy of ETSU Photo Lab.)

When coach Roy Frazier, a former All-OVC center and assistant coach at State, became head coach, he promised to create an interesting and aggressive style of football. He led the team for five seasons from 1973 through 1977, compiling a 16-36-2 record for the lowest winning percentage of any coach with five or more seasons at the helm. After leaving the team, he went on to run successful businesses in Johnson City, Tennessee, and Hendersonville, North Carolina, until his death in 2002. (Photograph courtesy Buc Football and Friends Foundation.)

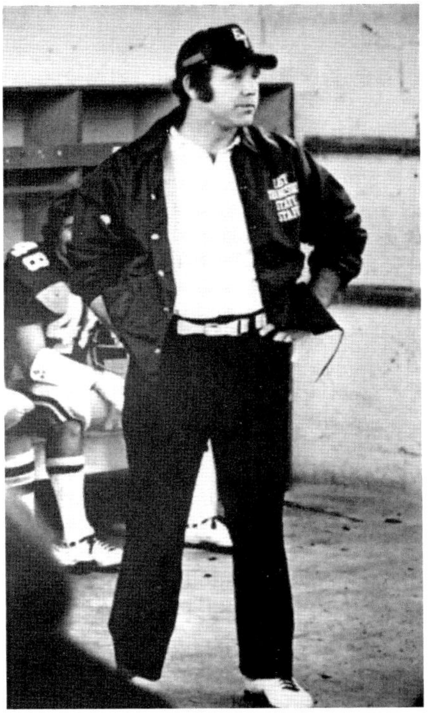

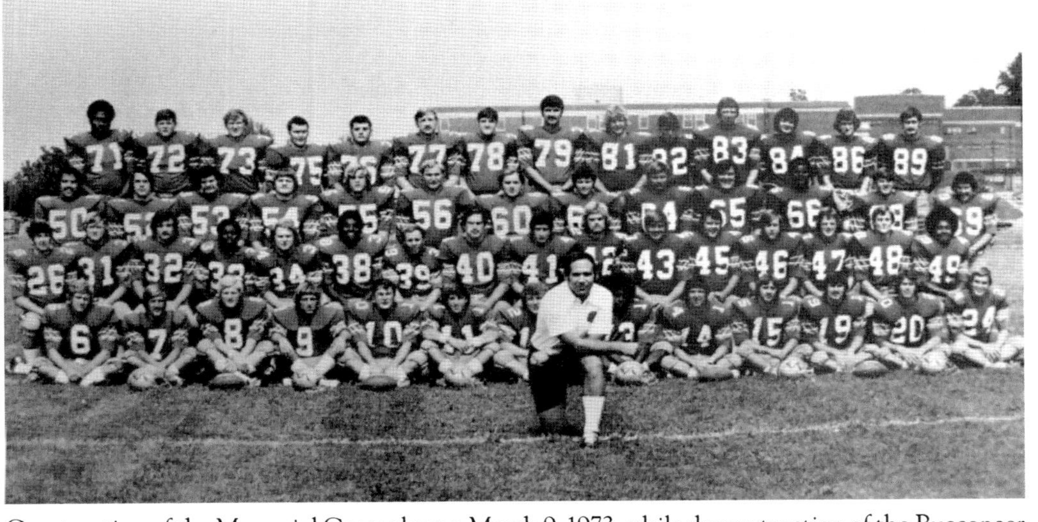

Construction of the Memorial Center began March 9, 1973, while deconstruction of the Buccaneer football team began with the first game, a 52-29 loss to Carson Newman. Former player Roy Frazier took over the mantle of head coach with similar results to the previous year. The team went 4-7 overall and 3-4 in the OVC and tied for fifth in the conference. The Bucs would share facilities with Science Hill at Roosevelt Stadium until completion of the "Mini-Dome." Quarterback Alan Chadwick was named OVC Offensive Player of the Year and made the All-Conference team along with defensive end Jeff Williamson. (Photograph courtesy Buc Football and Friends Foundation.)

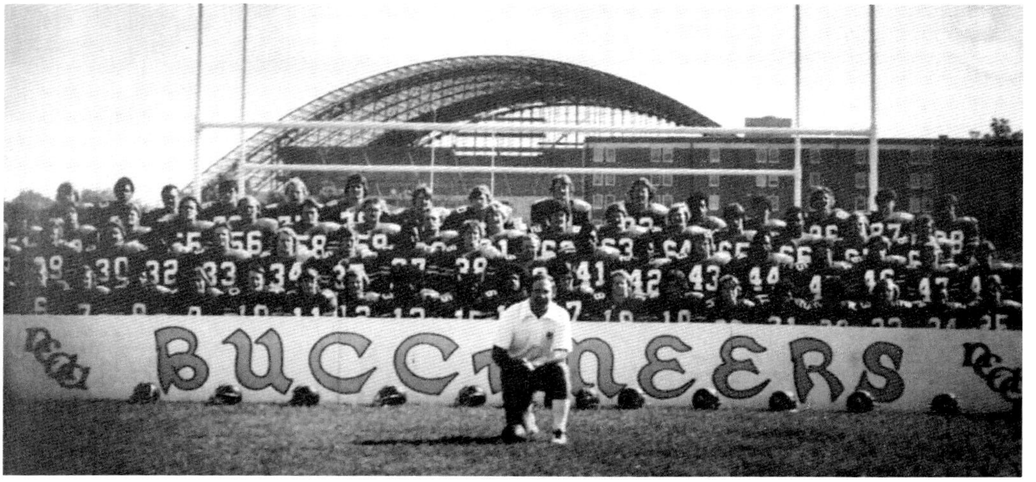

As the Dome era loomed, the Buccaneers finished another four-win season and fifth-place finish in the OVC in 1974. At 4-6-1 and 3-3-1 in the OVC, this would be the highwater mark for the Frazier era. Their lone All-Conference representative was defensive back Peppy McCary. (Photograph courtesy Buc Football and Friends Foundation.)

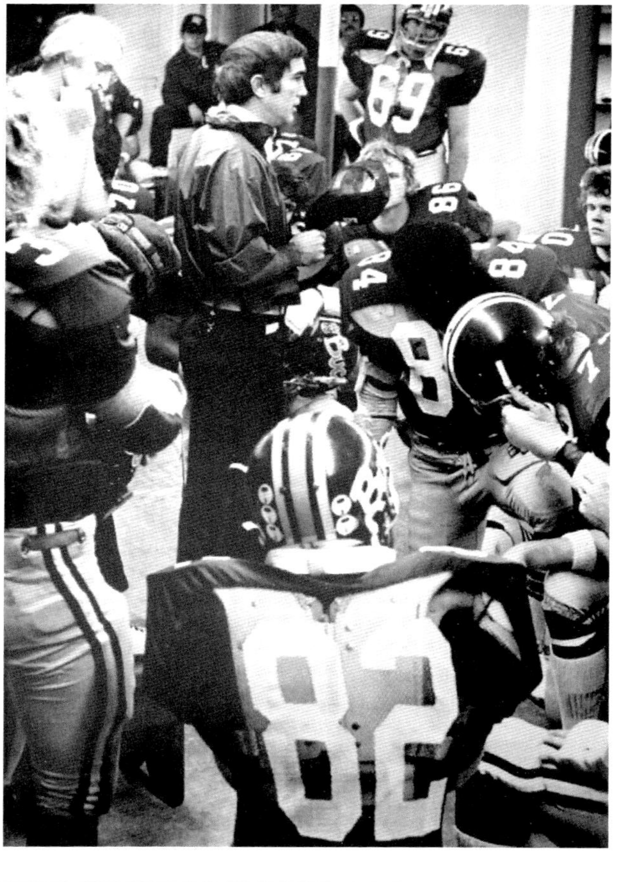

Despite losing only seven starters from the previous season, the 1975 Buccaneers had a rough season, finishing at 2-8-1 and in seventh place in the OVC at 1-5-1. Linebacker Pee Wee Brown was named to the All-OVC team. Pictured at left are coach Tommy Hundley (center) and coach L. T. Helton (far left), emphasizing the importance of concentration on the field. (Photograph courtesy Buc Football and Friends Foundation.)

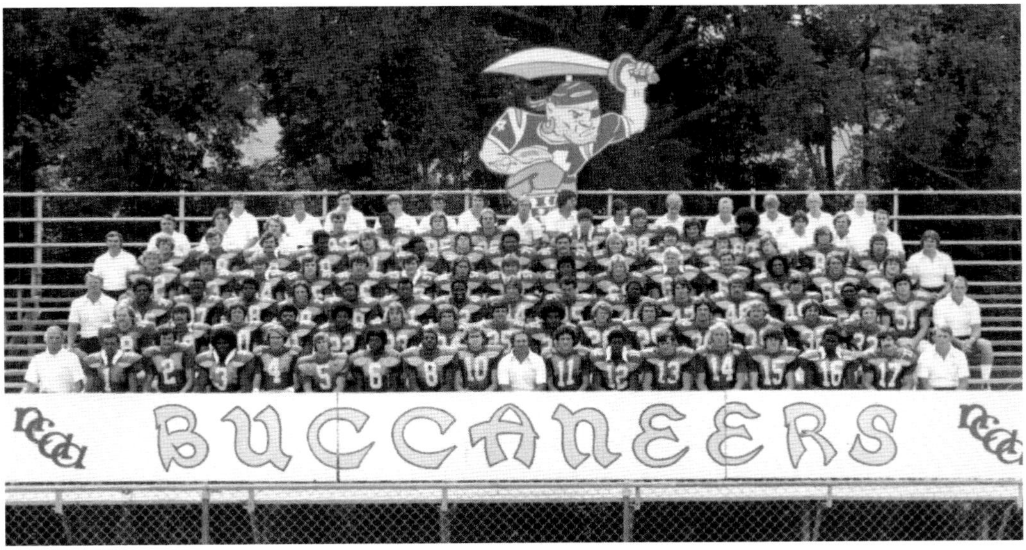

Not since 1969 was there excitement on the campus for Buc football. After beating top-ranked Tennessee Tech in the mud 18-7, the Buccaneers were 3-1 in the OVC and tied for second. The rest of 1976 would not go so well, with the team finishing 3-7 and in sixth place in the conference. (Photograph courtesy Buc Football and Friends Foundation.)

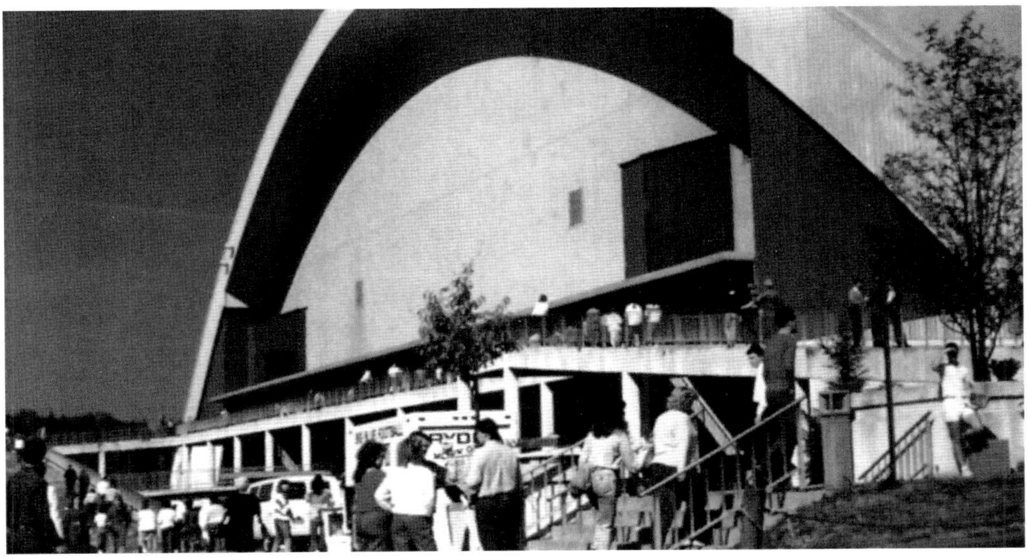

Memorial Center, better known as the "Mini-Dome" or "Dome," was based on a domed facility in Pocatello, Idaho. The Dome was constructed at a cost of about $8 million between 1973 and 1975, but the Bucs could not play in the facility until 1977 because of leaks in the roof. An effort to cut costs of the facility after Coach Bell retired shrank the sideline width, diminishing the view of the sidelines during football games. The mini-sizing of the "Mini-Dome" resulted in a stadium that was not fan friendly for football, and attendance declined. (Photograph courtesy Buc Football and Friends Foundation.)

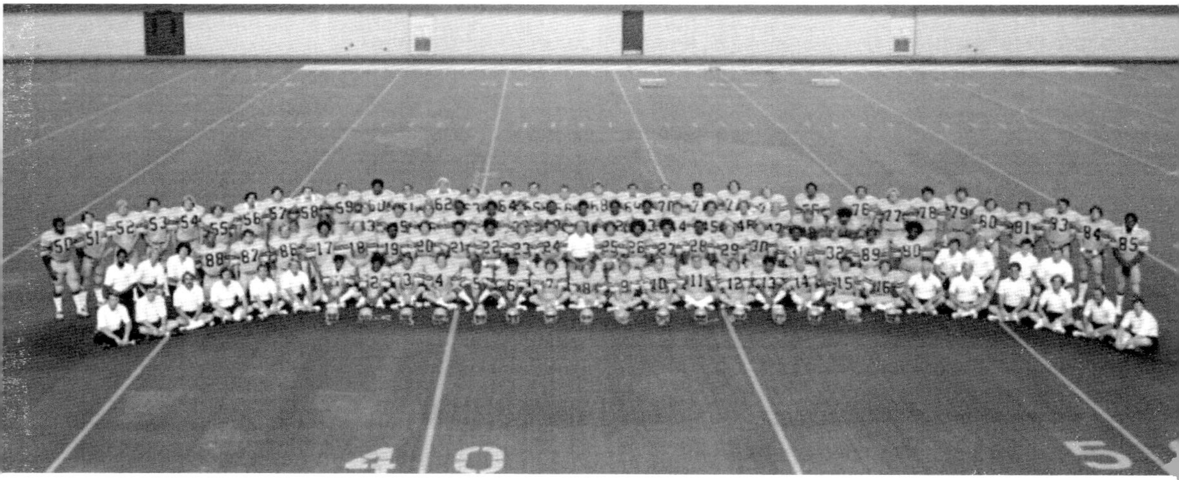

Frazier's last year was also the last year for the Buccaneers as a member of the OVC. It also marked the first year of play in the Mini-Dome. Despite the new state-of-the-art surroundings, the Bucs finished the 1977 season 3-8 overall and 2-5 in the OVC. The team's last All-OVC performer was wide receiver Dennis Law, who finished the year with 33 receptions for 488 yards and 4 touchdowns. (Photograph courtesy of ETSU Photo Lab.)

4

Southern Conference Comfort

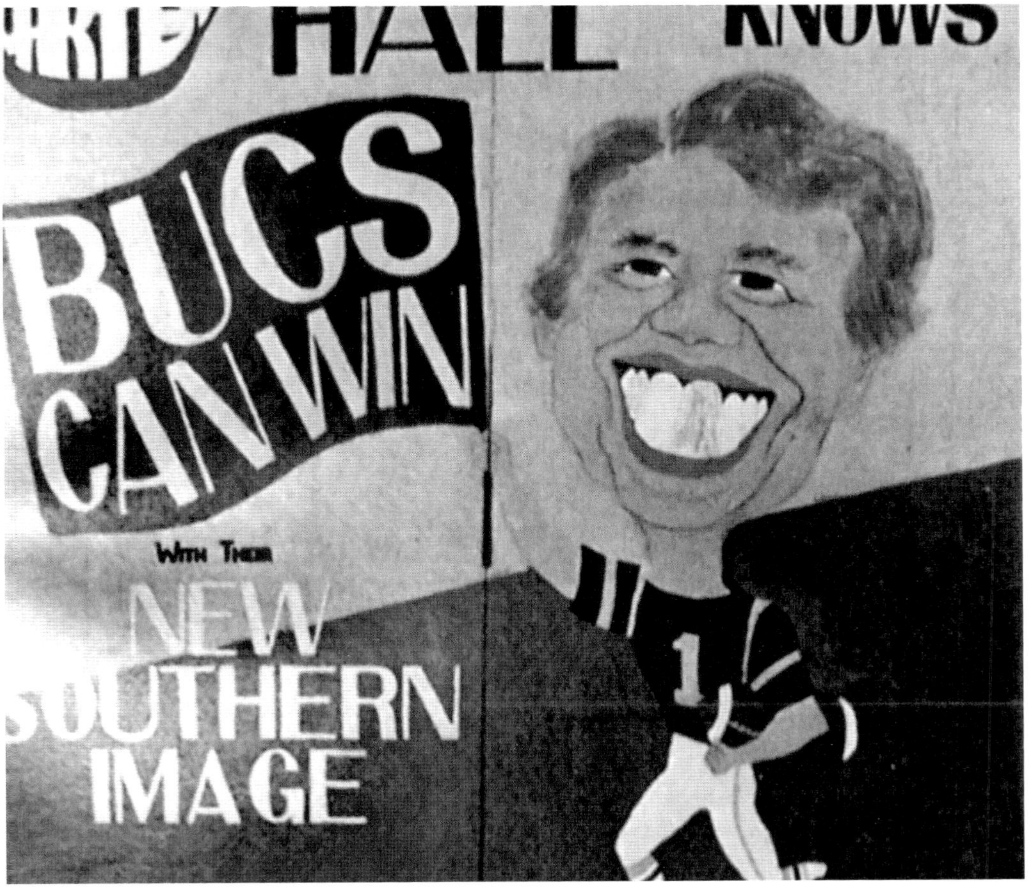

ETSU became the ninth member of the Southern Conference on July 1, 1978, after 21 years in the OVC. The move also marked the team's transition to Division I-A, but this would be short-lived when the conference was designated as I-AA in 1981. Since that time, the SoCon has been the premiere I-AA conference in football. When formed in 1921, the 23-team conference was tops, but many teams would leave as core members of the SEC (1932) and ACC (1953). (Photograph courtesy Buc Football and Friends Foundation.)

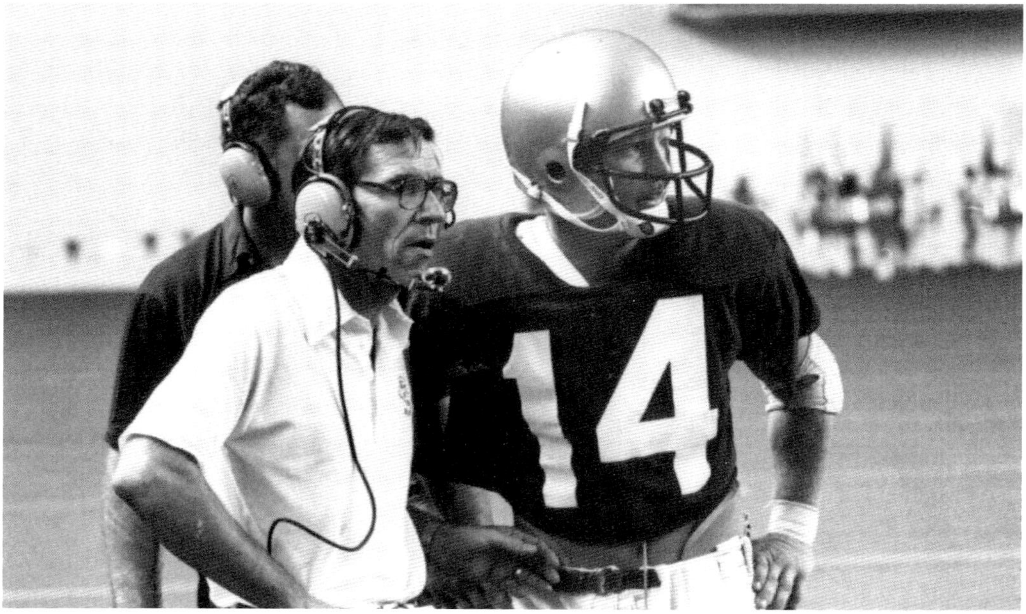

Jack Carlisle (with Mark Hutsell) took over as head coach of the Bucs after the final game of the 1977 season. He was lauded as a winner from Mississippi who would restore the sagging fortunes of ETSU football, but in his five years at State, 1978–1982, he compiled a 21-34 record. After leaving, he went back to coaching high school football and was inducted into the Mississippi Sports Hall of Fame in 2004. (Photograph courtesy of ETSU Photo Lab.)

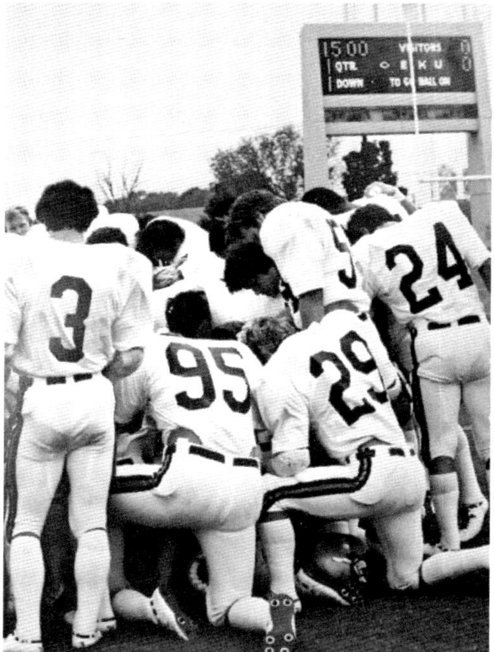

Excitement was in the air prior to the 1978 season. Having completed their first season at Memorial Center, getting a new coach, and being accepted into the Southern Conference as a I-A program were good reasons to herald a new era for the Buccaneers. However, the Bucs would play an OVC schedule and be considered an independent ineligible for conference championships until 1979. Newfound hope for the program would soon be dashed amid myriad injuries and a four-game skid to start the season. (Photograph courtesy Buc Football and Friends Foundation.)

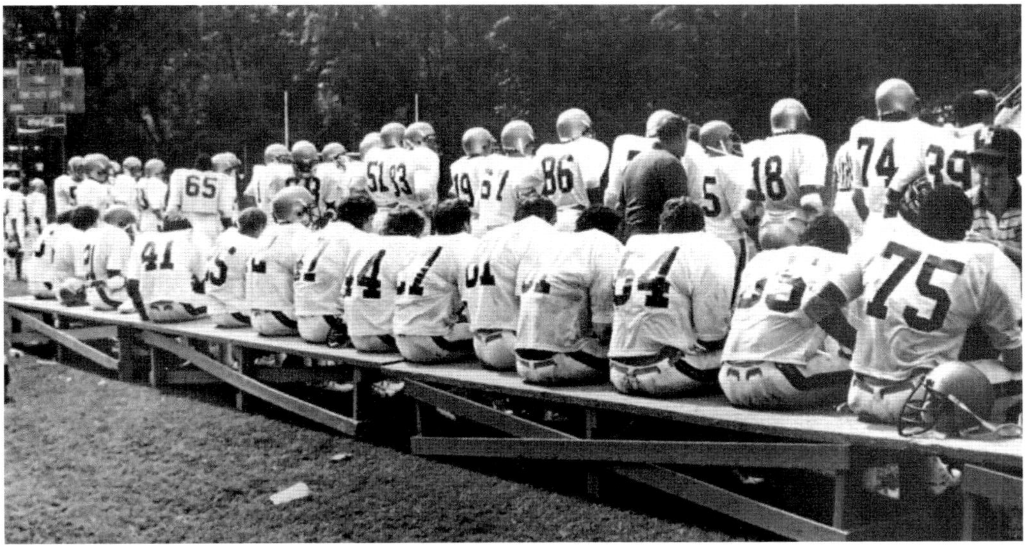

Turning their backs on their losing ways, the 1979 edition of the Buccaneers posted a 7-4 record for their first winning season since 1970. However, they were only 2-3 in conference play, good for only sixth place (of nine) in their first year of play in the Southern Conference. The overall strong team performance resulted in a number of team records being set (most points, most total yards) and All-Conference accolades for quarterback Mark Hutsell and defensive back Jay Megna. (Photograph courtesy Buc Football and Friends Foundation.)

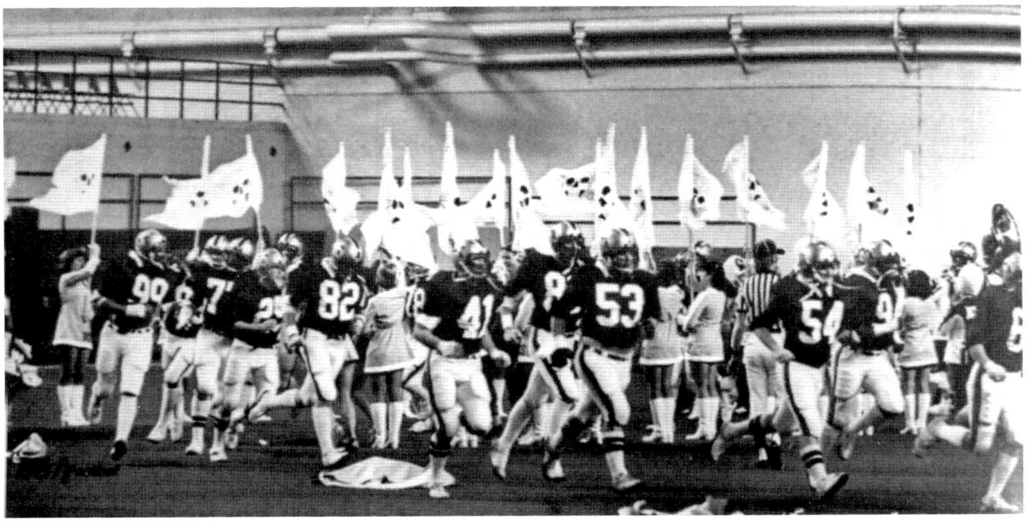

The loss of experienced players to graduation doomed the Bucs to an ugly rebuilding year and a final record of 2-9 (1-4 in the SoCon) in 1980. The loss to Wofford 9-16 in the first game of the season seemed to crush the team's spirit, causing a losing spiral that would not be corrected until the ninth game of the season, a 28-23 victory against James Madison. Their season-ending victory of 21-16 versus Marshall University would give some indication of things to come the following year. (Photograph courtesy Buc Football and Friends Foundation.)

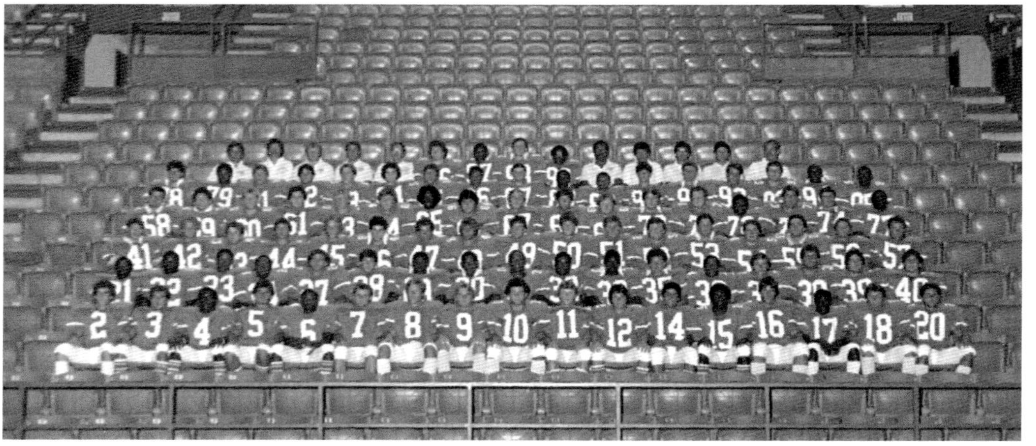

Big Blue had 34 letterman returning in 1981, eighteen on offense and 16 on defense, with a good recruiting campaign to bolster their expectations for the season. A lack of experience on the defensive line coupled with injury issues at secondary made the defense the biggest question mark, but the quarterbacks were unknown quantities as well, as they had little playing time coming into the season. The end result was a 6-5 season and a third-place finish (4-2) in the SoCon. Donnie Cook (10) stepped up in the secondary, answering questions about his ability to come back from injury by making the All-Conference squad. (Photograph courtesy of ETSU Photo Lab.)

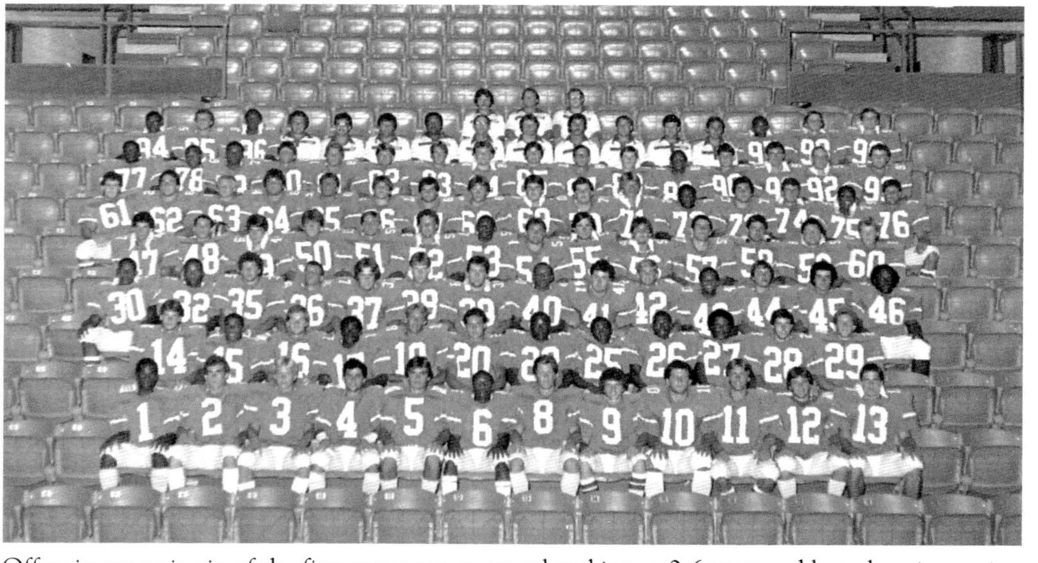

Offensive woes in six of the first seven games translated into a 0-6 start and last place in scoring nationally for part of that season. After losing the eighth game of the season, the firing of Coach Carlisle was announced. A 3-0 victory against the Citadel Bulldogs and a 28-0 pasting of the Marshall Thundering Herd left the Bucs at 2-9 for the 1982 season and in seventh place in the conference at 2-5. Bright spots for the year were Donnie Cook's selection to the All-Conference and All-American Teams and the strong offensive showing by Jerry Butler. (Photograph courtesy of ETSU Photo Lab.)

Dennie Cook, a strong safety, played his entire career (1979–1982) at ETSU under Coach Carlisle. During that time, he earned All-Southern Conference accolades twice, 1981–1982, and was considered the best strong safety in the SoCon for 1982, the same year he made All-American. He was team cocaptain and led the Bucs in interceptions his junior and senior seasons. After graduation in 1985, he started a successful career in business. (Photograph courtesy Buc Football and Friends Foundation.)

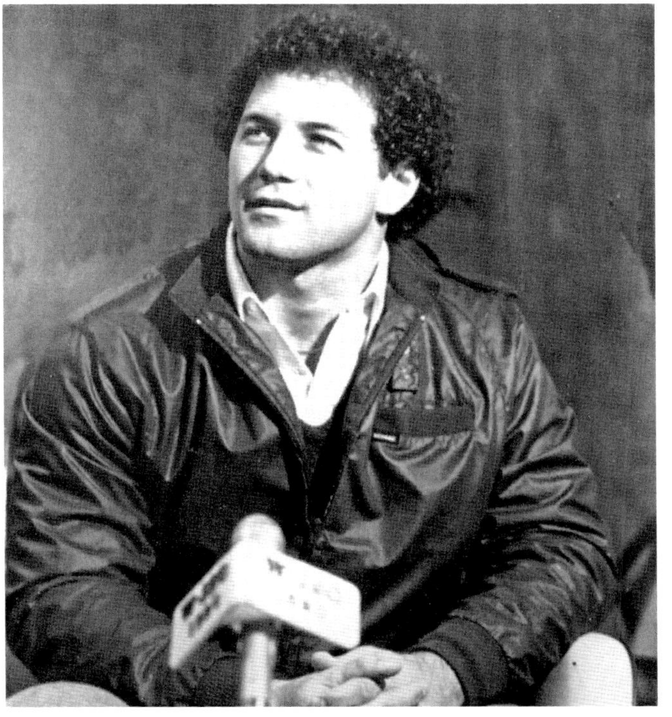

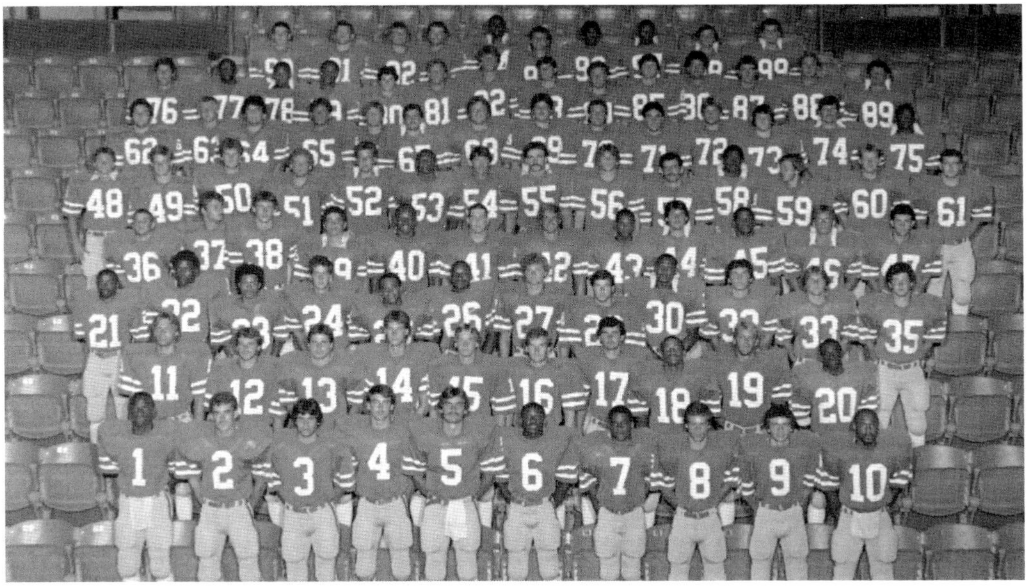

Another new beginning for the 1983 Buccaneers ended in a familiar way with a 3-8 record and a seventh-place (1-6) conference finish. New coach George F. "Buddy" Sasser finished with just one more win than the previous year, yet the team kept things tight in a number of games with tough opponents. Their lone conference win was a 45-0 smashing of the Citadel. (Photograph courtesy of ETSU Photo Lab.)

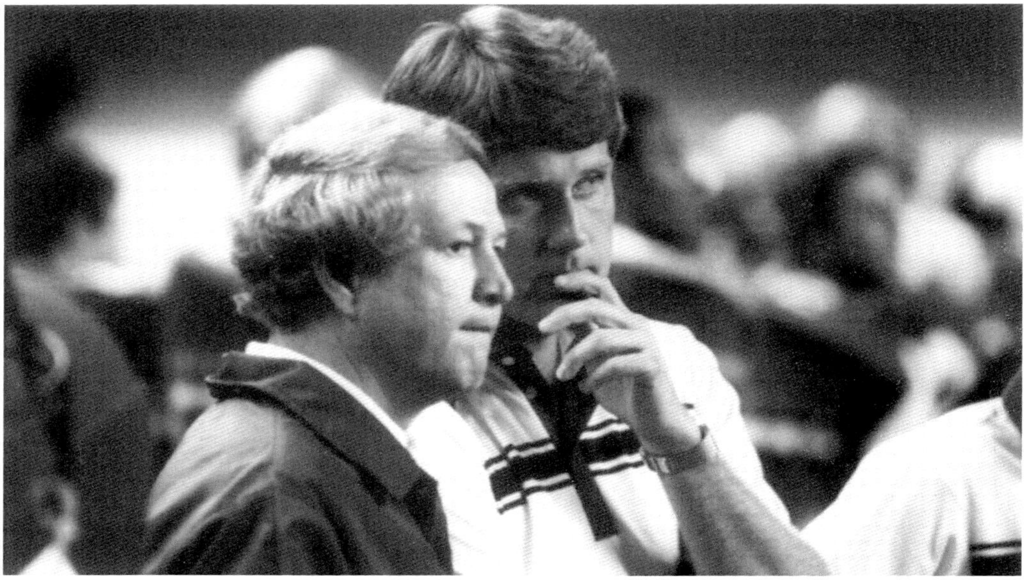

Buddy Sasser (left) started his reign as head coach December 1982. Over two seasons (1983–1984), he guided the team to a 9-13 mark. From 1984 to 1986, he served as athletic director. Prior to coaching the Buccaneers, he was the head coach at former rival Wofford College, where he turned the Terriers into an NAIA powerhouse with national rankings three of the six years he coached there. (Photograph courtesy Buc Football and Friends Foundation.)

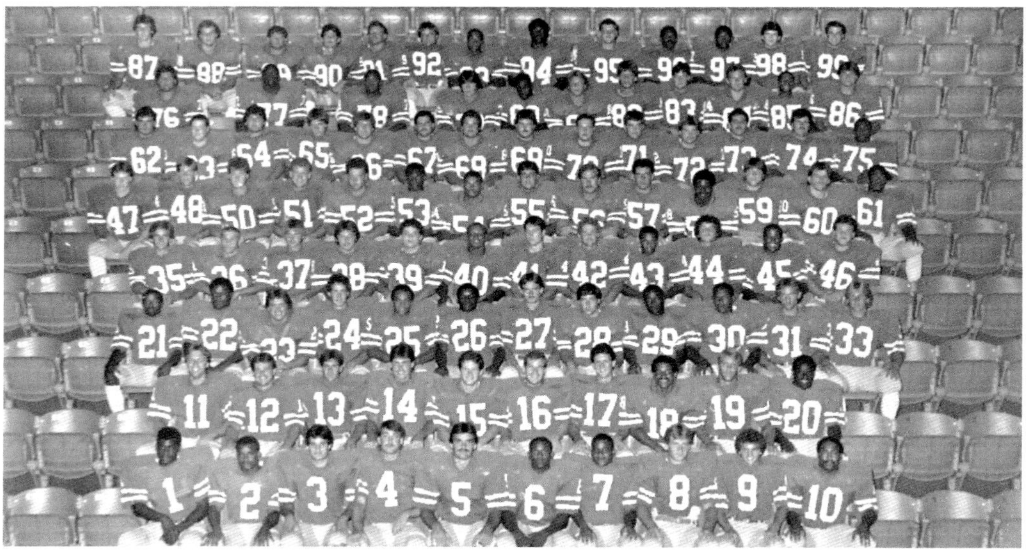

The school's annual summed up the 1984 campaign as "A Bucced Up Season." The team improved to 6-5 but only won two conference games, finishing tied for fifth place. The year started with wins in four of the first five games, bringing the Buccaneer "Blue Thunder" their first NCAA Division I-AA ranking. But things went south from that point on with only two wins out of the final six games; neither win was against a conference foe. (Photograph courtesy of ETSU Photo Lab.)

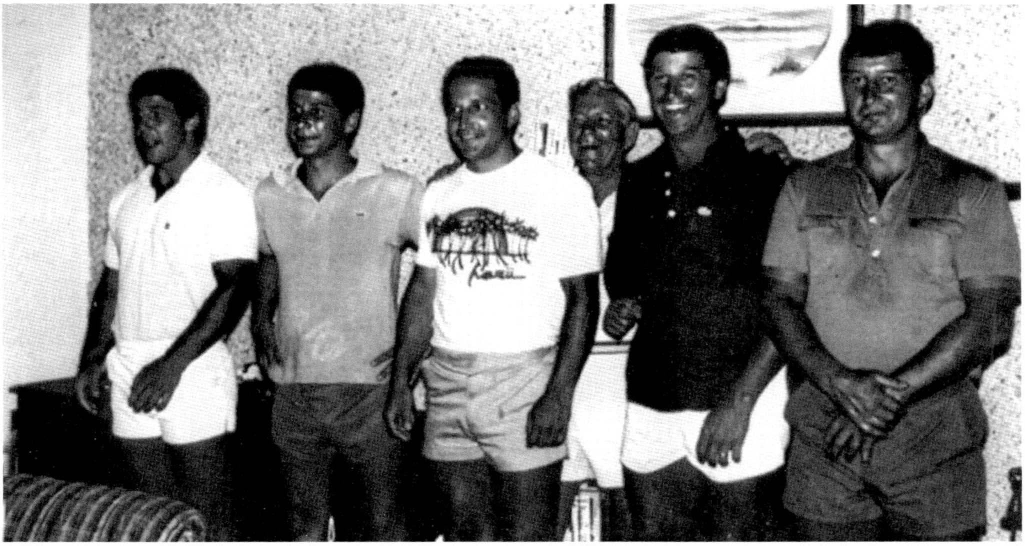

The Big Blue football program celebrated the end of the Trawick era in 1984 when Guy, the last of five brothers, played his final season for the Buccaneers. Starting in 1969 with Bill, the ETSU football team had a Trawick brother playing for 16 consecutive seasons. In between the oldest and youngest, Lee, Steve, and Don played. All but Steve, who served as starting quarterback for most of his four years, played defensive back. (Photograph courtesy Buc Football and Friends Foundation.)

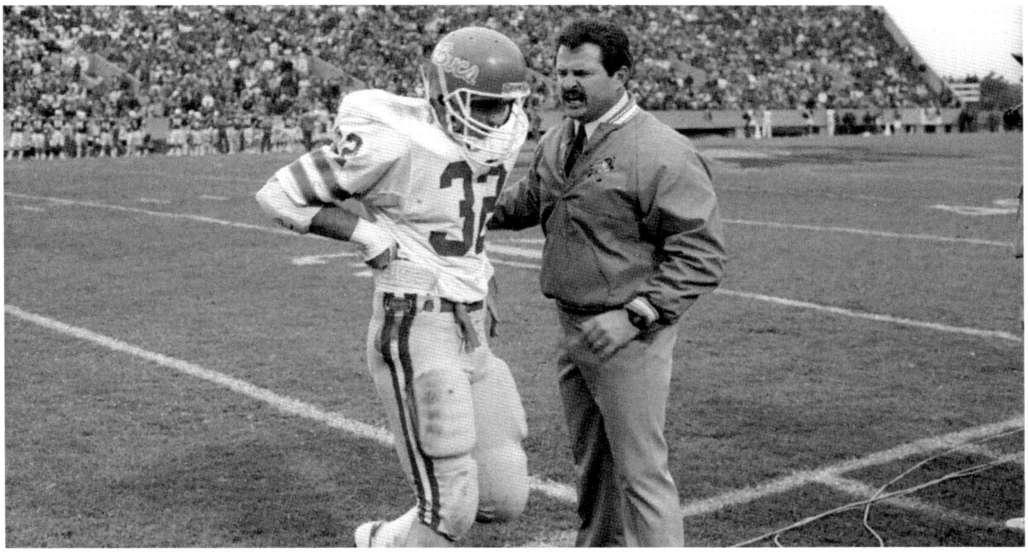

Coach Mike Ayers was promoted from within when newly appointed athletic director Buddy Sasser gave up the job July 12, 1985. Ayers came over with Coach Sasser from Wofford where he also served as defensive coordinator. As 12th head coach of the Buccaneers, Ayers, known as an excellent recruiter with contacts throughout the South and Midwest, lasted three years (1985–1987) and compiled an 11-21-1 record and a .348 winning percentage. Ayers left State to take the head coach position at Wofford. (Photograph courtesy of ETSU Photo Lab.)

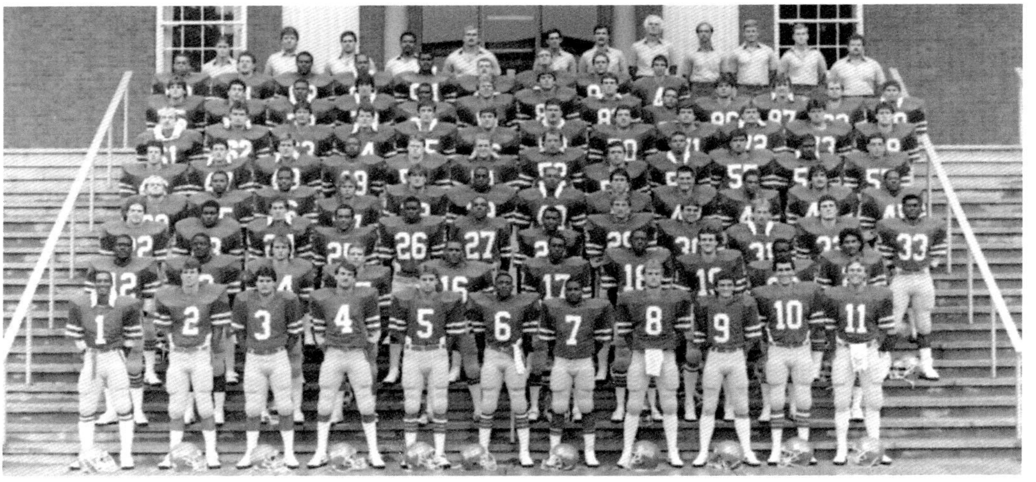

Despite 35 returning lettermen and veterans in every position on offense and welcoming back offensive coordinator L. T. Helton in 1985, the Big Blue had trouble scoring and finished their third winless season 0-10-1. The year would also mark their first time in last place in the Southern Conference. All but three of the games were close, but when the Bucs scored a lot of points, so did their opponents. Individually punter George Cimadevilla (3) garnered All-Conference and All-American honors. (Photograph courtesy of ETSU Photo Lab.)

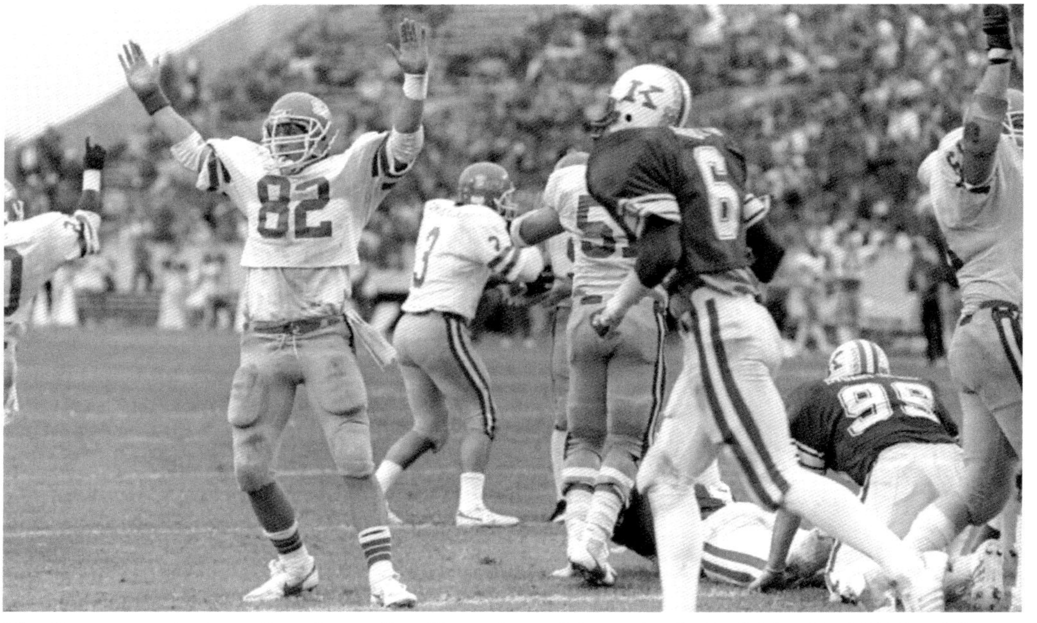

The Buccaneers had another close call in Kentucky on November 2, 1985. Tom Dodd (82) celebrates the Herbie Campbell extra point for a 13-10 third-quarter lead against Kentucky. The Bucs would lose the lead and the game in the fourth quarter as the Wildcats reeled off 13 unanswered points to win the game 23-13. All-American punter George Cimadevilla (3), who would hold the ball for extra points, can be seen in the background. (Photograph courtesy of ETSU Photo Lab.)

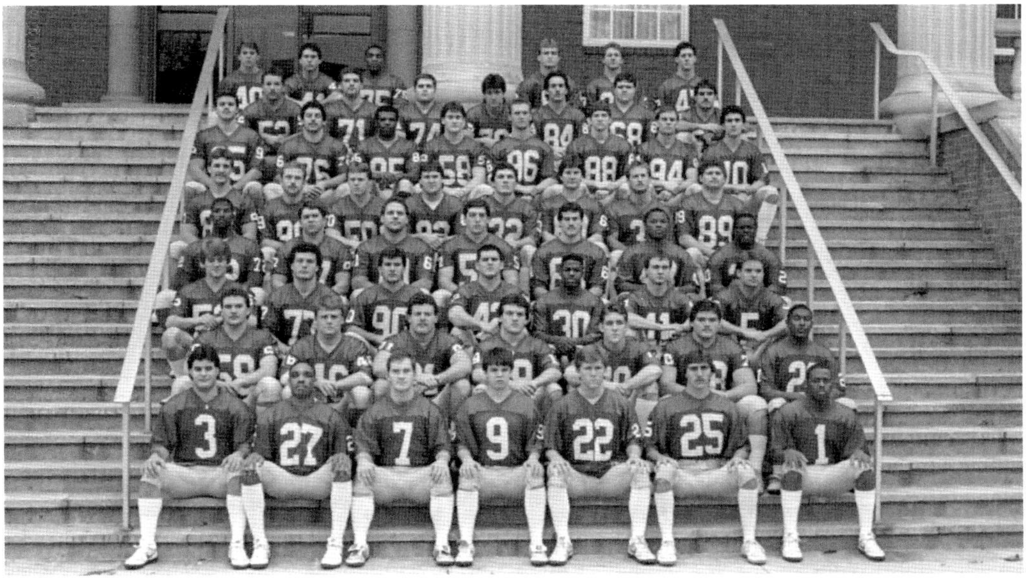

After a disappointing season of turnovers and lost opportunities, Coach Ayers's team turned things around in 1986, finishing fourth in the conference (4-3) with an overall record of 6-5. The rebound was due in large part to an experienced offensive line that created opportunities for running back Herman Jacobs, quarterback Jeff Morgan, and All-American punting by George Cimadevilla (Associated Press or AP first team) to maintain field position. (Photograph courtesy of ETSU Photo Lab.)

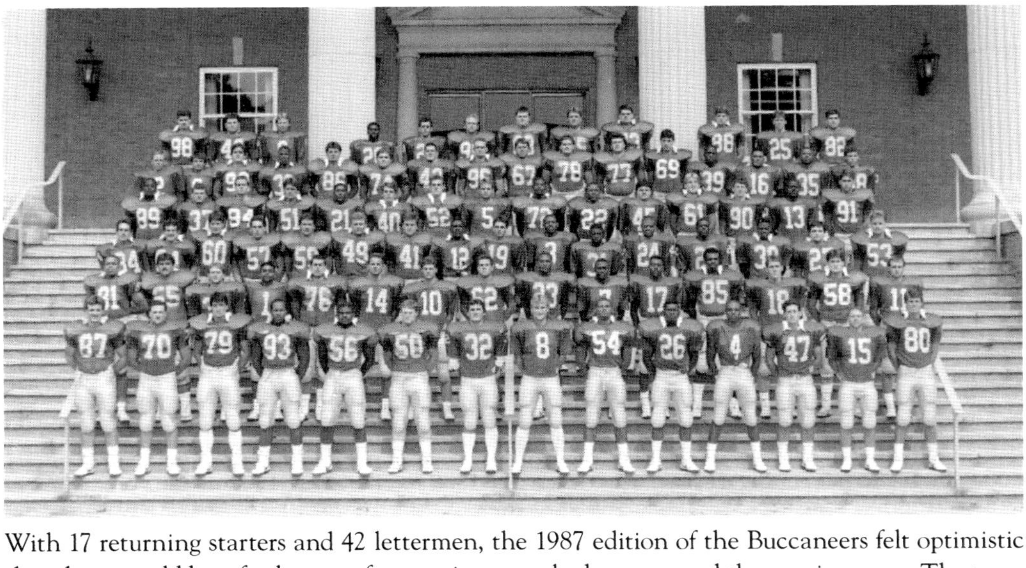

With 17 returning starters and 42 lettermen, the 1987 edition of the Buccaneers felt optimistic that there would be a fresh start after posting a marked turnaround the previous year. The team opened the year with three wins but then quickly matched that with three losses and then traded wins and losses until ending the season with a two-game skid. They finished the year 5-6, with a 2-5, seventh-place conference finish. (Photograph courtesy of ETSU Photo Lab.)

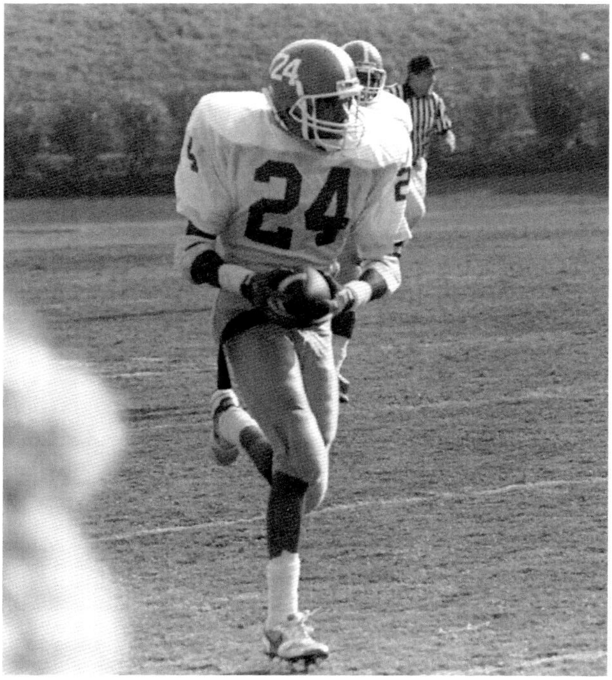

An unexpected victory lifted Buccaneer spirits when the Bucs traveled to Raleigh, North Carolina, to take on the North Carolina State Wolfpack. The Bucs beat the Wolfpack 24-19 with the back-breaking play coming on a Rick Harris (24) interception, which he returned 56 yards for a touchdown. The play was indicative of Harris's year, in which the defensive back was named to the Sports Net All-American first team. (Photograph courtesy of ETSU Photo Lab.)

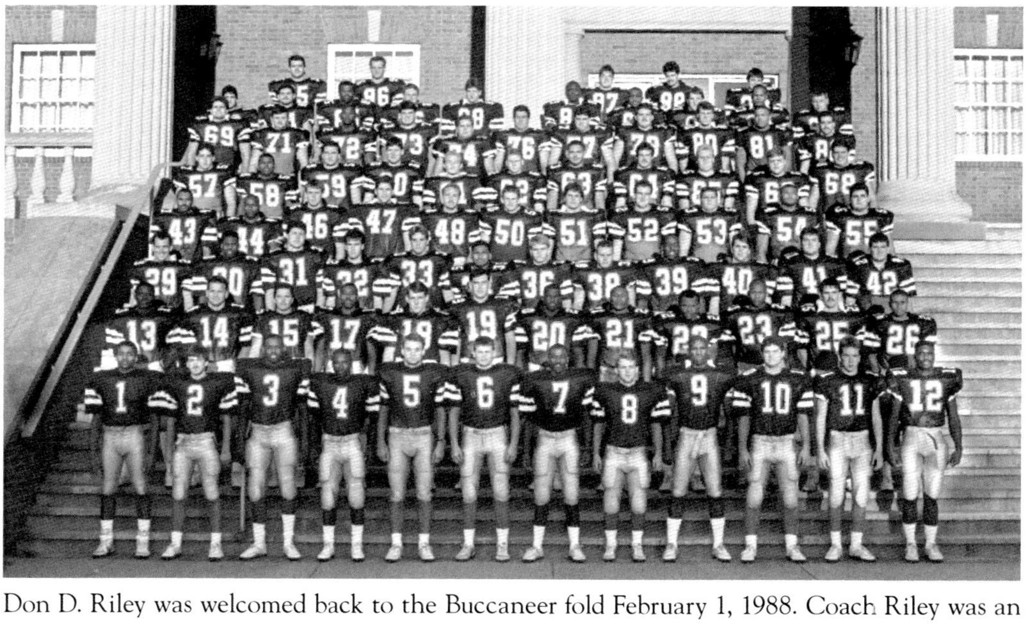

Don D. Riley was welcomed back to the Buccaneer fold February 1, 1988. Coach Riley was an ETSC player and graduate in 1956. He went on to coach high school in Greenville, Tennessee, and then on to Oklahoma State University and Vanderbilt prior to joining UCLA as line coach in 1976. During his time with the Bruins, they won three Rose Bowls (1983, 1984, and 1986). It was from that last position at UCLA that he left to take over at his alma mater where he went 10-34 from 1988–1991. (Photograph courtesy of ETSU Photo Lab.)

New coach Don Riley inherited a tough schedule that included North Carolina State again as well as tough division foes, including eventual 1988 cochampions Marshall and Furman. The season started well with wins against VMI and Wofford, led by former Buc coach Mike Ayers, but the Bucs' luck ran out as they lost the next seven games by a combined score of 287-88. Their final victory came against Davidson, and the Bucs ended the season 3-8 and tied for seventh place in the conference. (Photograph courtesy of ETSU Photo Lab.)

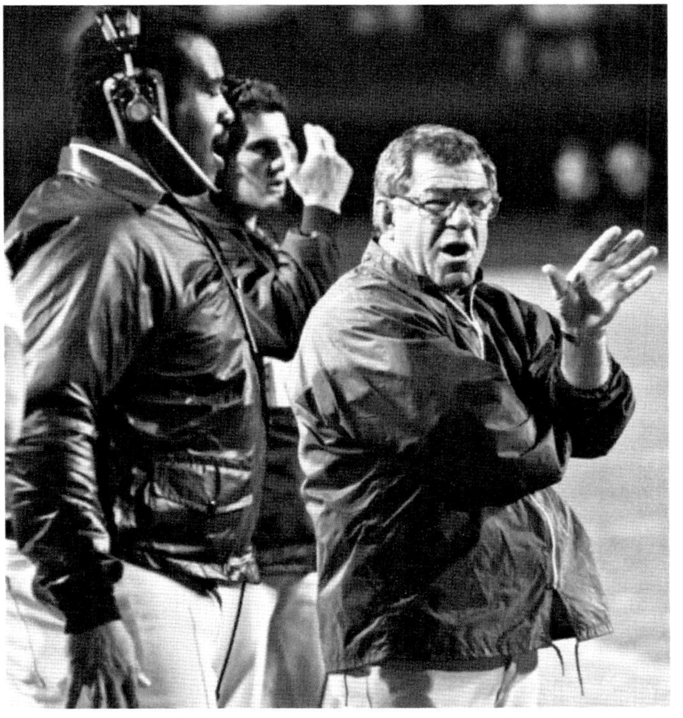

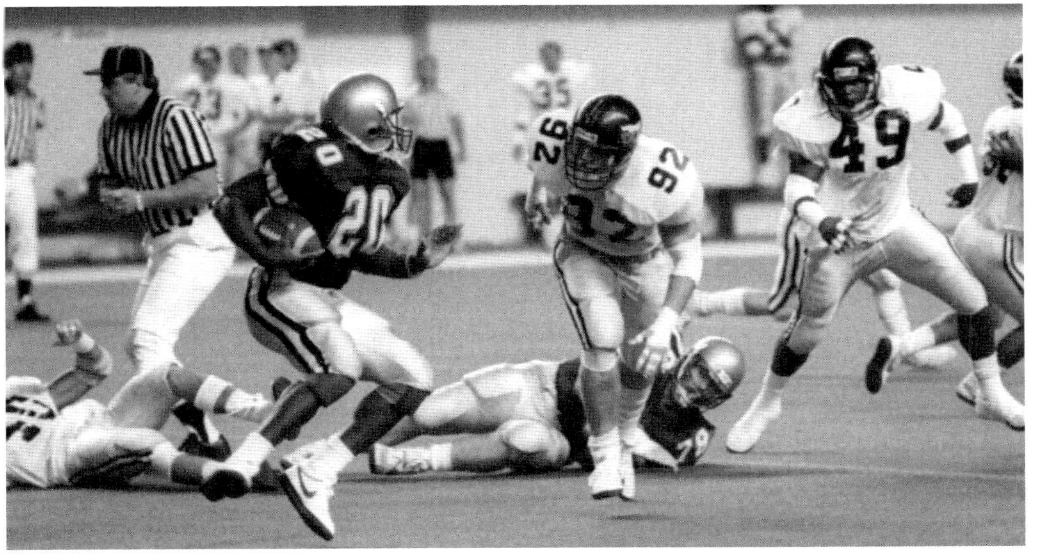

Star running back George Searcy, pictured eluding University of Central Florida (UCF) tacklers in a 1988 game, was the Bucs first official 1,000-yard rusher in 1989. His 1,324 yards on 275 tries set the current Buccaneer single-season record for yards. He also set records for points scored, with 108 on 18 touchdowns, and for rushing touchdowns, with 17. His 108 points broke Hal Morrison's record of 87 set in 1953. Searcy went on to play professionally in the World League of American Football and the Canadian Football League. (Photograph courtesy of ETSU Photo Lab.)

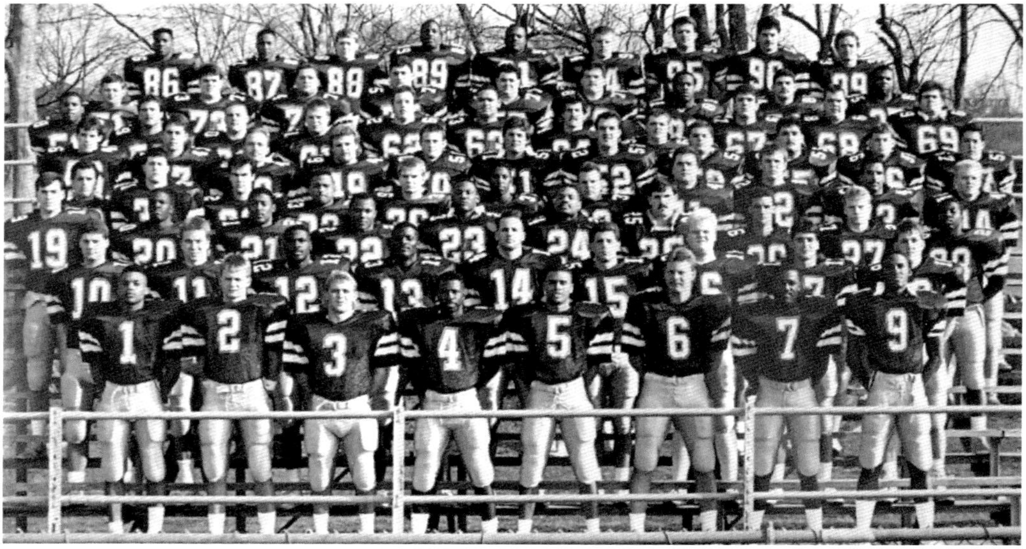

For the third time since joining the SoCon, the Buccaneers had a winning record (4-3) against conference foes, which placed them third in 1989. The bad news was that the total win column for the year would top out at four versus seven losses. The most exciting game of the season was State's homecoming comeback against UT-Chattanooga. Trailing 23-3 at the half, George Searcy (AP second team All-American and SoCon Offensive Player of the Year) scored three touchdowns in the second half to eke out a 24-23 victory. (Photograph courtesy Buc Football and Friends Foundation.)

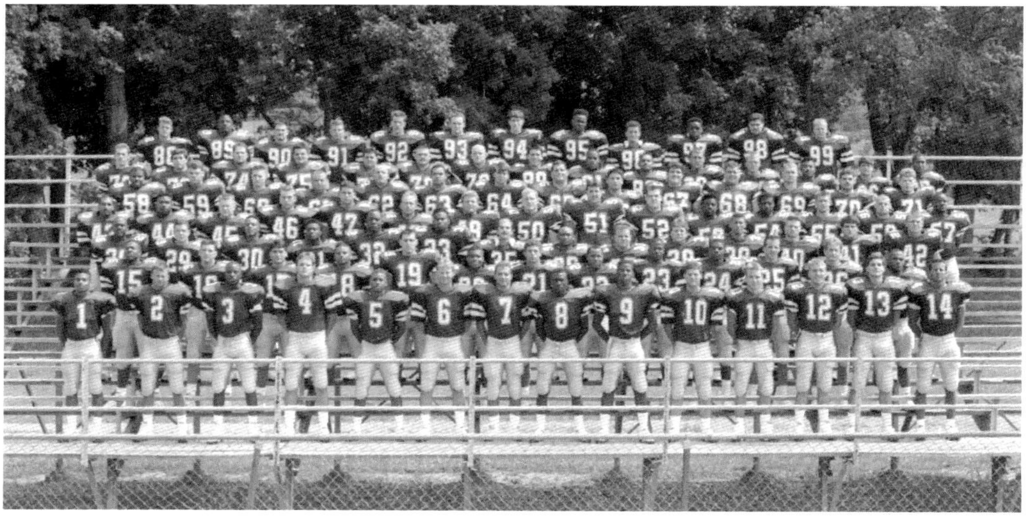

An injury-plagued year kept the Buccaneers down and out in 1990, assuring them of a fourth consecutive losing season and a 2-9 finish and eighth place in the conference. Highlights for the year were the 38-17 victory against Marshall where All-Conference tailback Derrick Hollins (18) hid the ball on a trick play for a surprise score and the 37-22 homecoming victory over Valdosta State. Offensive tackle David Ewart (75) and place kicker Mike Shoun (6) were also named to the All-Conference squad for 1990. (Photograph courtesy of ETSU Photo Lab.)

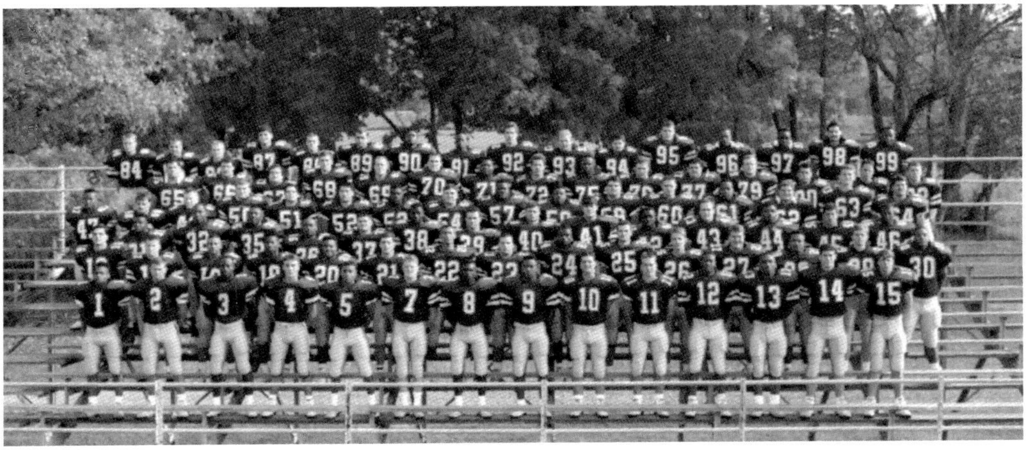

The 1991 season brought another painful 10-loss performance balanced against a lone victory at home September 28 against the Division II Newberry College Indians. The Buccaneers lost all their conference games for only the second time since joining the SoCon, which placed them in last place out of eight for the second year in a row. Linebacker Murphy Duckett (57) was an All-Conference selection. (Photograph courtesy of ETSU Photo Lab.)

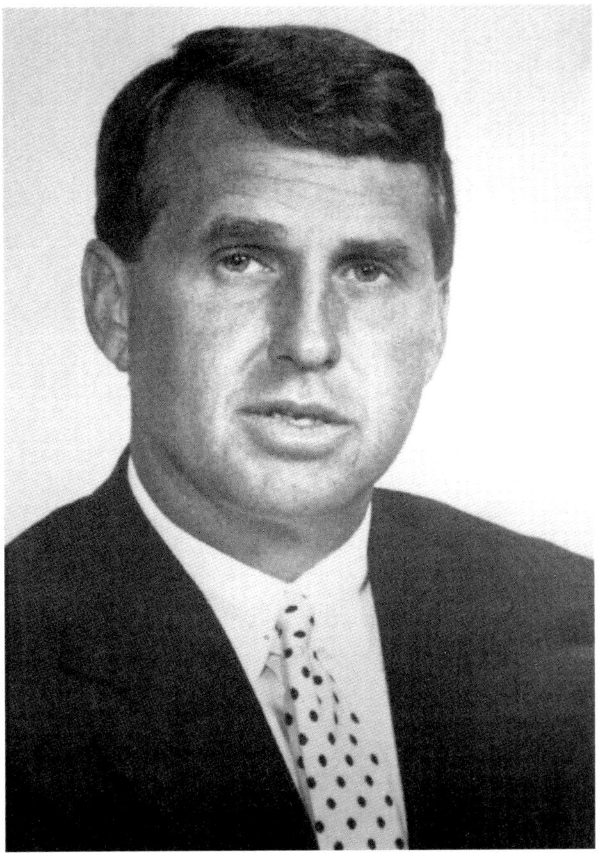

Head coach Mike Cavan brought bold talk of playing for and winning championships at ETSU. His plan was to accomplish this through a renewed focus on recruiting, but he did warn that it would take a good two to three years. Unlike some before him, the pronouncements of this coach from Georgia rang true. In his third year (1994), the Bucs had a winning record, which had not been seen since 1986, and in his fifth year, they were indeed pursuing a championship. In Cavan's five years (1992–1996) at the helm of the Buccaneer ship, he steered them to a 30-27 record and a .526 win percentage, the fourth-best in team history. (Photograph courtesy Buc Football and Friends Foundation.)

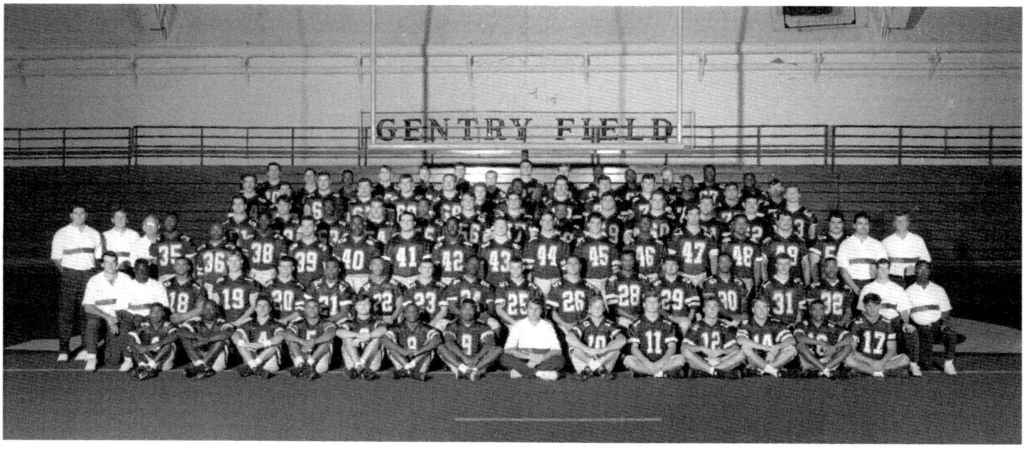

Fans were beginning to forget what winning football looked like in Johnson City when the 1992 season started. But the addition of a new coach coupled with a first game win versus the VMI Keydets encouraged fans to let feelings of new hope for a new era of Buccaneer football creep in. While the final record was not a winning one at 5-6, there were four home victories and the first road victory in five years. (Photograph courtesy of ETSU Photo Lab.)

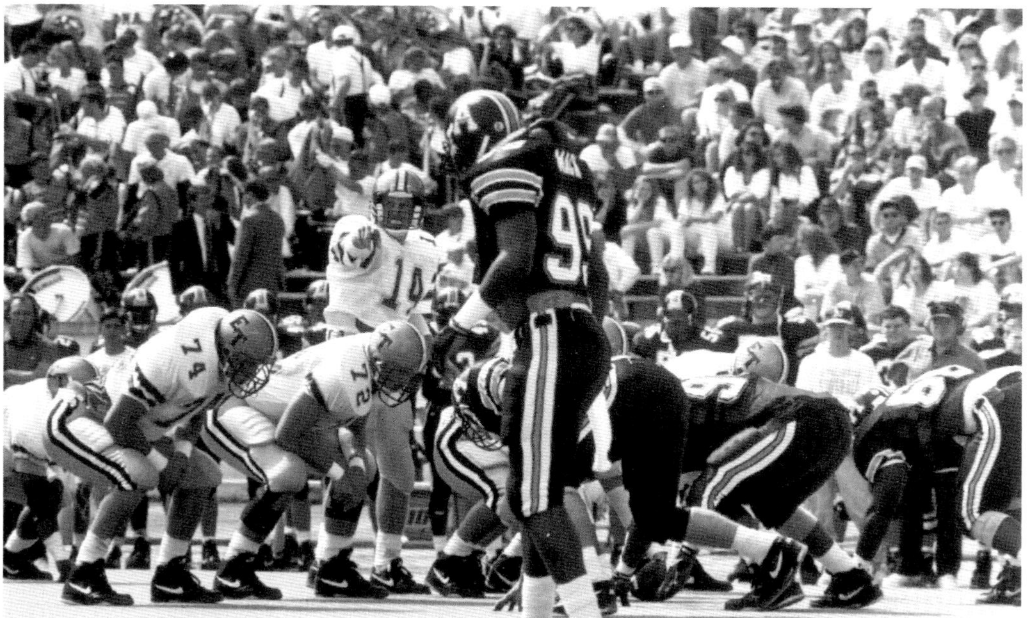

It was déjà vu in 1993 as the Buccaneers finished with a 5-6 overall record and wins against VMI, Mars Hill College, and UT-Chattanooga. But their conference record did improve by one game despite losing a place (seventh) in the conference standings. Wide receiver Jeff Johnson was selected by both the media and coaches to the All–Southern Conference Team for his sterling play and acrobatic pass-catching ability. (Photograph courtesy of Aaron Fenimore.)

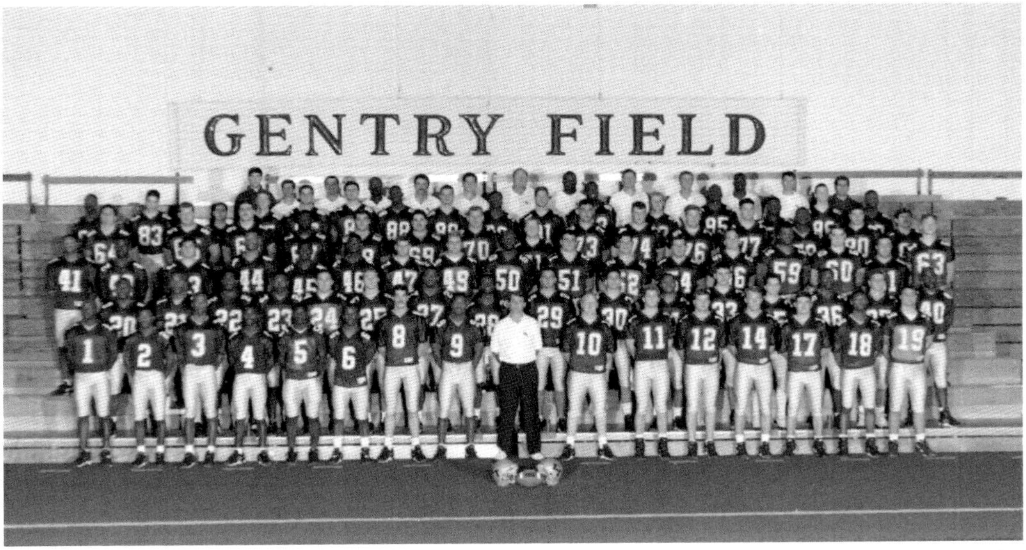

Great expectations were set for the 1994 Buc squad when pre-season polls ranked ETSU in the top 25. Everything was proceeding as expected as the Big Blue won their first three games, but the fourth game, a 0-38 pouncing at Auburn in historic Jordan-Hare Stadium, reversed fortunes in such a dramatic way that the Bucs could only manage one win (versus the Citadel) over the course of the next six games. They finished the season 6-5. (Photograph courtesy of ETSU Photo Lab.)

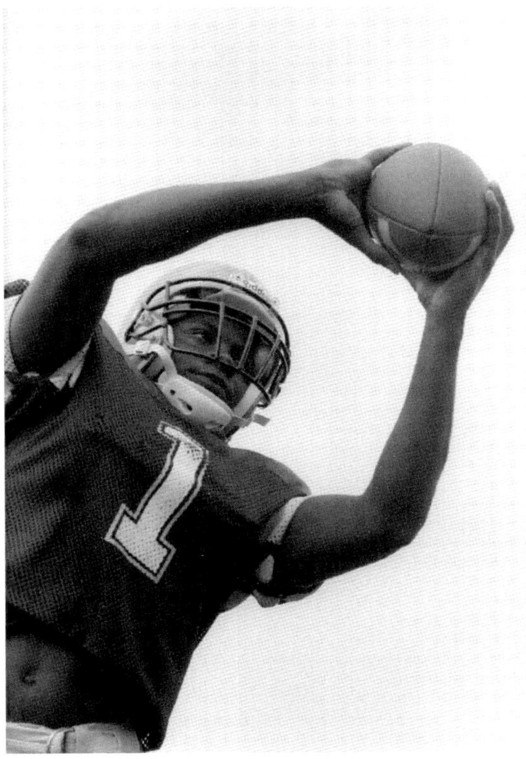

Wide receiver Jeff Johnson, pictured, was selected to the All-Conference squad again in 1994 along with defensive end James Russell. Johnson's 73 catches (the single-season record) for 857 yards and 8 touchdowns were good enough to earn him invitations to three All-American teams. During his career, Johnson tied Hal Morrison's record of 11 touchdown receptions in 1993 and broke Morrison's single-game reception record of 13 by pulling down 16 in a 1994 game versus VMI. (Photograph courtesy of ETSU Photo Lab.)

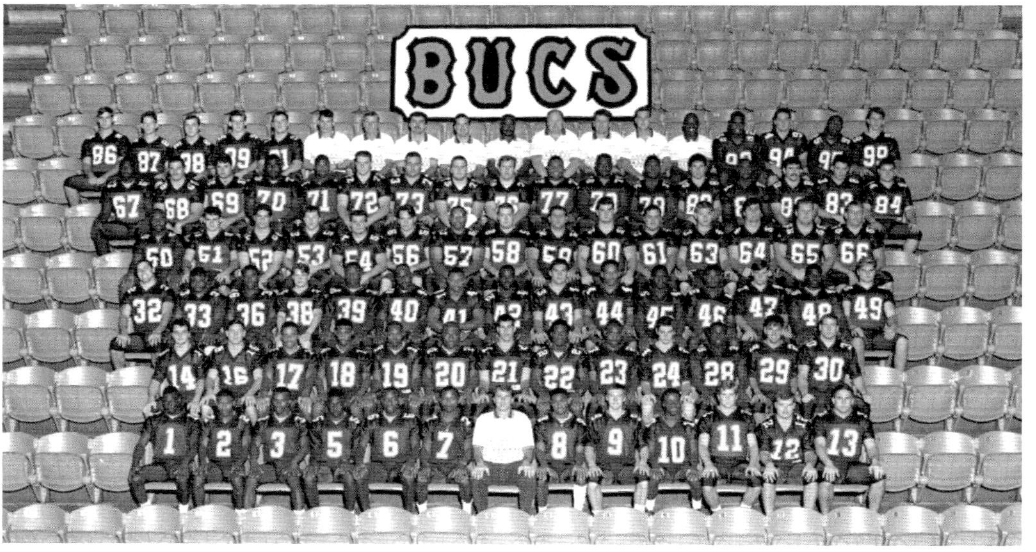

Because things had improved so much under Coach Cavan, 1995 was a letdown as the team finished with an overall 4-7 record and 4-4 (fifth-place) finish in the SoCon. On the bright side, the Bucs did win every one of their home games, one of which was against number 13–ranked Georgia Southern (21-16). Defensive standouts James Russell and Donnie Abraham were selected to both the media and coaches' All–Southern Conference teams. (Photograph courtesy of ETSU Photo Lab.)

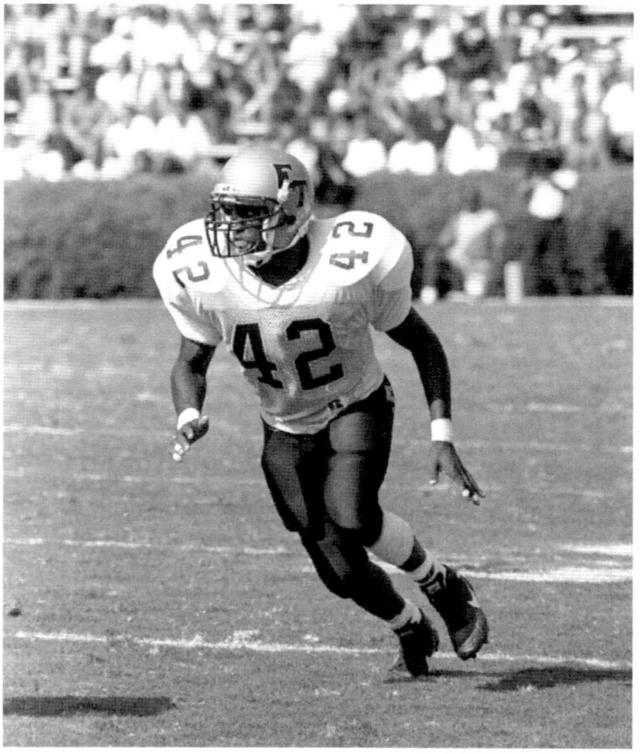

Cornerback Donnie Abraham was a standout defensive back for the Bucs from 1992 to 1995. After graduation, he played for the Tampa Bay Buccaneers (1996–2001) and the New York Jets (2002–2004) and has had the best professional career of any of the Bucs to date. He finished his nine-year professional career with 451 tackles and 38 interceptions and played in the Pro Bowl in 2000. (Photograph courtesy of ETSU Photo Lab.)

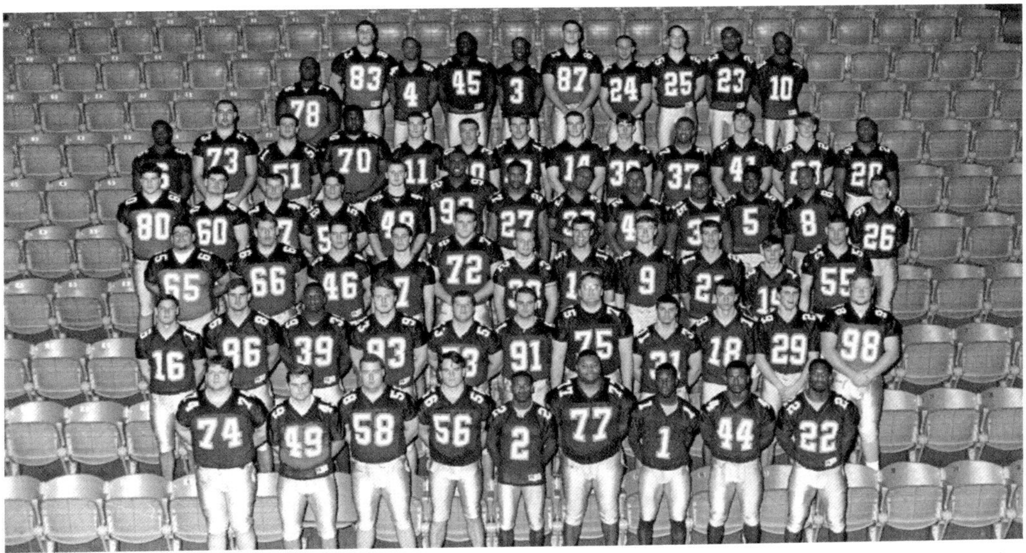

A glimpse of the glory experienced by the 1969 Grantland Rice Bowl champs was realized by the 1996 Buccaneers. Although they placed second (at 7-1) in the Southern Conference to Marshall, they did manage to win 10 games on the season. Their journey through this special season also saw them beat three other ranked foes: number 14 Liberty 24-20, number 4 Appalachian Sate 31-10, and number 8 Furman 21-19. (Photograph courtesy of ETSU Photo Lab.)

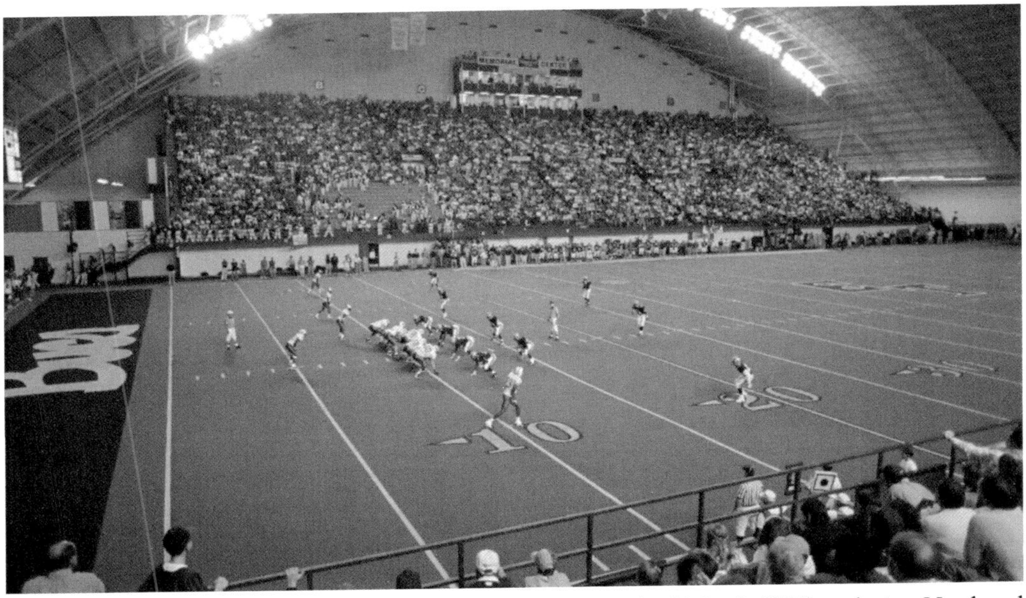

On November 9, 1996, the Buccaneers took on the top-ranked Marshall Thundering Herd and their star receiver, Randy Moss. Moss (88), on the far right on the 10-yard line, set NCAA records that year for most touchdown receptions and receiving yardage by a freshman. The Herd won the game 34-10 and went on to an undefeated season and their second I-AA National Championship since 1992. (Photograph courtesy of ETSU Photo Lab.)

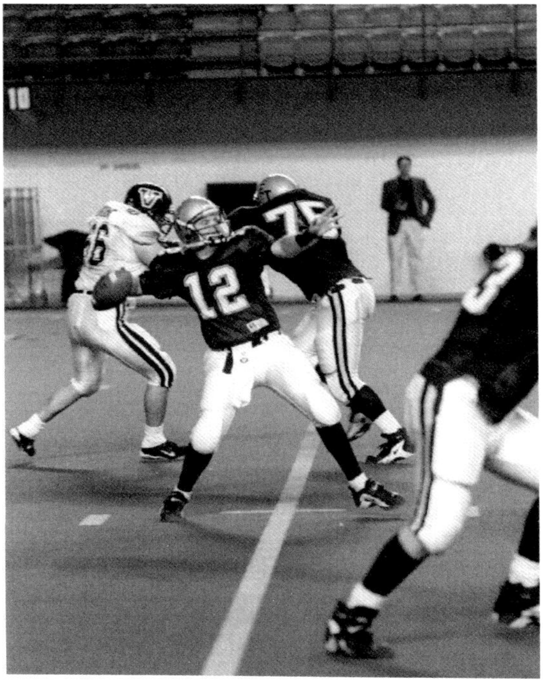

ETSU earned their first berth in the NCAA I-AA playoffs and an eighth-place ranking with their outstanding 9-2 performance. In the first round of the playoffs, ETSU met the 14th-ranked Villanova Wildcats at home in the Dome on November 30, 1996. The result was a 35-29 victory for the hometown fans. Senior quarterback Greg Ryan was 20-37 for 237 yards and two touchdowns. (Photograph courtesy of ETSU Photo Lab.)

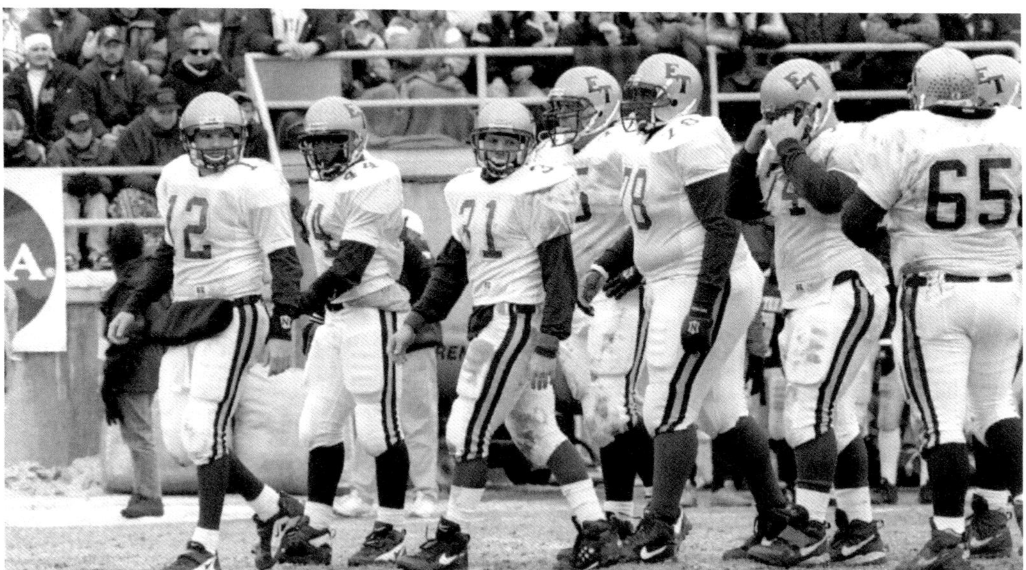

After their first-round victory, the Bucs traveled to snowy Missoula, Montana, to take on the number-two ranked Montana Grizzlies in the quarterfinals at Washington-Grizzly Stadium. Greg Ryan had another strong game, throwing for 313 yards and 2 touchdowns, but the Grizzlies prevailed 44-14. They went on to meet Southern Conference foe Marshall in the finals. It was the first time in the I-AA playoff that two undefeated teams matched up. (Photograph courtesy of ETSU Photo Lab.)

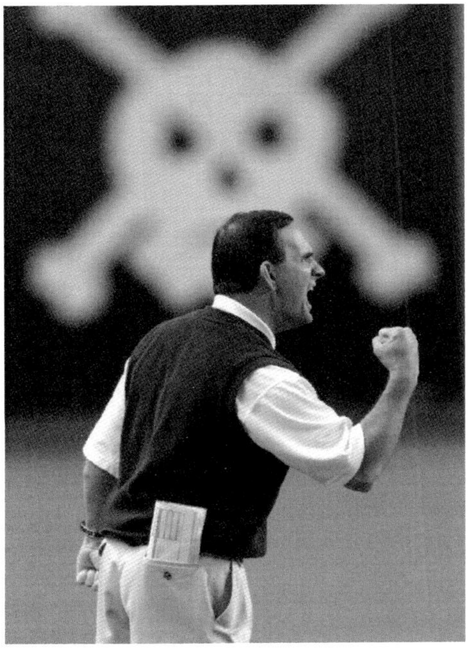

At this printing, Paul Hamilton was the 16th and final coach of the ETSU Buccaneers. Over his seven seasons (1997–2003) as head coach, he compiled a 38-41 mark and a .481 win percentage. The wins are third on the all-time list and his Southern Conference won-loss totals (24-32) are both highs at ETSU. In 1983, he was first hired as receivers coach at ETSU by Buddy Sasser and was promoted to quarterbacks coach by Mike Ayers in 1986. He followed Mike Ayers to Wofford College in 1988 and then went on to the Air Force Academy in 1990 before coming back to ETSU. (Photograph courtesy Buc Football and Friends Foundation.)

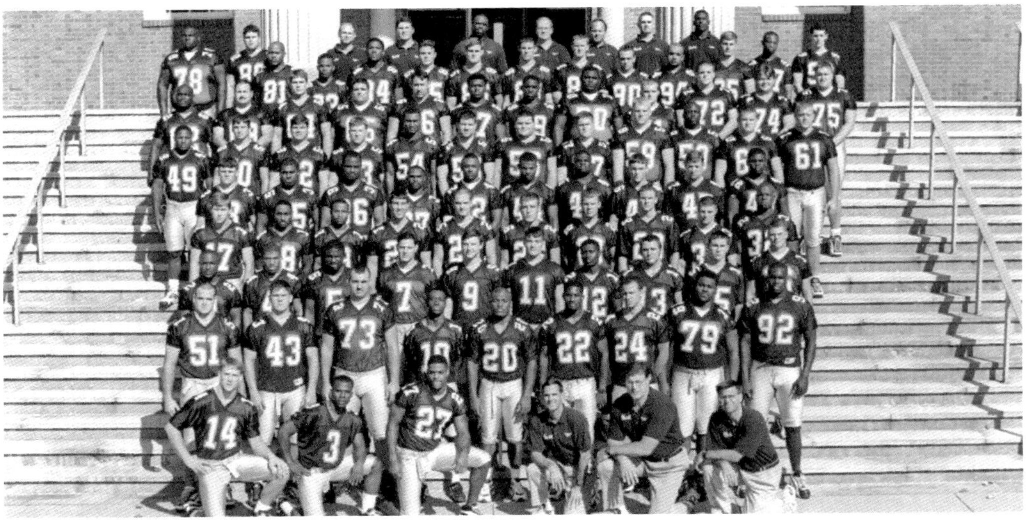

Under new coach Paul Hamilton, State continued winning and was ranked in the top 25 for most of 1997. The final tally for the year was a 7-4 record overall and a 5-3 mark (third) in the SoCon. This was the best record ever posted under a new coach in ETSU's history. The Bucs led the conference in total offense and total defense and boasted of the league's Male Athlete of the Year and Player of the Year (B. J. Adigun), Defensive Player of the Year (Mario Hankerson), and Rookie of the Year (Todd Wells). In addition, Adigun and Hankerson were both named to three All-American Teams, and fullback Brian Edwards, return specialist Anthony Stringfield, and offensive tackle Sam Haynie were named along with Adigun and Hankerson to the All-SoCon team. (Photograph courtesy of ETSU Photo Lab.)

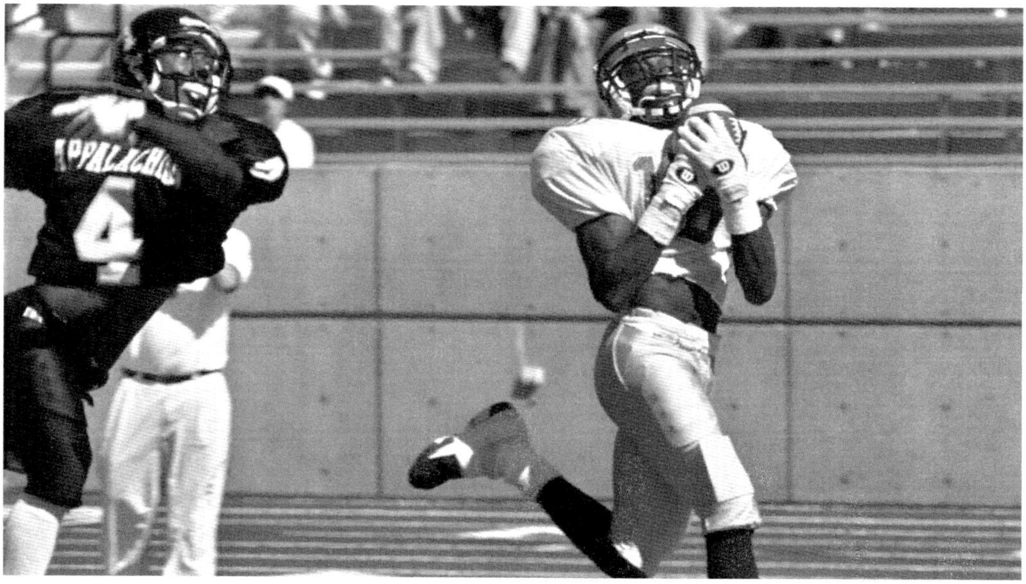

Wide receiver B. J. Adigun finished the 1997 season as one of the most decorated Buccaneers of all time. He was named the SoCon Athlete of the Year, SoCon Offensive Player of the Year, first-team All-American on three teams, and All-SoCon, and he was a National Player of the Year finalist in addition to ranking second nationally in receiving. He finished his career with the Bucs as their career leader in receptions (172), receiving yards (2,802), and touchdowns (26). (Photograph courtesy of ETSU Photo Lab.)

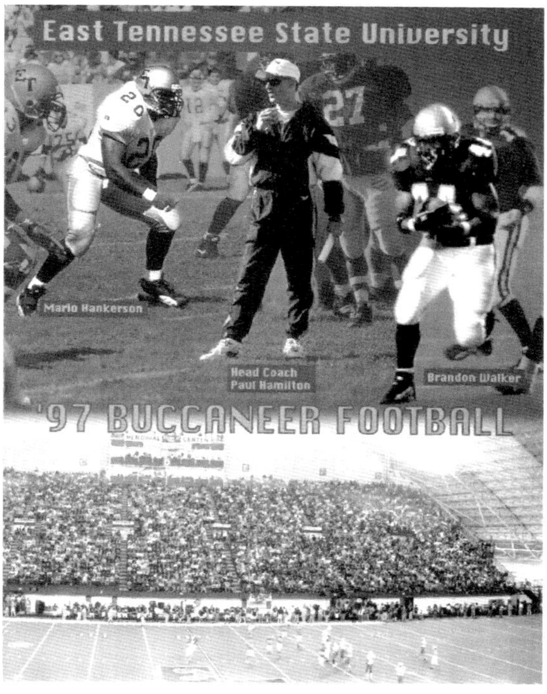

Two of the best to play under coach Paul Hamilton, Mario Hankerson and Brandon Walker, are pictured on the 1997 Media Guide. Hankerson, a linebacker, was All-SoCon and Defensive Player of the Year, First Team All-American, and a finalist for the National Player of the Year in 1997. He finished his career as the all-time leading tackler. Walker, a running back, was the 1996 SoCon Freshman of the Year and finished as ETSU's career leader in rushing yardage and scoring. (Photograph courtesy Buc Football and Friends Foundation.)

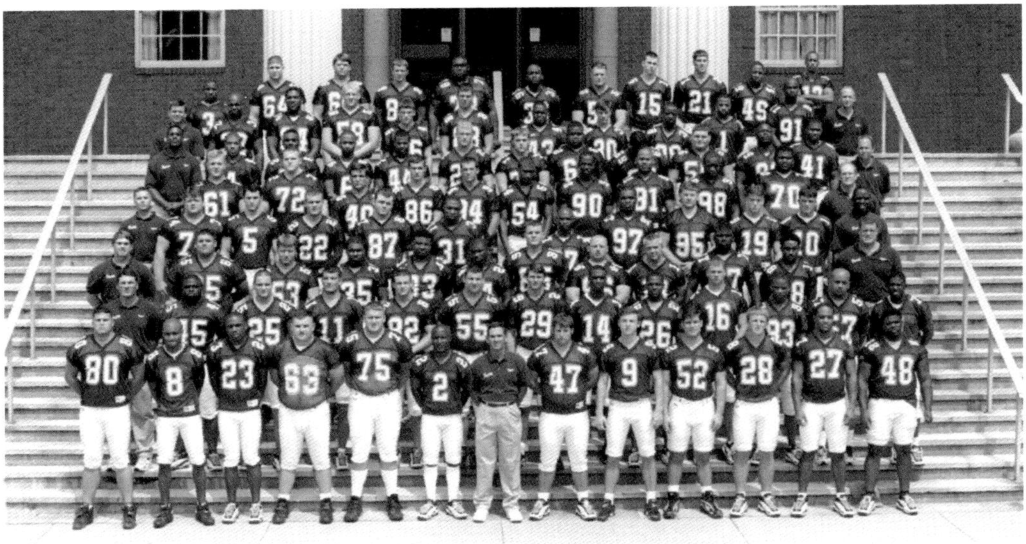

Loosing two All-Americans is bound to have repercussions. For the Buccaneers, the loss of these key players along with other experienced players left the Bucs short in 1998. The Bucs faced two I-A teams and the I-AA top-ranked Georgia Southern Eagles. The final result of this adversity was a 4-7 overall record and sixth-place finish in the conference. Individually the Bucs placed four on the All-Conference team: wide receiver Lamar Cooper, linebacker Kevin Peterson, offensive tackle Sam Haynie, and place kicker Jerry Chapman. (Photograph courtesy of ETSU Photo Lab.)

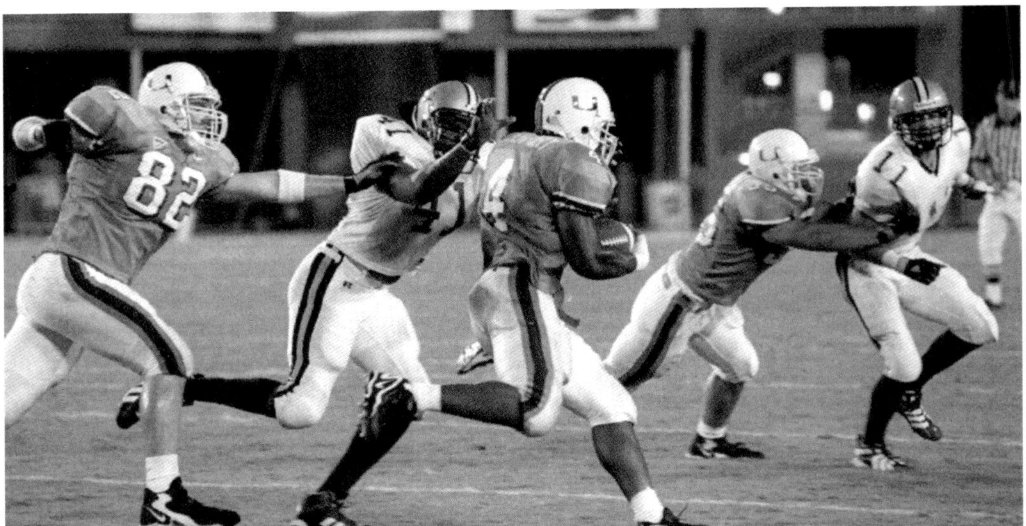

The season started in a bad way September 5 when the Bucs were severely drubbed 17-66 at the hands of the Miami Hurricanes in the Orange Bowl. Miami, a perennial powerhouse, would go on to a 9-3 record and a win in the Micron PC Bowl. Pictured are defensive end Fernando Gant (41) and free safety Adam Walton (11) in pursuit of Miami running back Najeh Davenport. (Photograph courtesy of ETSU Photo Lab.)

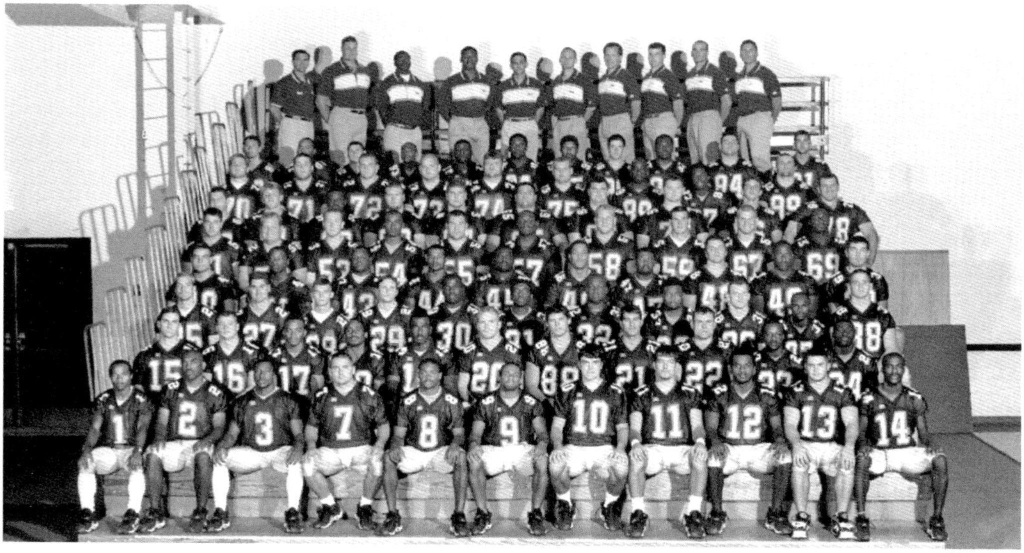

The first of three consecutive 6-5 overall finishes and three 4-4 SC (fifth-place) finishes occurred in 1999. The Bucs would go on to meet and lose to three top-ten I-AA teams: Appalachian State (3rd), Furman (14th), and Georgia Southern (3rd). Linebacker Kevin Peterson was named to two third team All-American squads and also garnered All-SC honors with center Jim Beverly and linebacker Derek Fudge. (Photograph courtesy of ETSU Photo Lab.)

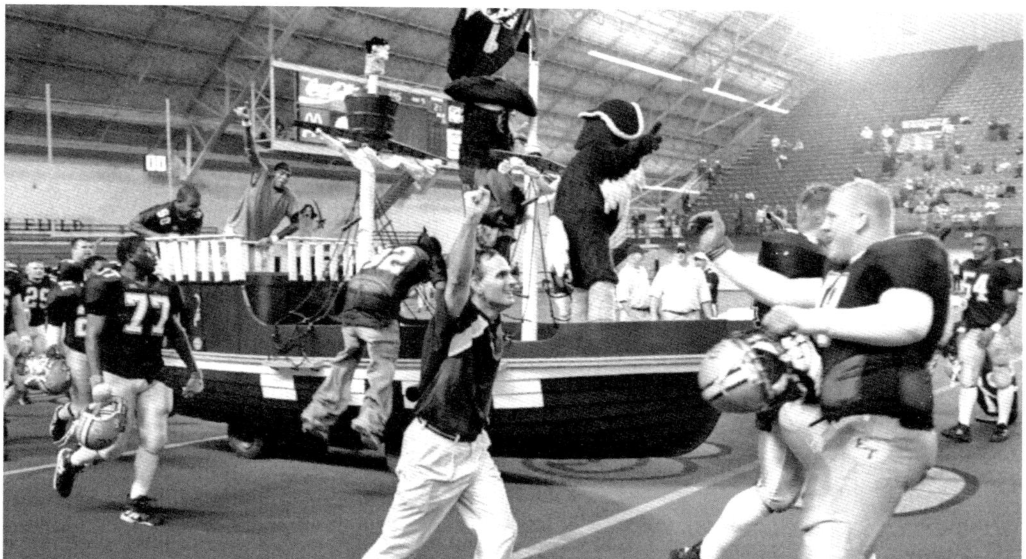

In 2000, the Buccaneers would go 6-5 again and play three top-ranked teams, losing to two. However, they would play sixth-ranked Furman at home and defeat them 23-21. Two defensive players would earn All-Conference honors: linebacker Rahim El Amin and defensive back Denario Smalls. Rahim, Smalls, wide receiver Cecil Moore, and quarterback Todd Wells would also get the *Don Hansen's Weekly Football Gazette* (*DH*) Honorable Mention. (Photograph courtesy of ETSU Photo Lab.)

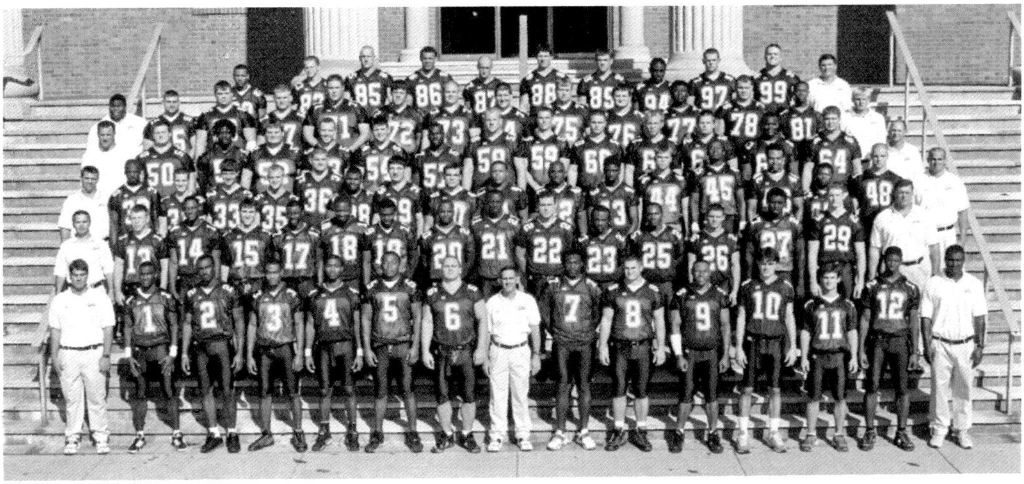

The 2001 squad had an exciting close to their season, reeling off four wins in their last six games. Most significantly, the Bucs defeated their first top-rated team, the Georgia Southern Eagles, at home in front of the Big Blue fans and a regional television audience. Both the coaches and media named wide receiver Cecil Moore to All-SoCon teams. He, defensive back Tony Tiller, and defensive lineman Brandon Calton also were listed to the honorable mention All-American Team. (Photograph courtesy of ETSU Photo Lab.)

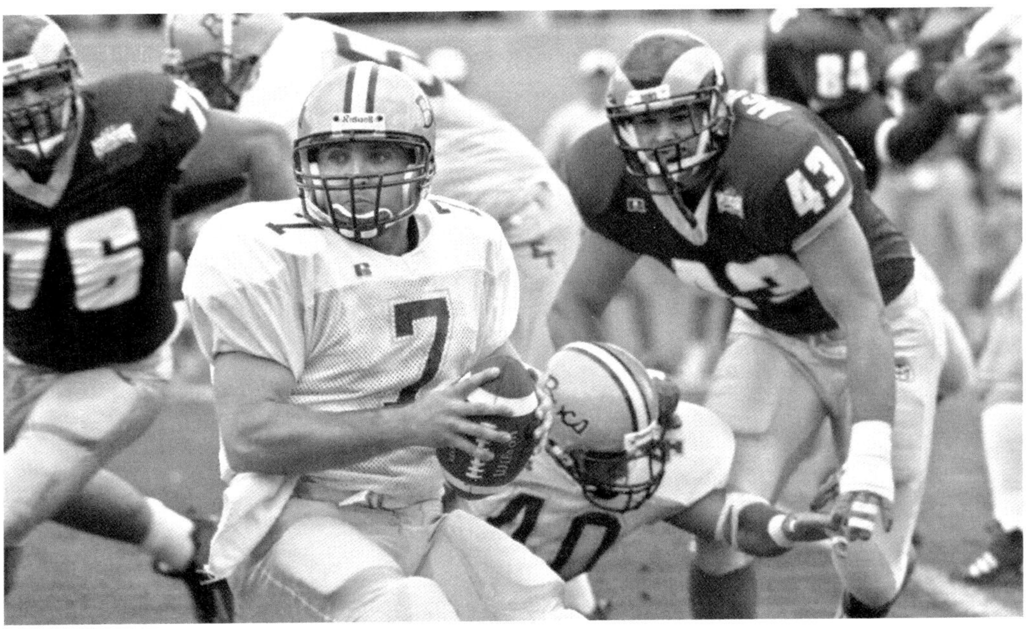

Quarterback Todd Wells finished his outstanding career as a Buccaneer in 2000 with numerous accolades. He was the 1997 SoCon Freshman of the Year, All-SoCon, and Honorable Mention on the 2000 DH All-American Team. Statistically, he is the all-time total offense leader in the SoCon, ETSU's single-season passing record holder, and State's single-game offense record holder. He was elected to the ETSU Athletic Hall of Fame in 2007. (Photograph courtesy of ETSU Photo Lab.)

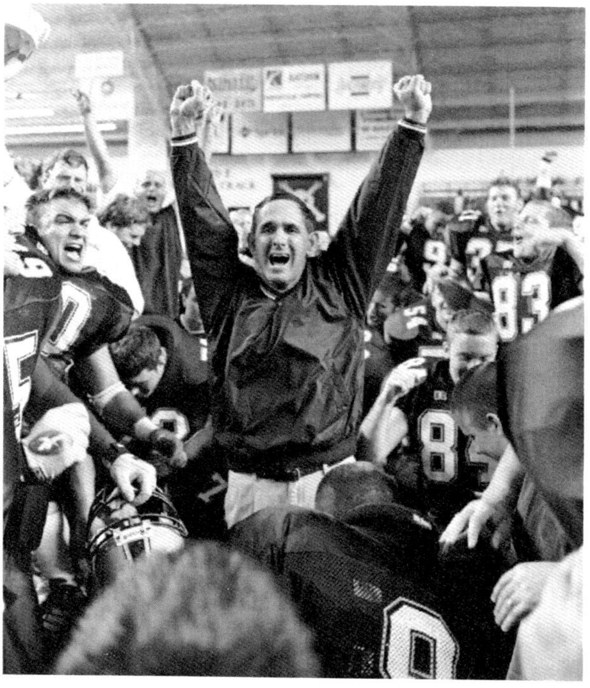

On October 19, 2001, quarterback Matt Wilhjelm and wide receiver Cecil Moore combined on a pair of touchdown passes and the Buccaneer defense took away four Georgia Southern turnovers to lead ETSU to their first ever defeat of a number-one ranked team. The final score was Bucs 19 and Eagles 16. (Photograph courtesy of ETSU Photo Lab.)

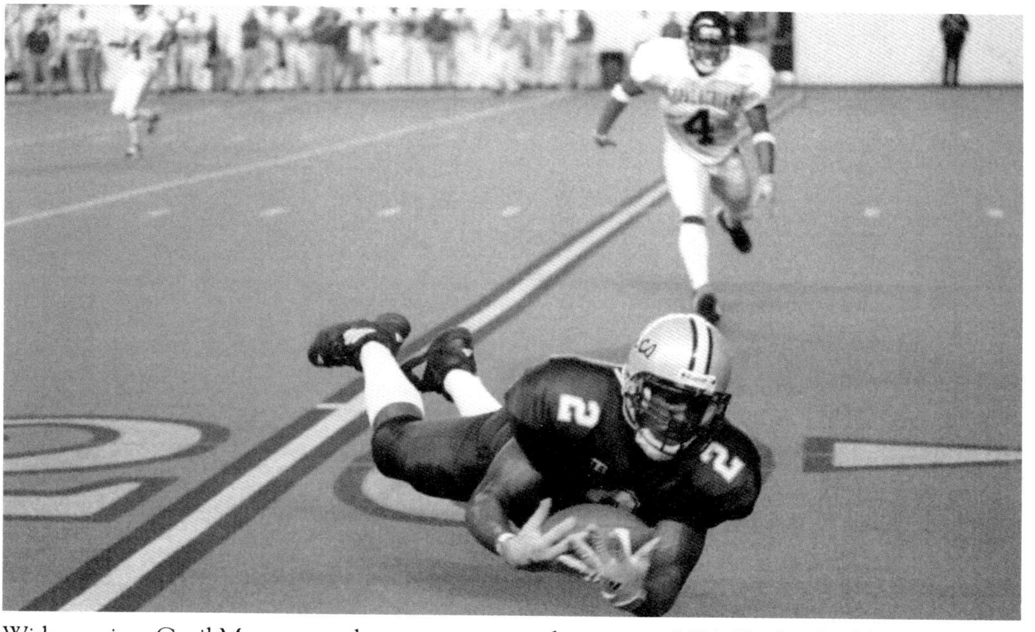

Wide receiver Cecil Moore stretches out to get another pass in 2001. He finished his stellar, All-American career at ETSU as the number-two man behind B. J. Adigun in career receiving yards (2,488) and receptions (161). He is only the second person to eclipse the 2,000-yard plateau for his career after leading the Bucs in receiving for three consecutive years, 2000–2002. (Photograph courtesy of ETSU Photo Lab.)

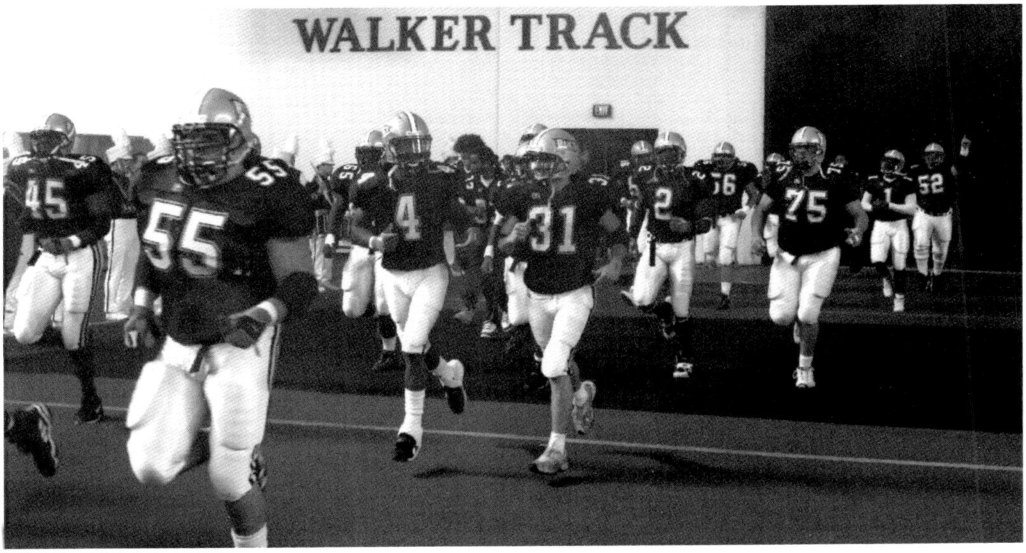

Coming off their third-straight winning season, the Buccaneers were quietly optimistic about challenging for a Southern Conference title in 2002. But with only two starters returning on offense, the cause for optimism was unfounded when the Bucs finished 4-8 overall and 2-6 (tied for seventh) in the SoCon. The Bucs did place two defensive stars on the All-SoCon team and the DH All-American (honorable mention) Team: defensive back Tony Tiller (4) and defensive back Gerald Sensabaugh. (Photograph courtesy of ETSU Photo Lab.)

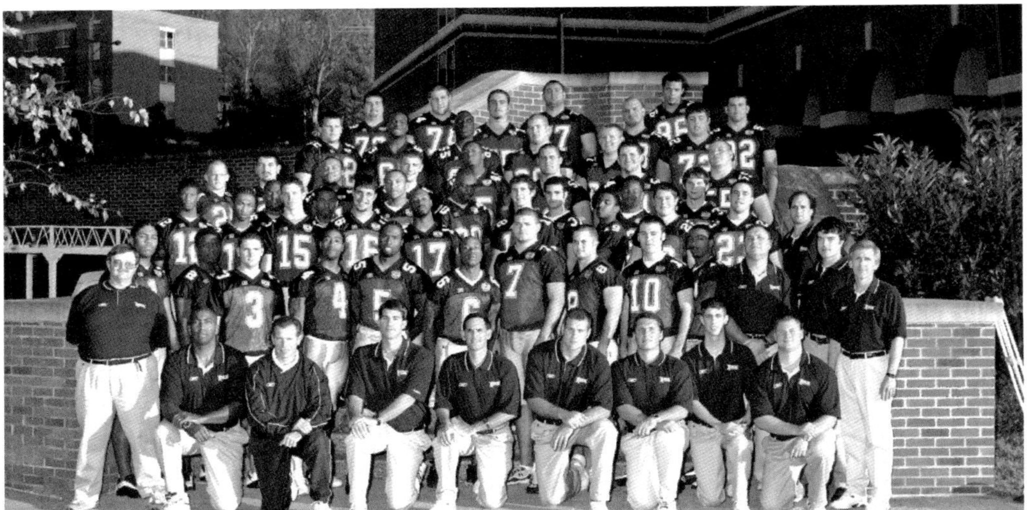

The final Buccaneer football team in the school's history (to date) finished the 2003 season 5-7 overall and 2-6 (seventh) in the SoCon. Hoping to erase a disappointing season in 2002 and trying to leave good memories for the final season, the Bucs strived mightily to go out winners. They did so in a way by winning their final game in dramatic fashion—on a last-second field goal to defeat the Citadel 16-13. (Photograph courtesy of ETSU Photo Lab.)

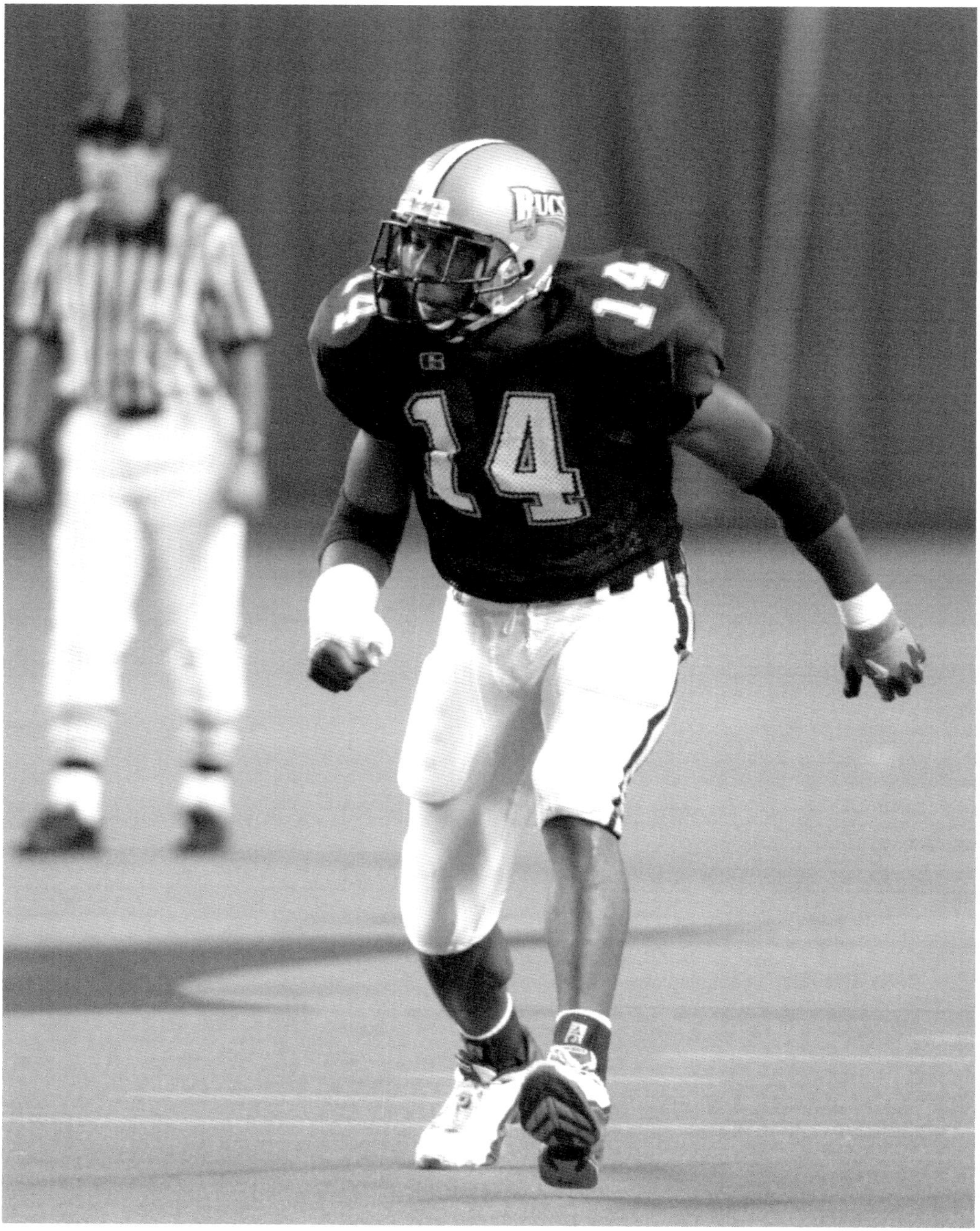

In 2003, Tony Tiller, Gaven Varner, and Gerald Sensabaugh (pictured) were All-SoCon picks, and Sensabaugh, Brandon Calton, and Aaron Bass were All-American picks. Sensabaugh, a two-time All-Southern Conference selection, transferred to North Carolina for his senior year after ETSU dropped its football program and was selected by the Jaguars in the fifth round of the 2005 NFL Draft. He tied an NCAA game-record after blocking three punts in one game versus Georgia Southern. (Photograph courtesy of ETSU Photo Lab.)

5

Spirited Support

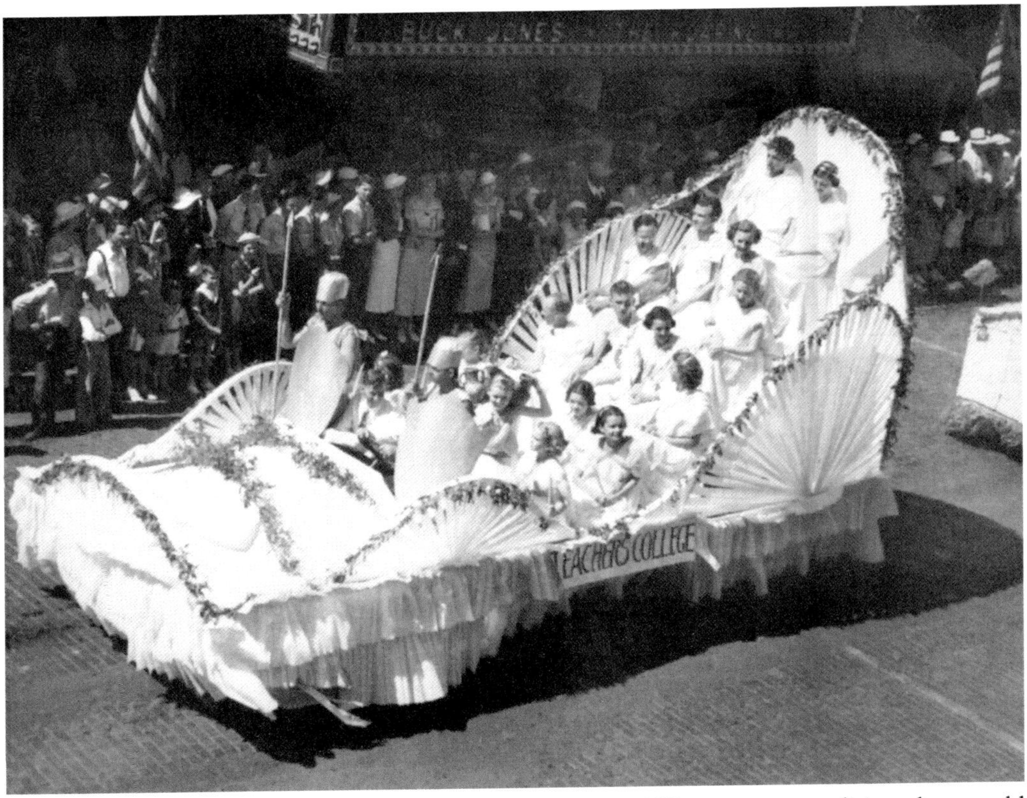

The first homecoming game and day was November 28, 1925, starting a tradition that would expand to one of the biggest events of the school year. Homecoming parades traveled down Main Street for many years. The movie marquee in the background of this photograph advertises a 15-episode Buck Jones serial movie, *The Roaring West*, which was released in 1935. (Photograph courtesy Buc Football and Friends Foundation.)

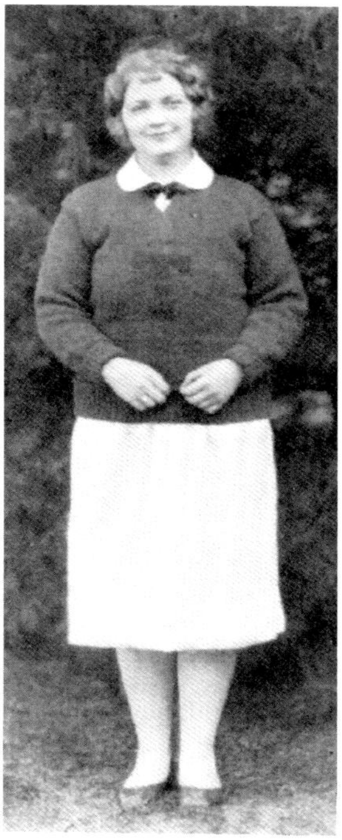

The first reference in the school's annuals to cheerleading appears in the 1926 edition of *Old Hickory* and consists of a lone picture of Bonnie Shell and the designation "cheerleader." Shell, a 1927 graduate, was proud of the fact that she periodically attended classes from the time the school was a Normal through its designation as a University. Luntsford (her married name) Hall was named in her memory in 1974. (Photograph courtesy Buc Football and Friends Foundation.)

The "Yells" and "Songs" seen below are early examples of cheers led by students and early cheerleaders like Bonnie Shell and Virginia Parker at ETSC football games. These cheers were printed in the 1928 edition of the school annual, the *Old Hickory*. (Photograph courtesy Buc Football and Friends Foundation.)

Old Hickory

Yells

T-E-A-C-H-E-R-S
Teachers! Teachers!
Rack-Kack-Kack-Kack! Rack-Kack-Kack-Kack!
Hold 'em! Hold 'em! Hold 'em!
Let's Go!

* * *

Blue team, Gold team,
Blue and Gold team
T. C. Ball Team
Fight! Fight! Fight!

* * *

Fight, team, fight, fight, team, fight.
Fight, team, fight, team,
Fight, fight, fight!

* * *

T. C. rah! rah!
T. C. rah! rah!
Rip-rah! rip-rah!
T. C. rah! rah!
(*Repeat*)

* * *

Hit 'em high, hit 'em low,
Come team, let's go.

* * *

Yea Team, Yea Team,
Fight, Fight, Fight.
Yea Team, Say Team,
We're betting on you!

* * *

He's a wonder
He's a dream
He's the Captain
Of our team.

* * *

We love you, we like you,
We stick to you tight
But ole T. C.
You must fight! fight! fight!

* * *

2 — 4 — 6 — 8
Whom do we appreciate?
Team! Team! Team!

Old Hickory

Songs

-------------- --------------, Bum!
What you gonna do since the Teachers come
What you gonna say, how you gonna play
Never win a game 'til the Judgment Day.
Oh, you know, I know we play ball!
Something you can't do at all.
Oh! --------------, --------------, bum!
What you gonna do since the Teachers come?

* * *

Ain't they sweet, ha ha, neat ha, ha, handsome and fair?
They are jim dandies, we girls all declare.
Then it's high road rolicking well,
Look at our team—say, don't they look swell?

* * *

Hi-yi-ye-yik-us!
Nobody like us.
We are the gang from E. T. C.
Always a winning
Always a grinning
Always a feeling fine.
Hi-Yi!

* * *

We're backing our team E. T. C.
We're blue, and we're gold, E. T. C.
We'll back you to stand 'gainst the best in the land,
For we know you have sand E. T. C. rah! rah!
So crack out that ball E. T. C.
We're backing you all E. T. C.
Our team is our fame, protector on boys for we expect a touchdown from you E. T. C.

* * *

On E. T. C., on E. T. C.
Plunge right through that line
Run the ball clear round old--------------
Touchdown sure this time.
On E. T. C., on E. T. C.

* * *

Fight team for your fame
Fight, fellows, fight and we will win this game.

Dr. Howell Hood Sherrod, a 1938 graduate of State, founded Watauga Orthopaedics, PLC, after returning from the U.S. Navy in 1950. Dr. Sherrod served as the first official team physician from 1950 to 1993, and his firm provided first-class sports medicine care for the Buccaneers until 2003. In 1960, Dr. Burgin Dossett Jr. became the team physician for internal medicine. Both men worked tirelessly serving the Bucs, and both were sons of past ETSU presidents. (Photograph courtesy Buc Football and Friends Foundation.)

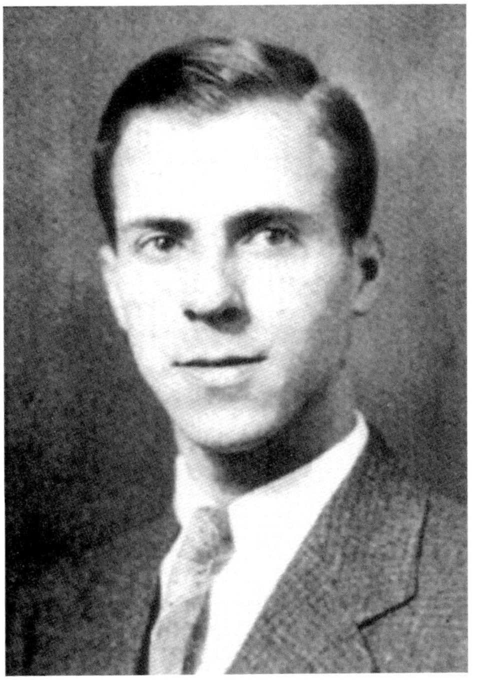

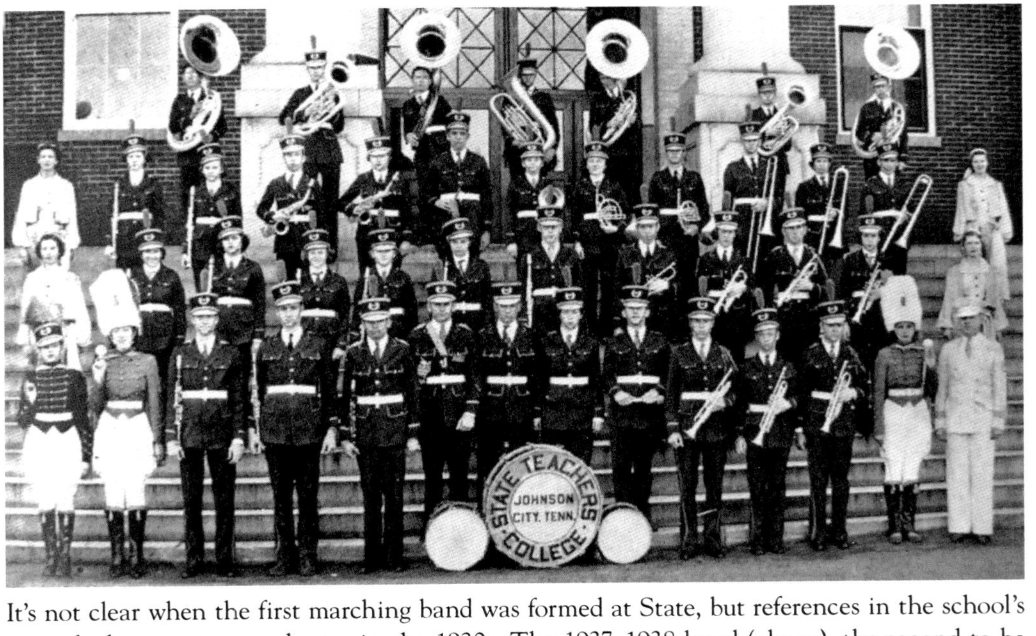

It's not clear when the first marching band was formed at State, but references in the school's annuals document an orchestra in the 1920s. The 1937–1938 band (above), the second to be recognized in the annuals, grew to about 50 members, gaining 20 members over the previous two years. They played in the homecoming parade and at football games and gave numerous concerts on and off campus throughout Johnson City. (Photograph courtesy Buc Football and Friends Foundation.)

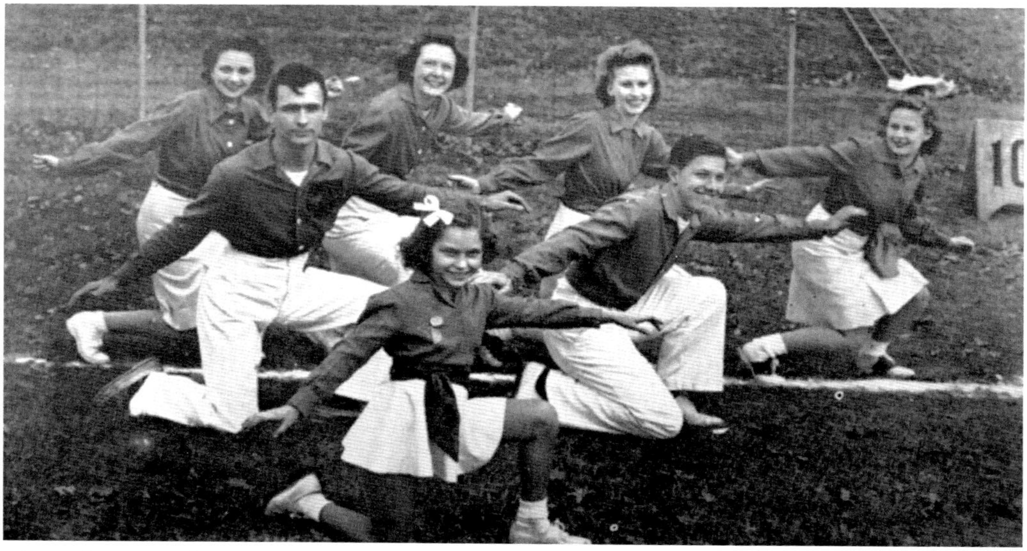

The 1939–1940 cheerleading squad is the first team to be pictured in uniform in the school's annual, *The Buccaneer*. Pictured from left to right are (first row) Jeane Watkins; (second row) Carl Wheeler and Jack Britton; (third row) Kathryn Pye, Mable Wallin, Evelyn Denton, and Mary Ryburn. (Photograph courtesy Buc Football and Friends Foundation.)

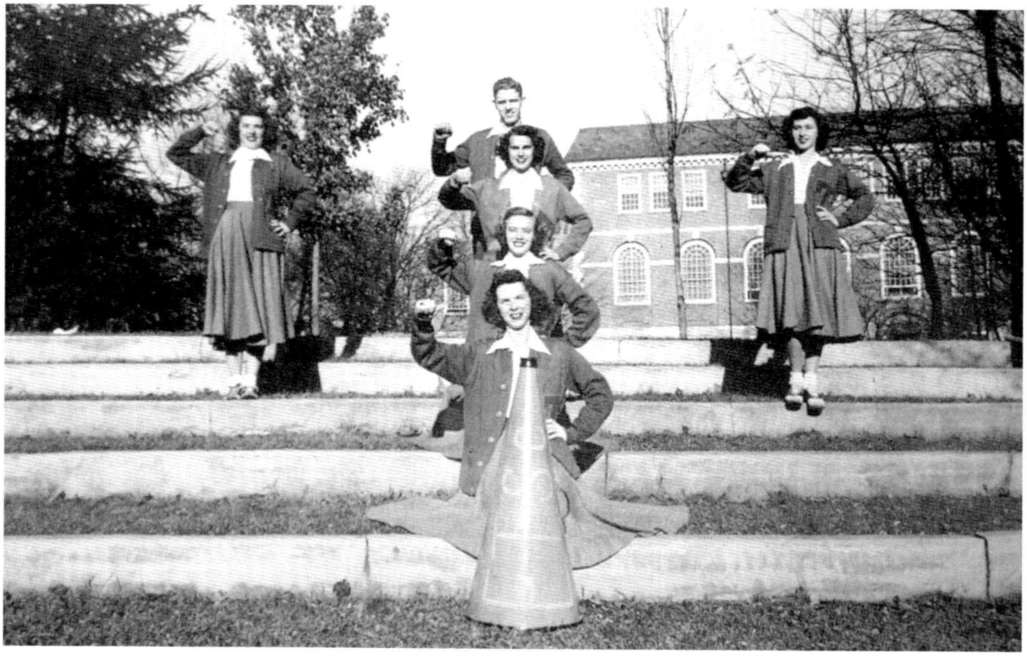

The ETSC cheerleaders for 1948–1949 are Jo Anderson, Nell Joy Brooks, Stanley Bunn, Laura Jo Ellis, Wanda Goode, and Betty Jean Stanton. The megaphone in front has been standard equipment for cheerleading since the early 1900s. (Photograph courtesy Buc Football and Friends Foundation.)

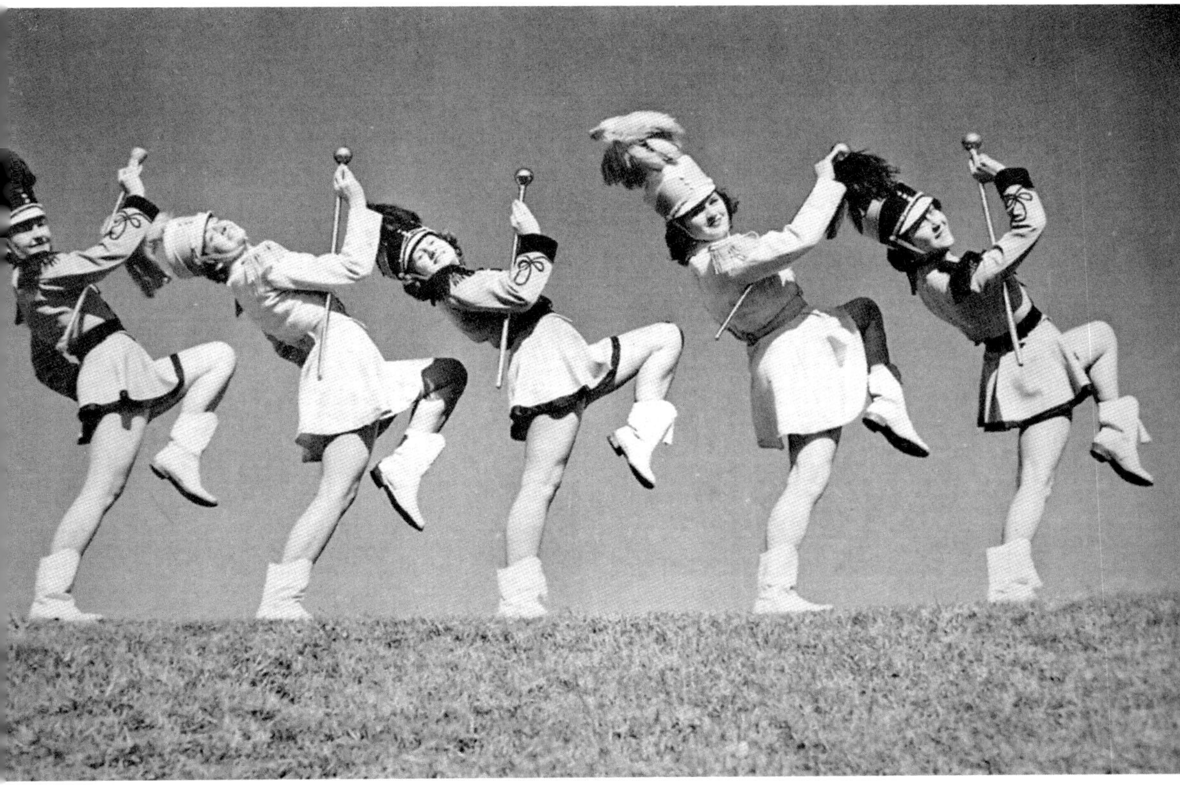

The 1950–1951 majorettes are pictured; from left to right, Gorman, Hale, Herron, Winter, and Alley strike a pose for the school annual. Known for high-stepping and twirling batons, majorettes have been a part of band performances from the early 1900s, and the practice is thought to have originated from juggling and/or flag-twirling acts of the late 19th century. One of the highlights of the 1950 season was the mass band performance at the State-Emory game. (Photograph courtesy Buc Football and Friends Foundation.)

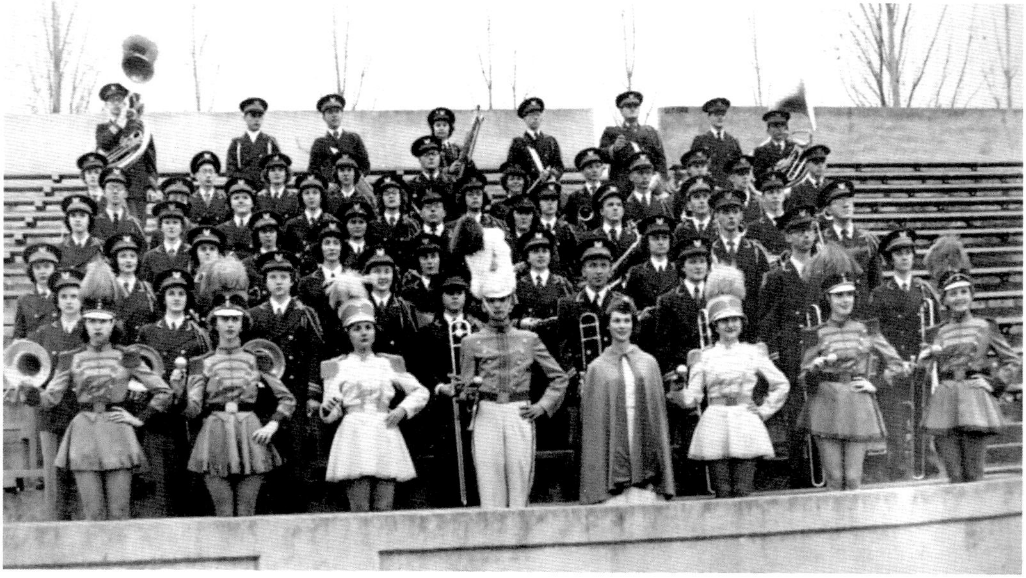

Directed by J. Marvin Lindley, the ETSC Band of 1952–1953 had grown to a 65-piece organization that was featured on the gridiron during football halftimes. The band also played at school basketball games and pep rallies. At the end of the marching season, the concert band would be organized and would play throughout the region. (Photograph courtesy Buc Football and Friends Foundation.)

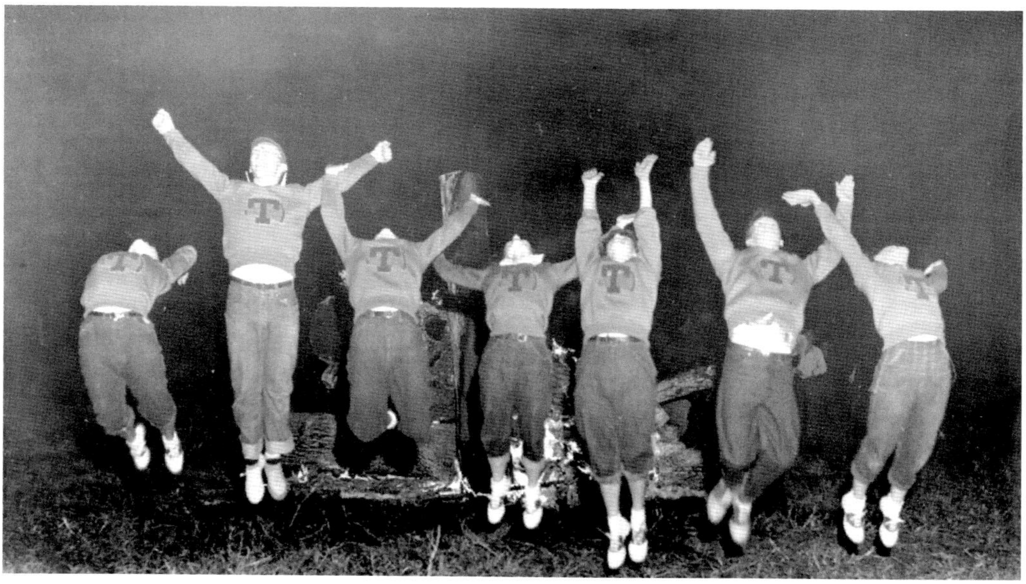

Leading the cheers at homecoming events such as this bonfire (believed to be during 1953) was a key job for the cheerleading squad. They would also ride in the homecoming parade and organize and lead pep rallies on the campus during football and basketball seasons. (Photograph courtesy Buc Football and Friends Foundation.)

"Billy the Kid," or "Captain Kidd," a beloved State mascot for many years, is pictured on the sidelines during a 1952 ballgame. Billy was the center of attention during Milligan-State matchups when State and Milligan students would make raids of the opposing school's campus in attempts to steal each other's mascots. After one Milligan raid, State supporters put detergent in the Milligan reservoir in retaliation, causing bubbles to discharge from the faucets. The State band played *I'm Forever Blowing Bubbles* at the game. (Photograph courtesy Buc Football and Friends Foundation.)

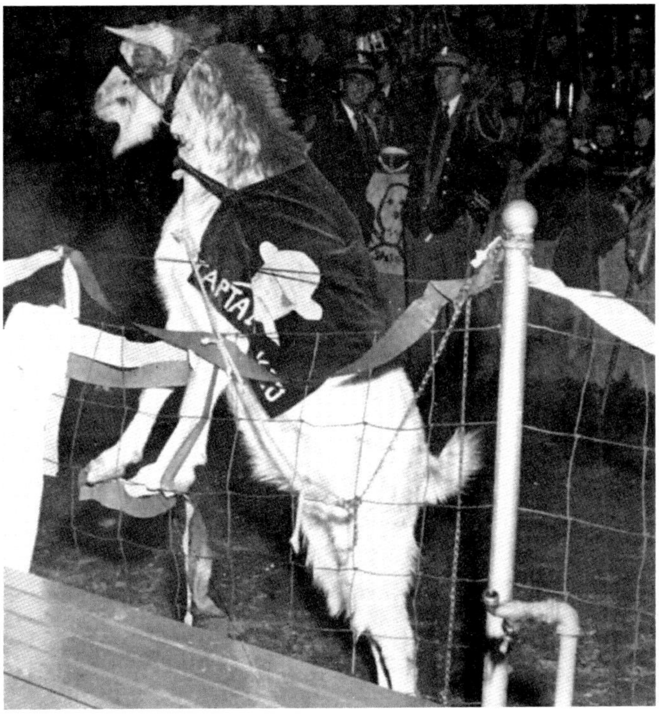

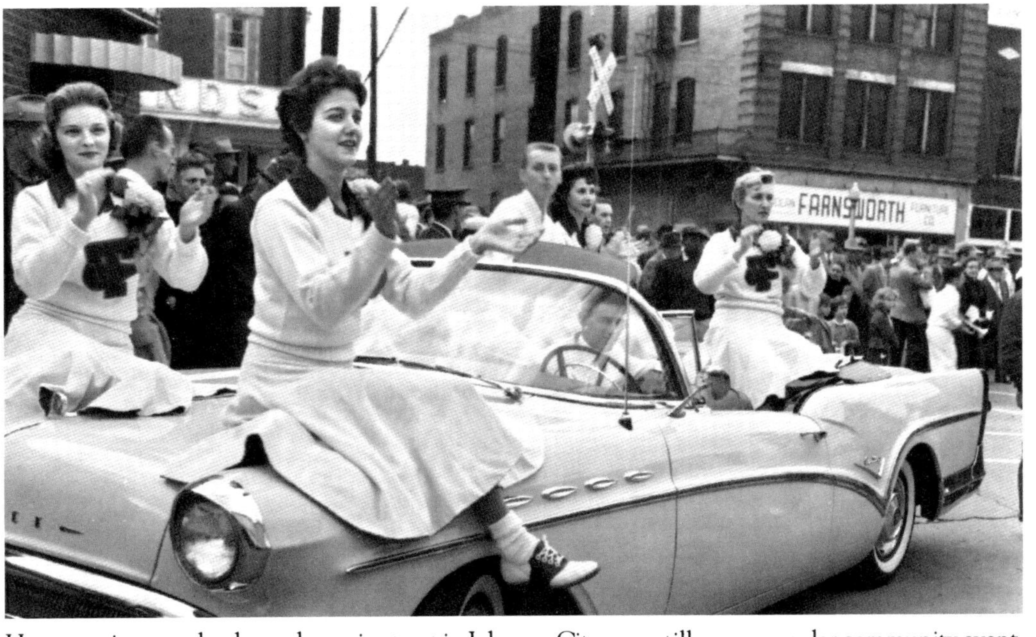

Homecoming parades down the main street in Johnson City were still a very popular community event. This would last for another decade or so until attendance and participation dwindled significantly. Pictured are members of the 1957–1958 cheerleading squad including Barbara Willingham (foreground) on the hood of the car. (Photograph courtesy of Barbara [Willingham] Hundley.)

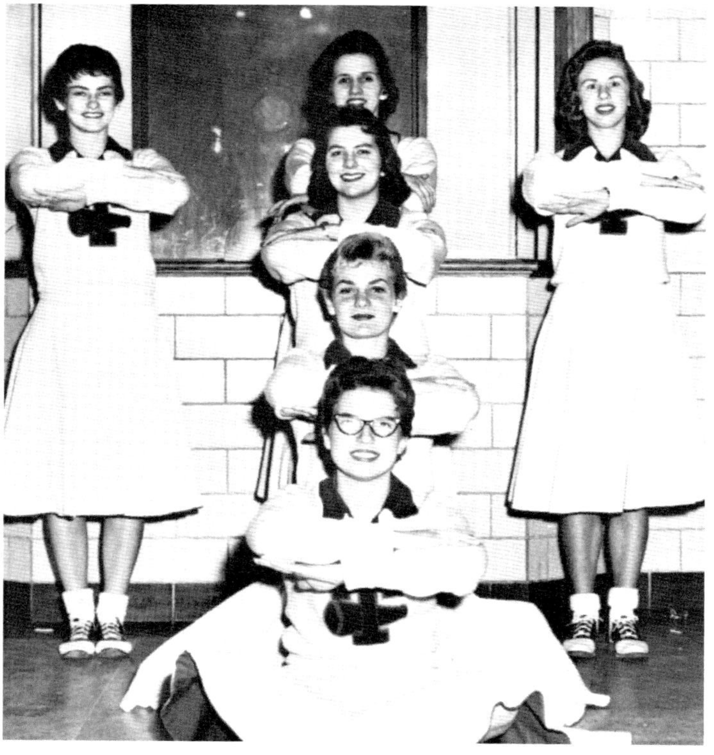

The 1958–1959 cheerleading squad is (from front to back) Winnie Gillespie, Judy Noblin, and Rhetta Belle Lyle; (second row, left to right) Joyce Leeper, Scotty Beach, and Mary Elizabeth Chambers. Tryouts for the team were before school started and would be judged by male and female members of the student body and faculty. At this time, approximately 20 to 30 girls would try out for the team sponsored by Dorothy Hicks, who was a physical education teacher until 1968. (Photograph courtesy Buc Football and Friends Foundation.)

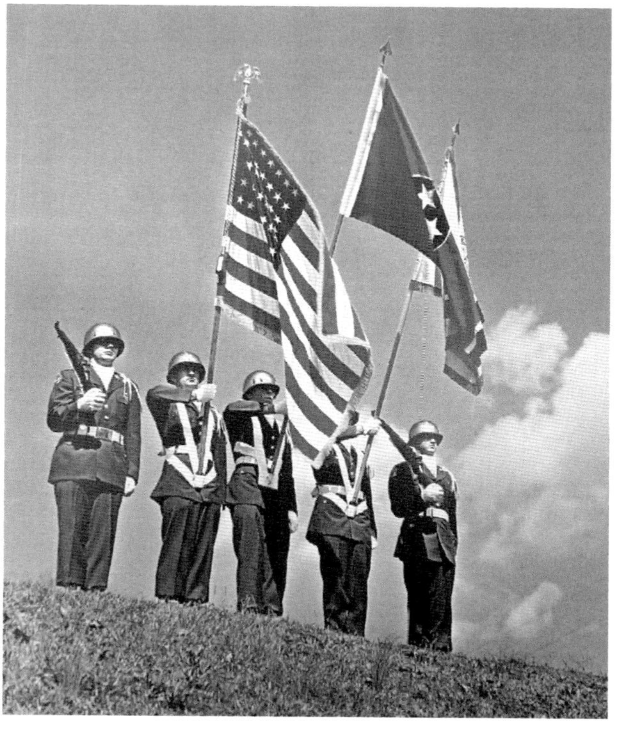

The color guard from 1962–1963 is shown carrying the National and State Colors. In addition to the flag bearers who are positioned in the center of the color guard, there are two individuals who carry rifles. Being assigned to the color guard is considered an honor because these individuals present and carry the symbols of their unit and country. (Photograph courtesy Buc Football and Friends Foundation.)

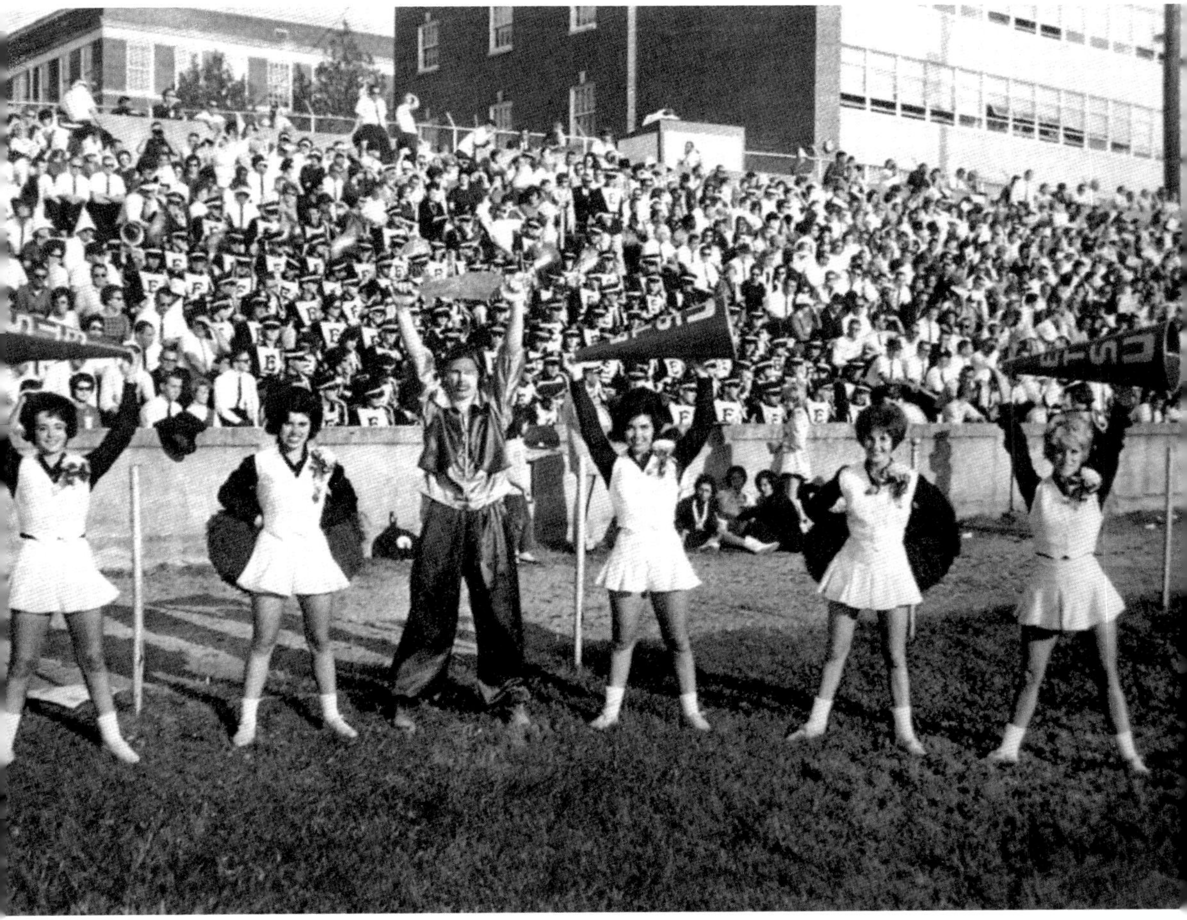

"Buc," a gaudily clad buccaneer that followed "Billy the Kid" as a mascot, ably assists the 1963–1964 cheerleaders; from left to right are Ann Duncan, Kaye Turbyville, Annie Lane (captain), Linda Gray, and Annette Roach (Carol Alexander was not pictured). At halftime, the cheerleaders would frequently extend a welcome to the visiting cheerleaders and fans, and the visiting cheerleaders would sometimes perform cheers for the home team. (Photograph courtesy Buc Football and Friends Foundation.)

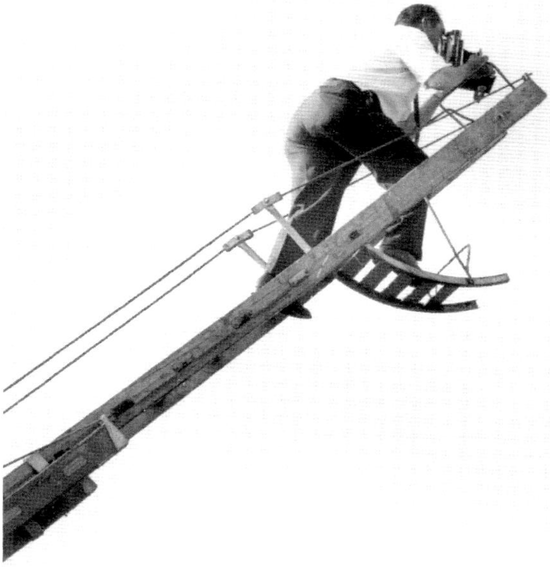

Louie Kinch provided photographic services for the school from the early 1950s to the late 1960s when the university hired Tom Daniel, the first full-time staff photographer. After Daniels left in the late 1970s, current staff photographer Larry Smith started his tenure. In this 1967 photograph, Kinch is shown going to great lengths (and heights) to get the best possible shot of the football team on the field. The ladder is mounted to the back of a pickup truck. (Photograph courtesy Buc Football and Friends Foundation.)

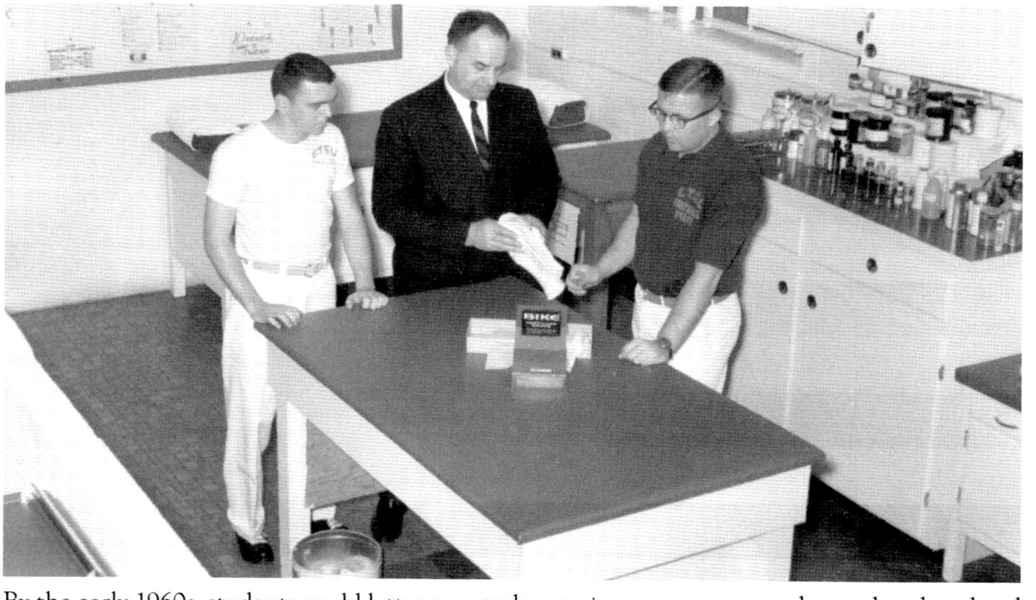

By the early 1960s, students could letter as a student trainer or manager and served under a head trainer starting in 1965. Pictured from left to right are Jay Shoop (assistant trainer), coach John Robert Bell, and Jerry Robertson (the first full-time head trainer). Shoop went on to be a trainer for a number of college and professional sports teams. He currently is director of sports medicine at Georgia Tech. (Photograph courtesy Buc Football and Friends Foundation.)

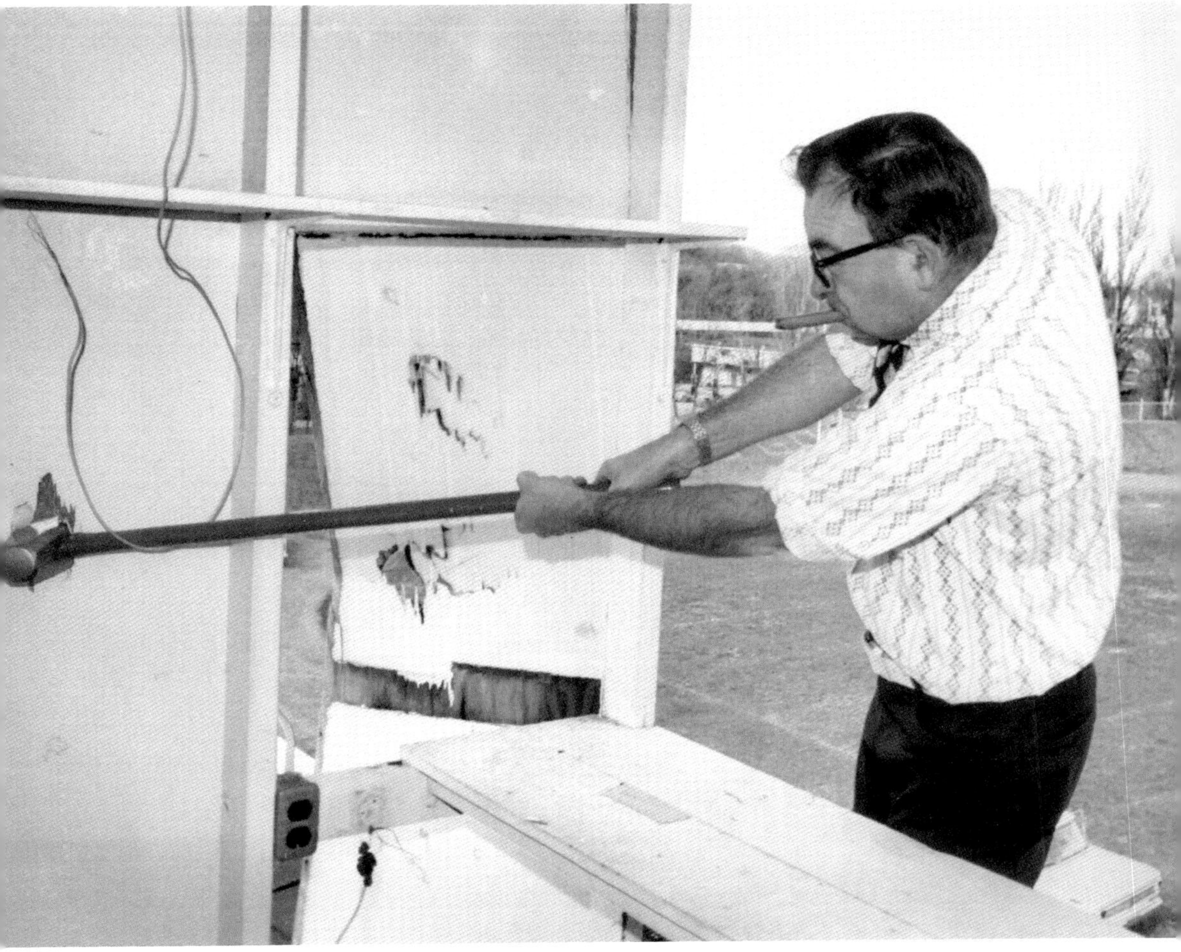

Legendary Sports Information Director (SID) John Cathey was known for his storytelling and cigars. He came to ETSU in 1969 to replace State's first SID, Bill Captain, and spent the next 25 years attending over 700 basketball games and working 271 consecutive football contests, a streak that ranked fifth in the nation among retired SIDs. Over his career, he was cited numerous times for excellence by College Sports Information Directors of America and received the College Football Centennial Award of SID. (Photograph courtesy Buc Football and Friends Foundation.)

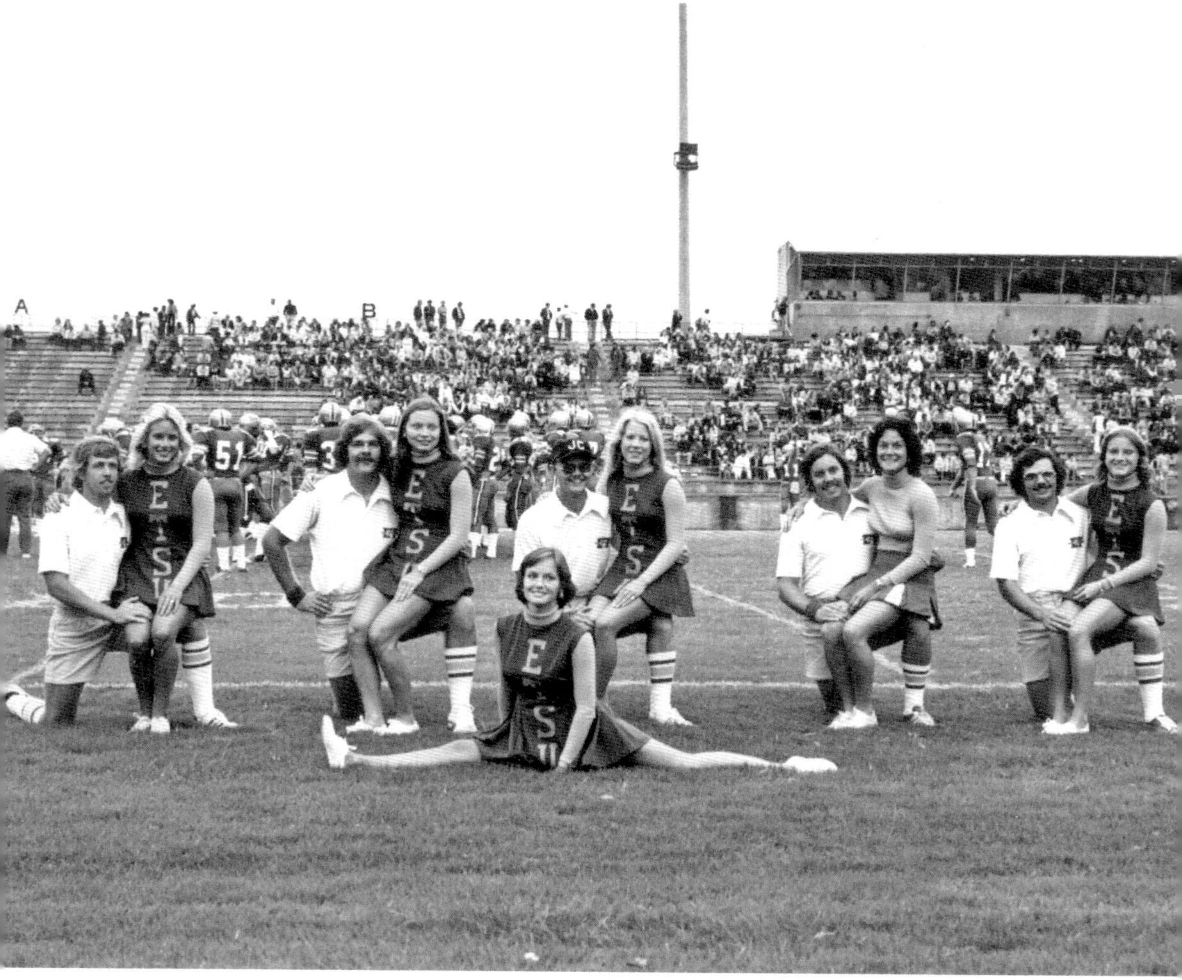

The 1974–1975 cheerleaders at Memorial Stadium are, from left to right, (first row) Kaye Green; (second row) Jerry Schuetz, Polly Wheelock, Rick Felts, Pat Earnest, Rigby Kind, Beth Foster, Steve Sitton, Debbie Cohen, Glen Smelser, and Lisa Piercy. Teammate Franklin Maples was not pictured. The main purpose of the squad is to promote school spirit. Duties include attending and cheering at all athletic events, making signs for each game, and conducting pep rallies. Members had to be undergraduates and had to maintain a 2.0 grade point average. (Photograph courtesy Buc Football and Friends Foundation.)

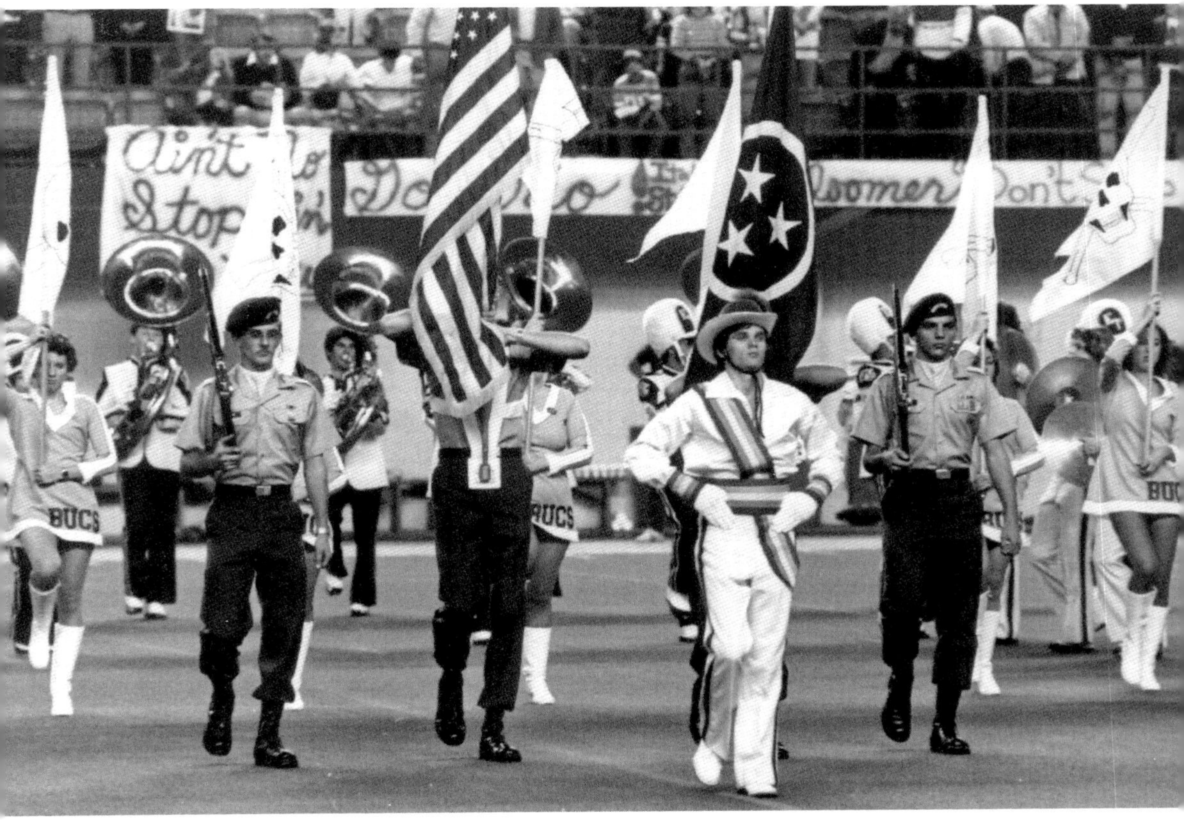

Modern color guard combines military drill, the use of flags, sabers, mock rifles, and other equipment, as well as dance and other interpretive movement. Traditional color guard first began in England around the time of the Civil War. Here they would play music to keep soldiers' spirits up and to keep them in beat. Today the guard uses choreography and equipment for added visual appeal during a marching band show. The ETSU Color Guard performs in Memorial Center during the late 1970s. (Photograph courtesy Buc Football and Friends Foundation.)

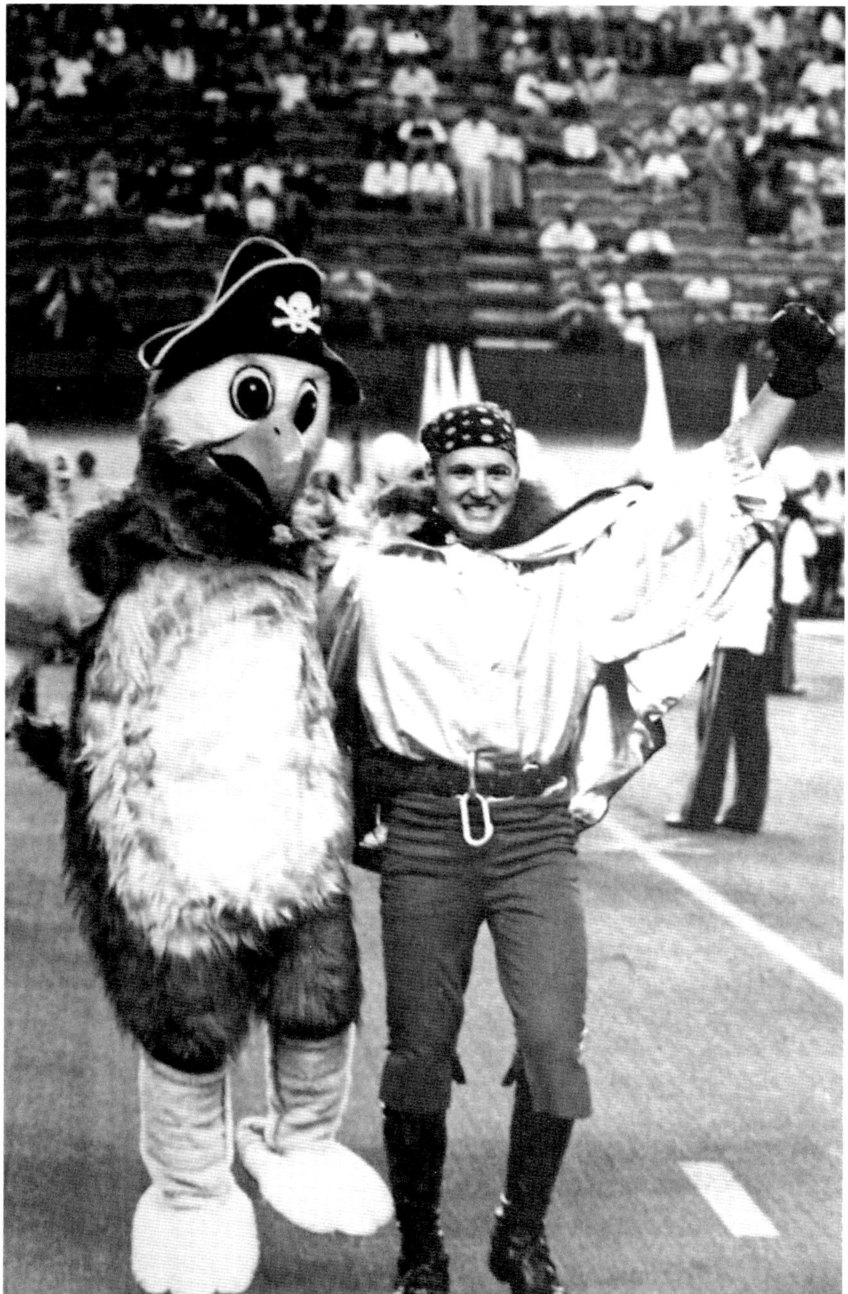

Bucky gained a companion during homecoming festivities on October 11, 1980, when Pepper the parrot hatched out of a big egg. As part of the Spirit Staff, Bucky and Pepper are always there supporting ETSU athletes and encouraging the crowd to cheer no matter how far ahead or behind the Buccaneers find themselves in a game. Both still work athletic events together. (Photograph courtesy Buc Football and Friends Foundation.)

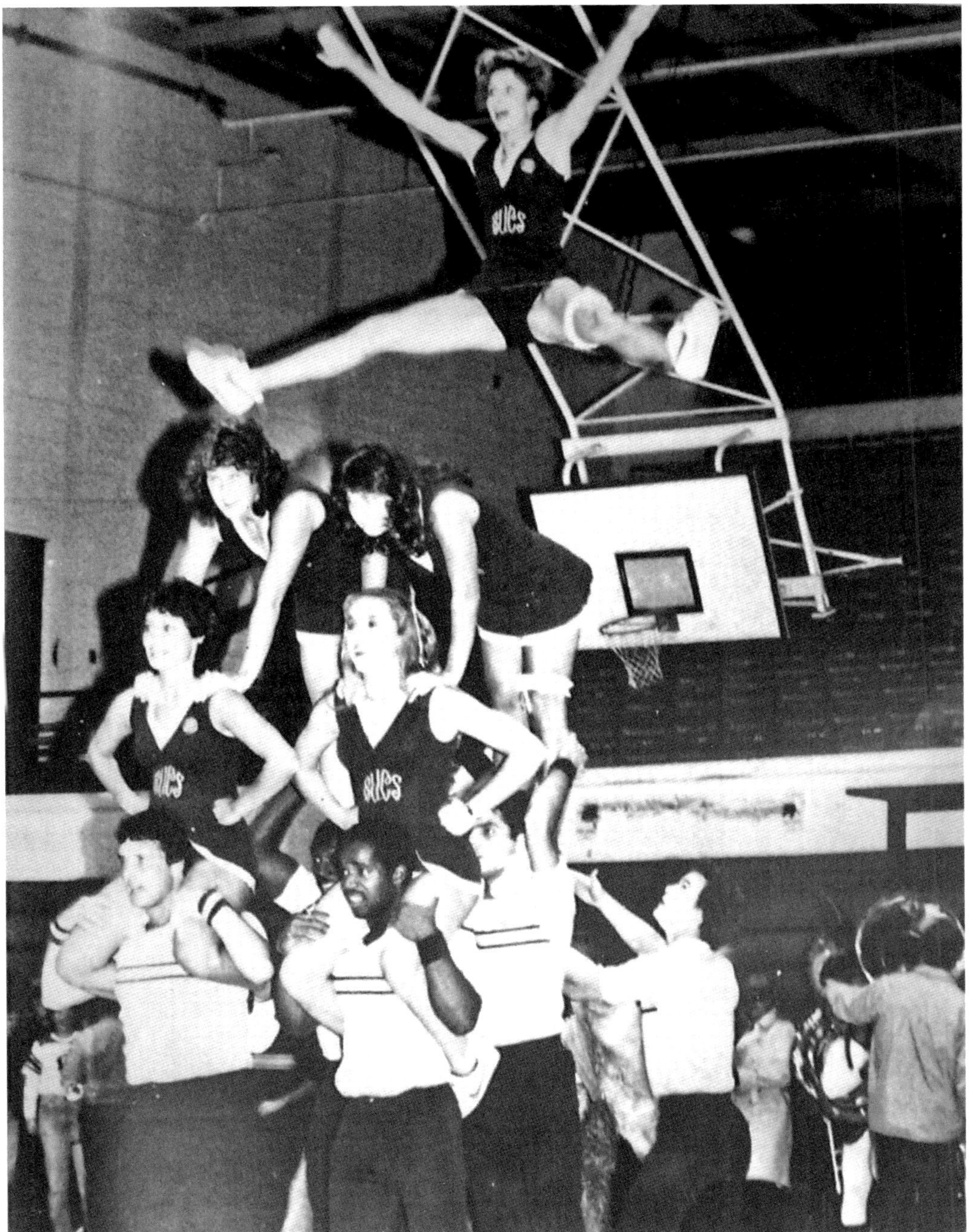

As can be seen in this photograph of the 1983–1984 cheerleaders, the skill and athleticism needed to perform had risen considerably from that needed in years past, where the main skill was to lead cheers, jump high, and do the occasional cartwheel. Modern cheerleading has evolved into a sport involving complex choreography combined with gymnastic skills. (Photograph courtesy Buc Football and Friends Foundation.)

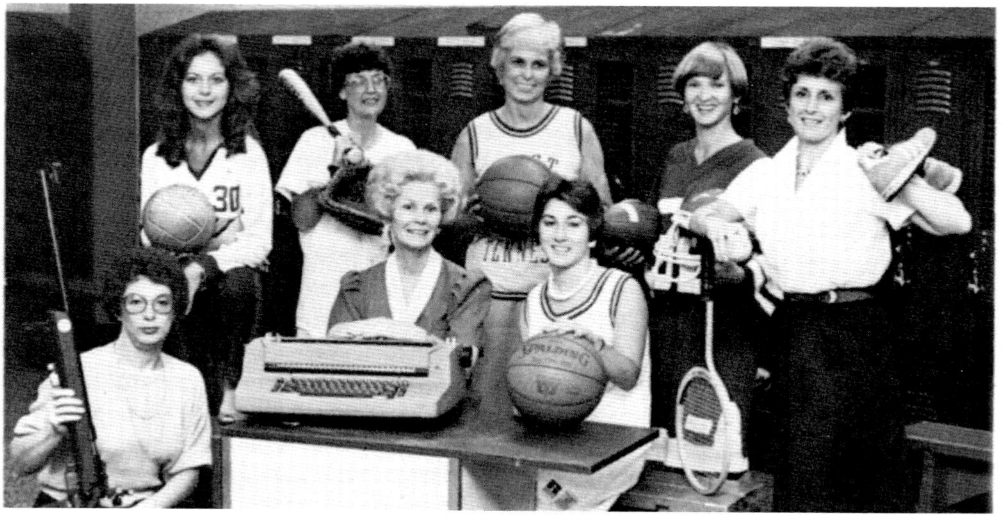

The sports secretaries did everything that needed doing behind the scenes of the sports program. Tasks accomplished by this able team would include: coordinating student workers, arranging travel plans, assisting with budgets, preparing copies of game and practice plans, preparing recruiting correspondence, and in the early days handling tickets. This 1985 photograph from the Media Guide demonstrates their multi-tasking abilities. (Photograph courtesy Buc Football and Friends Foundation.)

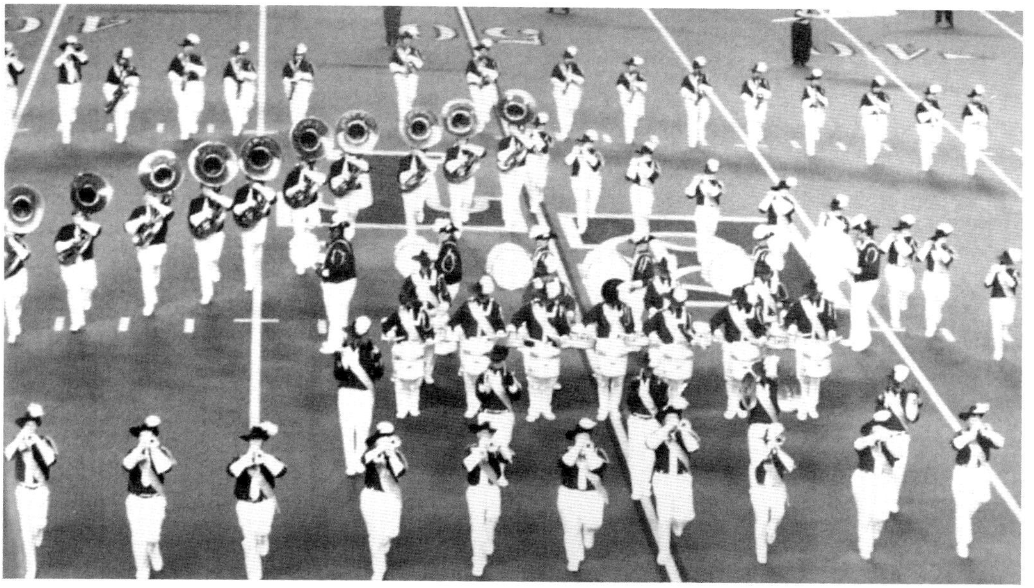

The marching band, like most programs at the university, has expanded significantly over time. The band program would have over 100 people perform well-orchestrated and choreographed numbers involving the band, majorettes, and color guard in elaborate costumes. The 1996–1997 marching band (above) performs for fans at halftime. (Photograph courtesy Buc Football and Friends Foundation.)

6

1969

A Year of Unrivaled Glory

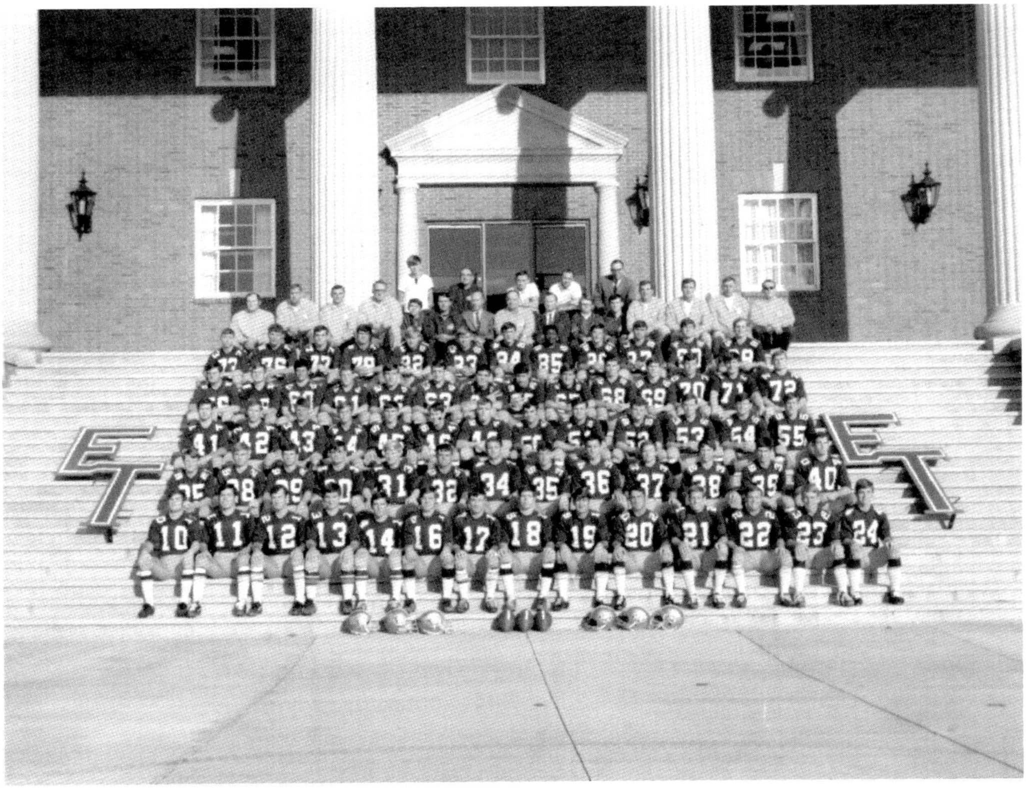

In addition to celebrating college football's 100th anniversary, the Buccaneers celebrated their finest year in history in 1969. The Bucs under John Robert Bell won the OVC crown and went undefeated, posting a 10-0-1 record. Defensive coach Buddy Bennett put together a monstrous secondary known as "Bennett's Bandits" that was led by Billy Casey and Al Guy, who combined for 20 interceptions on the year. The season record reflected a dominant defense and steady offense. The Buccaneers defense gave up only 93 points in 10 games and picked off 34 passes for the season. (Photograph courtesy of L. T. Helton.)

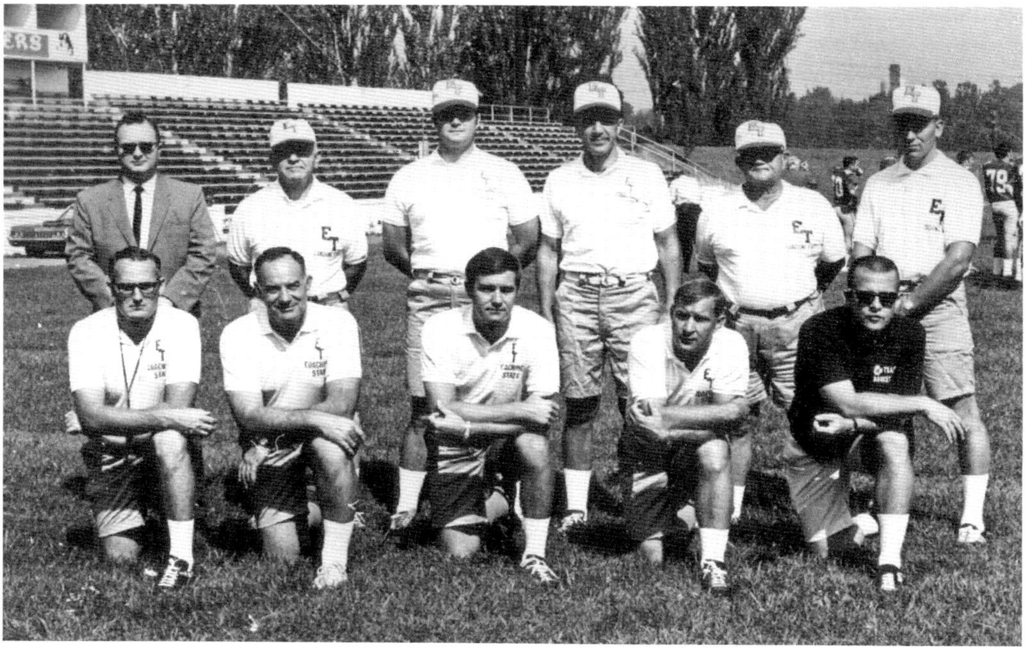

The 1969 coaching staff responsible for guiding the best edition of the Buccaneers, pictured from left to right, are (first row) L. T. Helton, John R. Bell, Larry Watson, Buddy Bennett, and Jerry Robertson; (second row) Dr. Burgin Dossett Jr., Julian Crocker, Bob Zolverian, Franklin Brooks, Calvin Frey, and Thurston Rose. (Photograph courtesy Buc Football and Friends Foundation.)

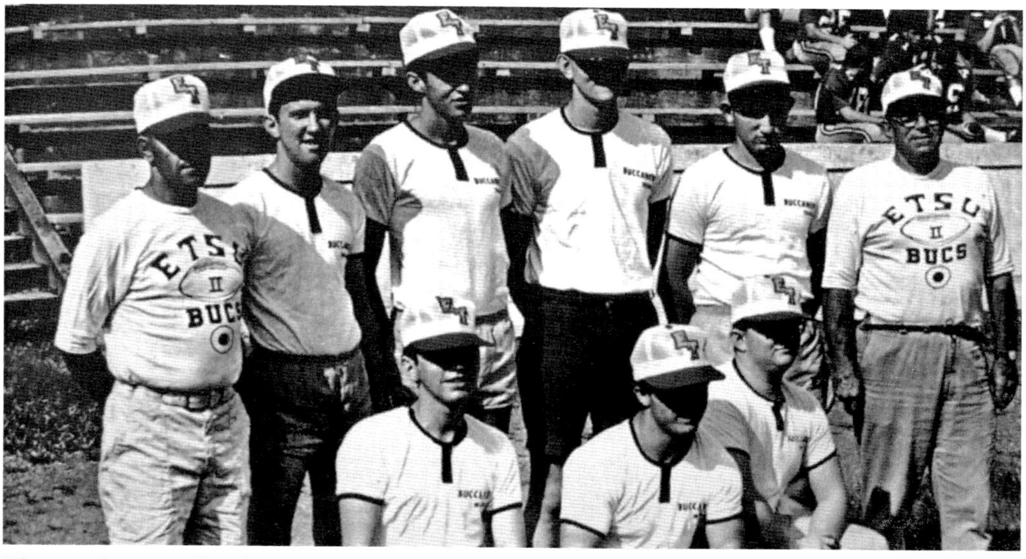

The coaching staff and team were assisted by an able and ready group of trainers and equipment managers. Pictured from left to right are (first row) Dan Collins, John Redmon, and Allen Haney; (second row) Jim Howard, Charles Lunsford, Ken Jenkins, Allen White, Ray Parlier, and equipment manager Jess Birchfield. (Photograph courtesy Buc Football and Friends Foundation.)

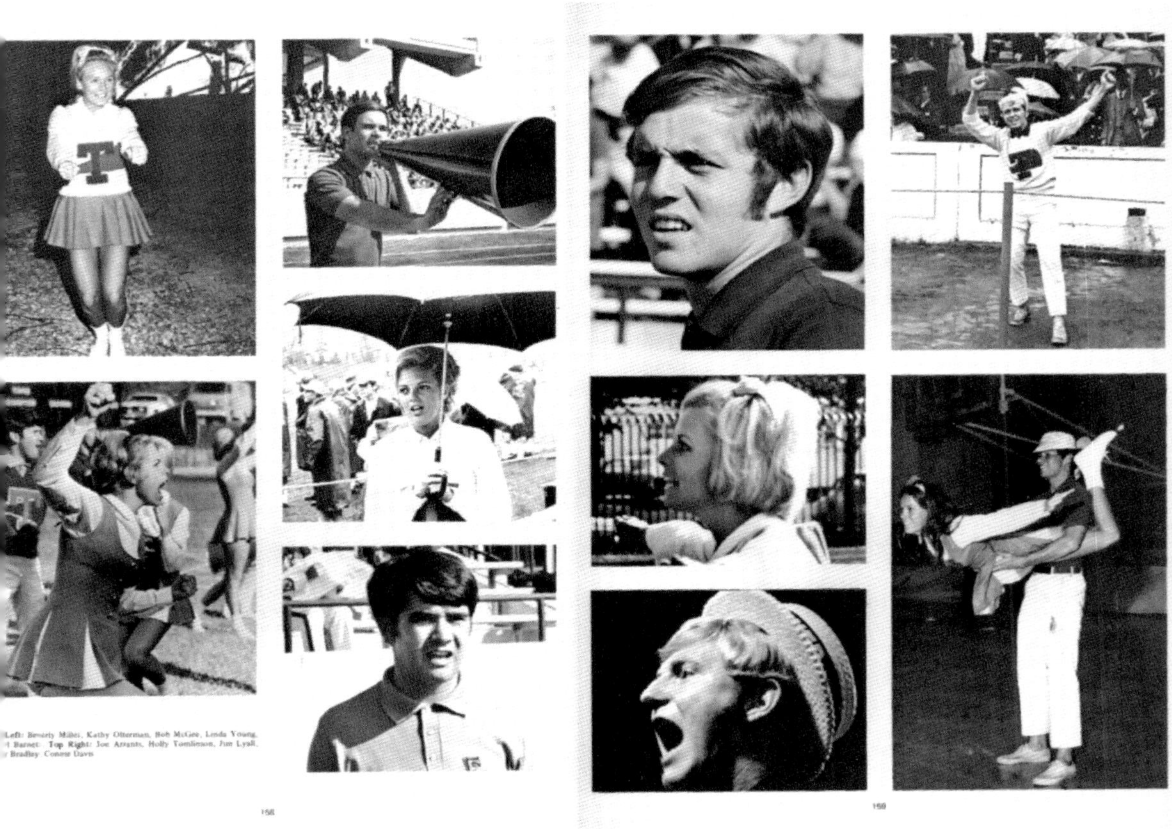

The 1969 cheerleading team—from left to right, (top row) Beverly Miller, Bob McGee, Joe Arrants, and Dicky Bradley; (second row) Kathy Olterman, Linda Young, Holly Tomlinson, and Connie Davis; (bottom row) Darryl Barnett and Jim Lyall—did their part during the season to keep spirits up, cheering the team to victory. The squad was active through the year at pep rallies, the homecoming parade and bonfire, and of course at games. (Photograph courtesy Buc Football and Friends Foundation.)

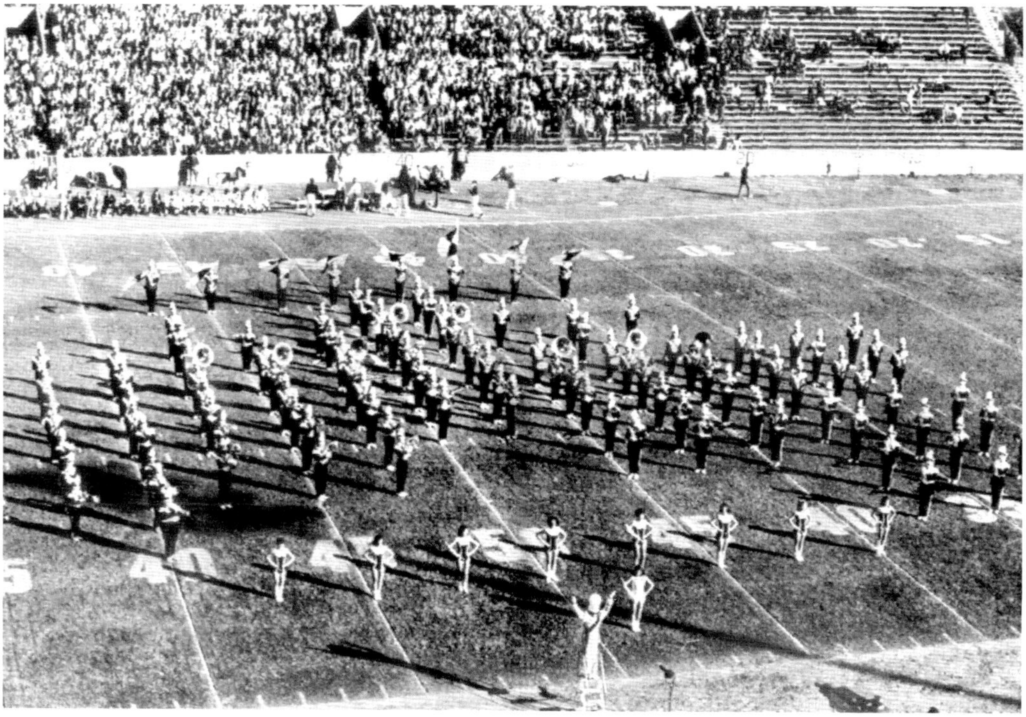

The Buccaneer Marching Band in its fully assembled glory was known in 1969 as the "Band with the Sound" and included a color guard and the Piratetts. Directed by Kenneth Large and Drum Major Mark Bays, they kept the crowds entertained and set the mood for the games. Without the "Sound," game days would not have been the same. (Photograph courtesy Buc Football and Friends Foundation.)

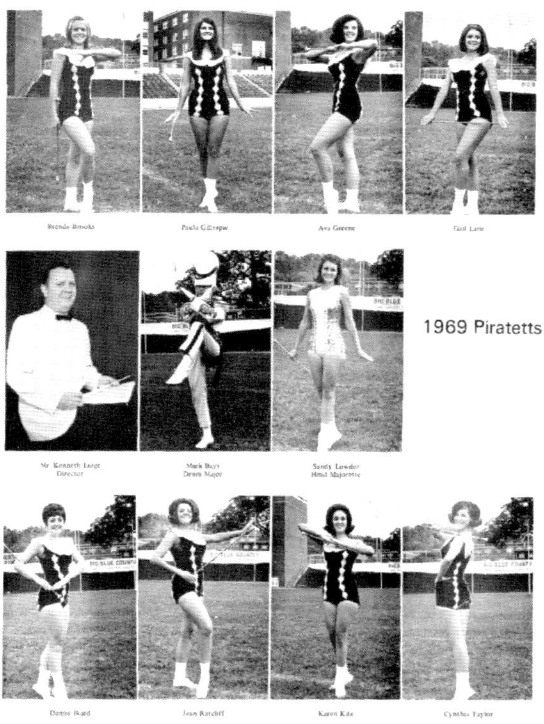

1969 Piratetts

Under the direction of Kenneth Large, the band increased in size to over 125 members including the 9-member Piratetts and increased in prominence. During his tenure, 1966–1974, the band performed throughout the region, garnering praise and recognition for their award-winning performances. (Photograph courtesy Buc Football and Friends Foundation.)

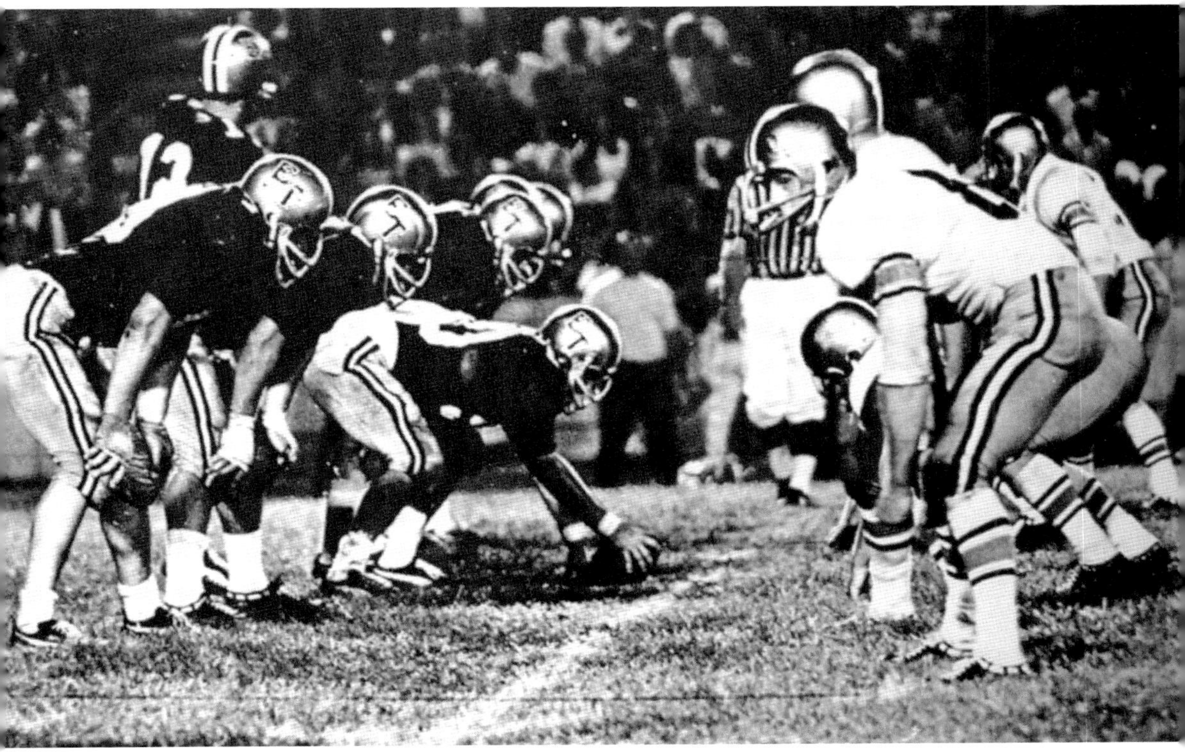

Fortunately for ETSU, the first play from scrimmage was not an omen of how things would turn out for the year. On that play, the Appalachian State quarterback connected with his receiver for a 67-yard touchdown pass. The Bucs trailed 16-7 with just six minutes remaining in the game, but the tide turned and the Bucs squeaked out an 18-16 home victory against the Mountaineers on September 13. (Photograph courtesy Buc Football and Friends Foundation.)

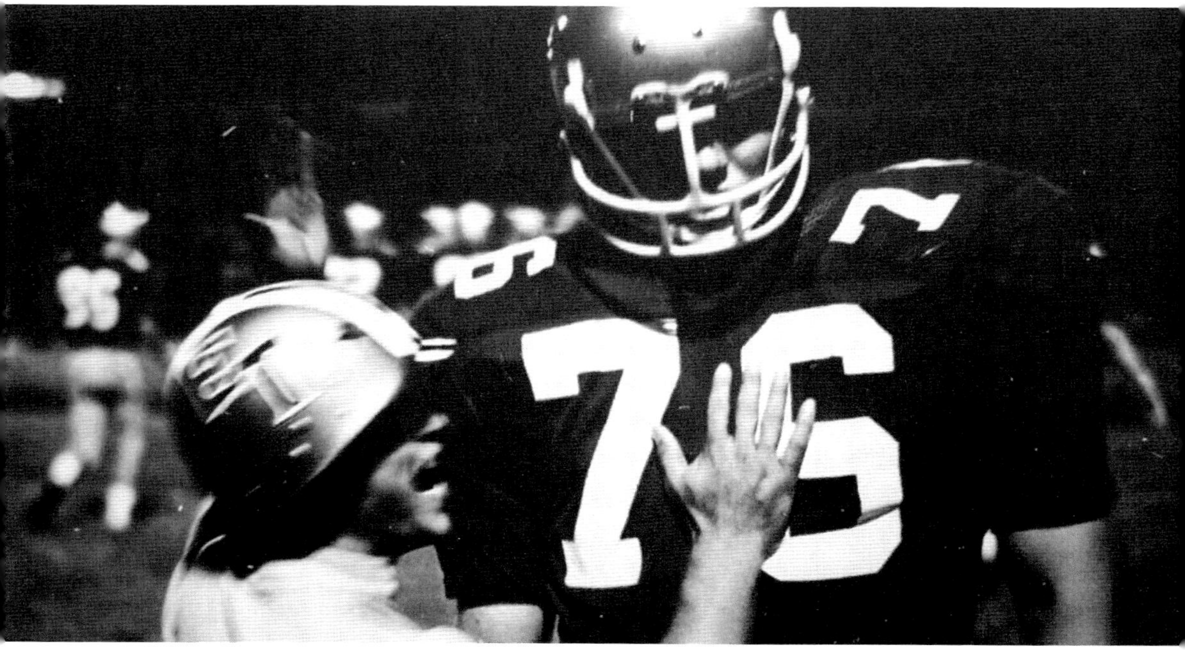

The Big Blue next met the East Carolina Pirates, a member of the Southern Conference, in another tight contest in front of a capacity crowd at University Stadium on September 20. The defense set the tone for the game by intercepting three passes and allowing the superior Corsair team to walk away with a 7-0 margin for their second home victory. Above, a fan congratulates Dennis Larkins. (Photograph courtesy Buc Football and Friends Foundation.)

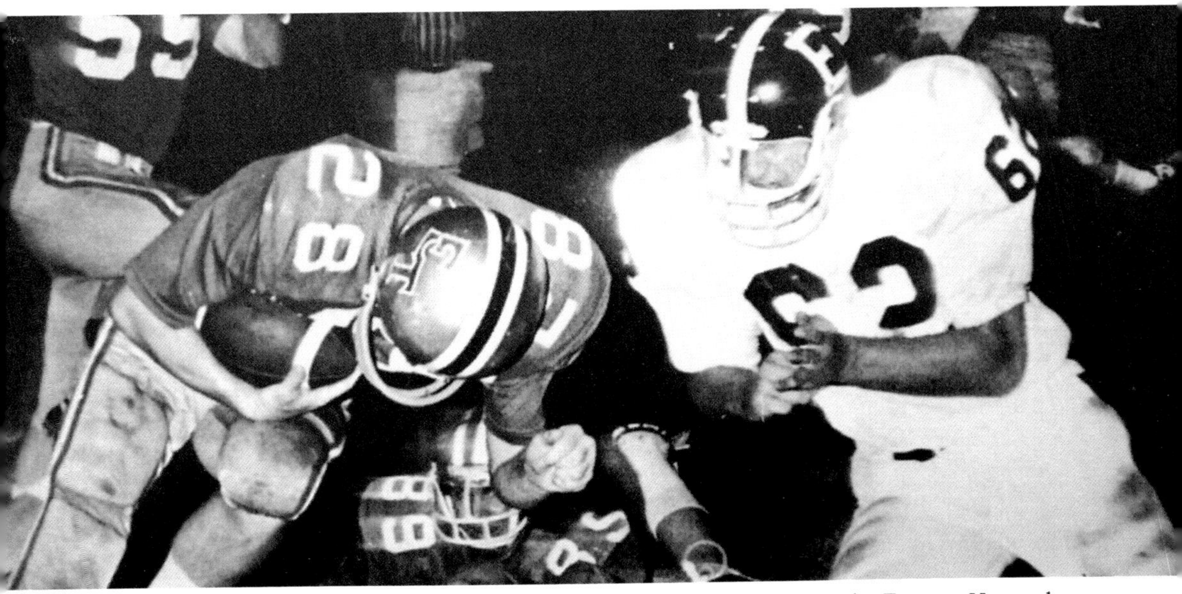

Jerry Weston and the Bucs put their heads down and pushed their way past the Eastern Kentucky Colonels to the tune of 19-7 for their third home victory and seventh win in a row, dating to the previous year. Bob Jones (55) and Ron Mendheim (89) are in the background trying to clear the way. Two late interceptions by Bill Casey preserved the lead and the game for the Bucs. (Photograph courtesy Buc Football and Friends Foundation.)

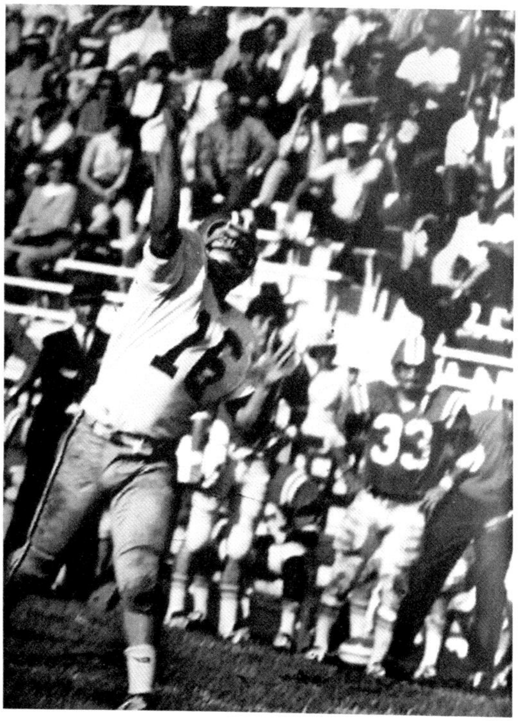

Starting an October road trip, Larry Graham and the Buccaneers aired it out against eventual OVC runner-up Western Kentucky, winning 16-7 before 7,500 fans at L. T. Smith Stadium in their first test away from home. The Western Kentucky Hilltopper team that year was led by captain Romeo Crennel, who went on to NFL coaching fame serving under Bill Parcels and Bill Belichik in six super bowls. Crennel is currently head coach of the Cleveland Browns. (Photograph courtesy Buc Football and Friends Foundation.)

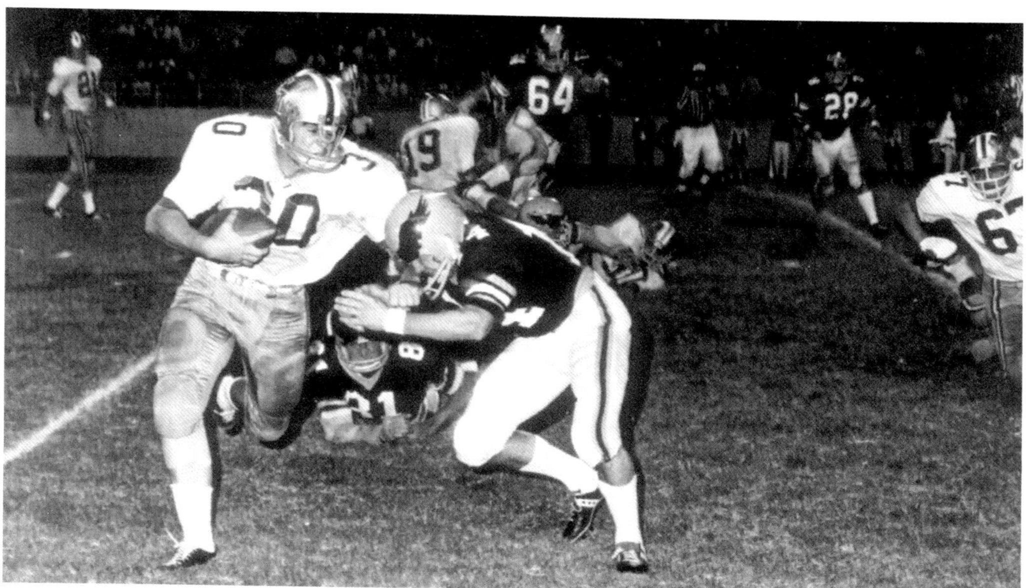

The fifth game of the season was played October 11 in Cookeville against the Tennessee Tech Golden Eagles. Both the Buccaneer offense and defense were hitting on all cylinders, generating a 30-7 rollover. Quarterback Larry Graham threw for two touchdowns (one for 51 yards to Pat Hauser) and ran for a third. Above, Mike Roberts (30) runs as Ed Harris (67) tries to get in front to block. (Photograph courtesy Buc Football and Friends Foundation.)

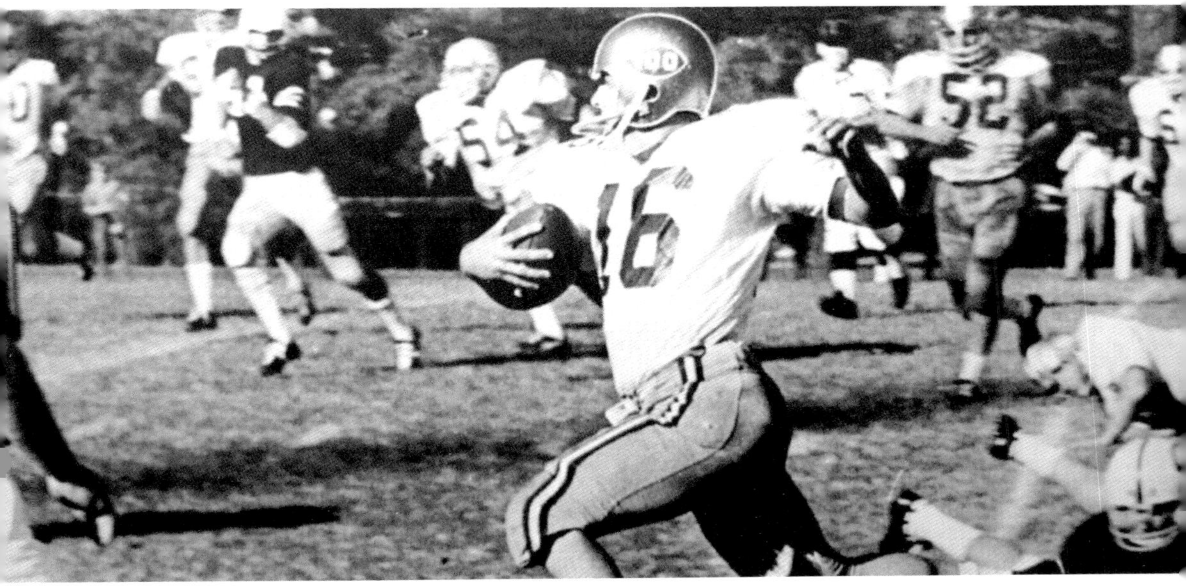

On the road again, the Buccaneers played University of Tennessee–Chattanooga at historic Chamberlain Field (opened in 1908), and like their first game, they came from behind to win 17-13. Larry Graham (16) scrambles for yardage against the Moccasins. His six-yard pass to end Ron Causey capped an 18-play, 84-yard drive for the win. (Photograph courtesy Buc Football and Friends Foundation.)

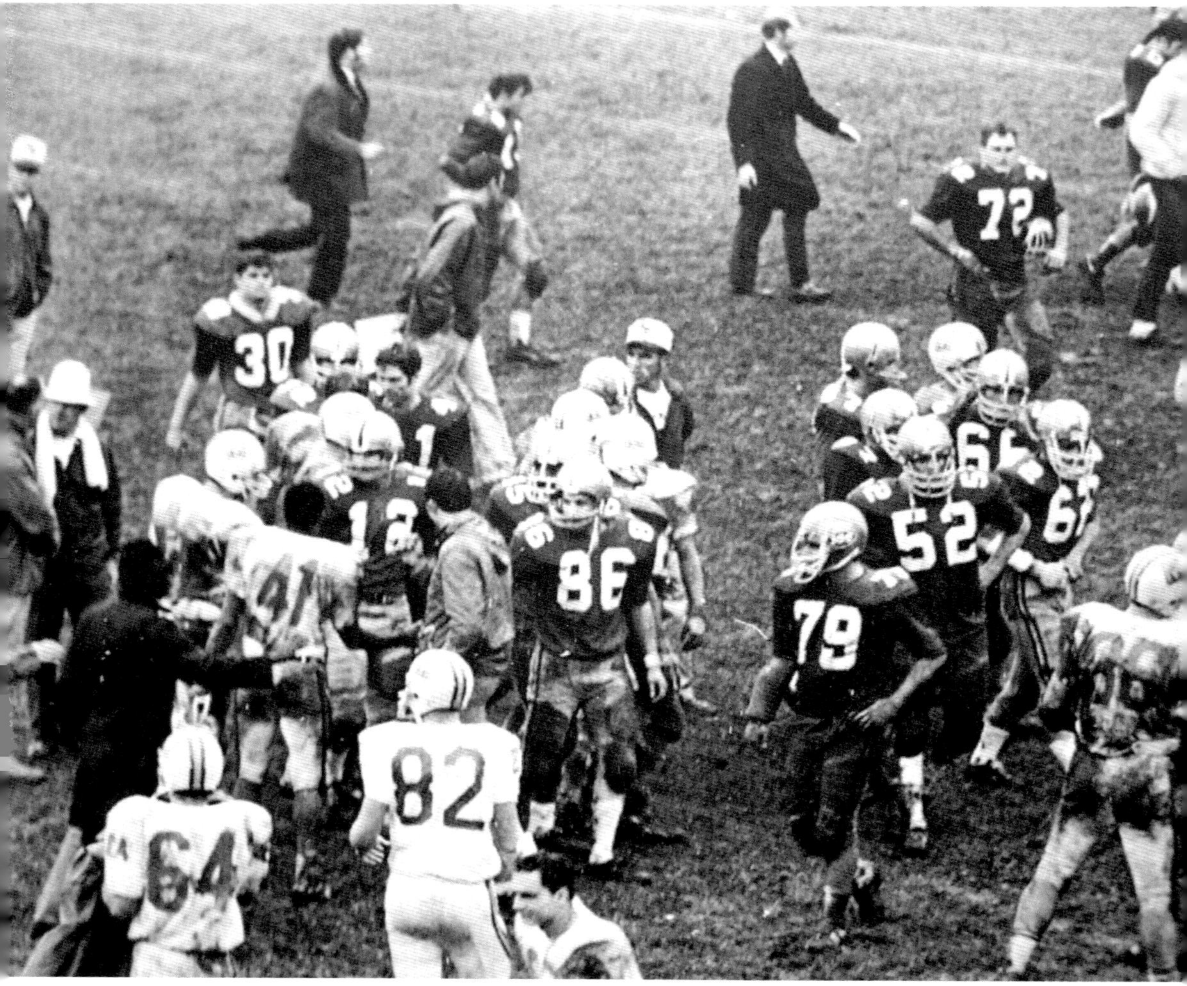

On October 25, the Bucs returned to Big Blue Country for a sloppy homecoming game against the Murray State Racers. On a dreary, cold, wet, and miserable day, the two teams sloshed to a 10-10 tie in front of rain-soaked fans sporting a sea of umbrellas. Murray scored first after a 50-yard run and 14-yard pass. State prevented other scoring opportunities on the strength of five interceptions and roared back to a 10-7 lead by halftime but missed two field goals in the second half that would have put the game away. (Photograph courtesy Buc Football and Friends Foundation.)

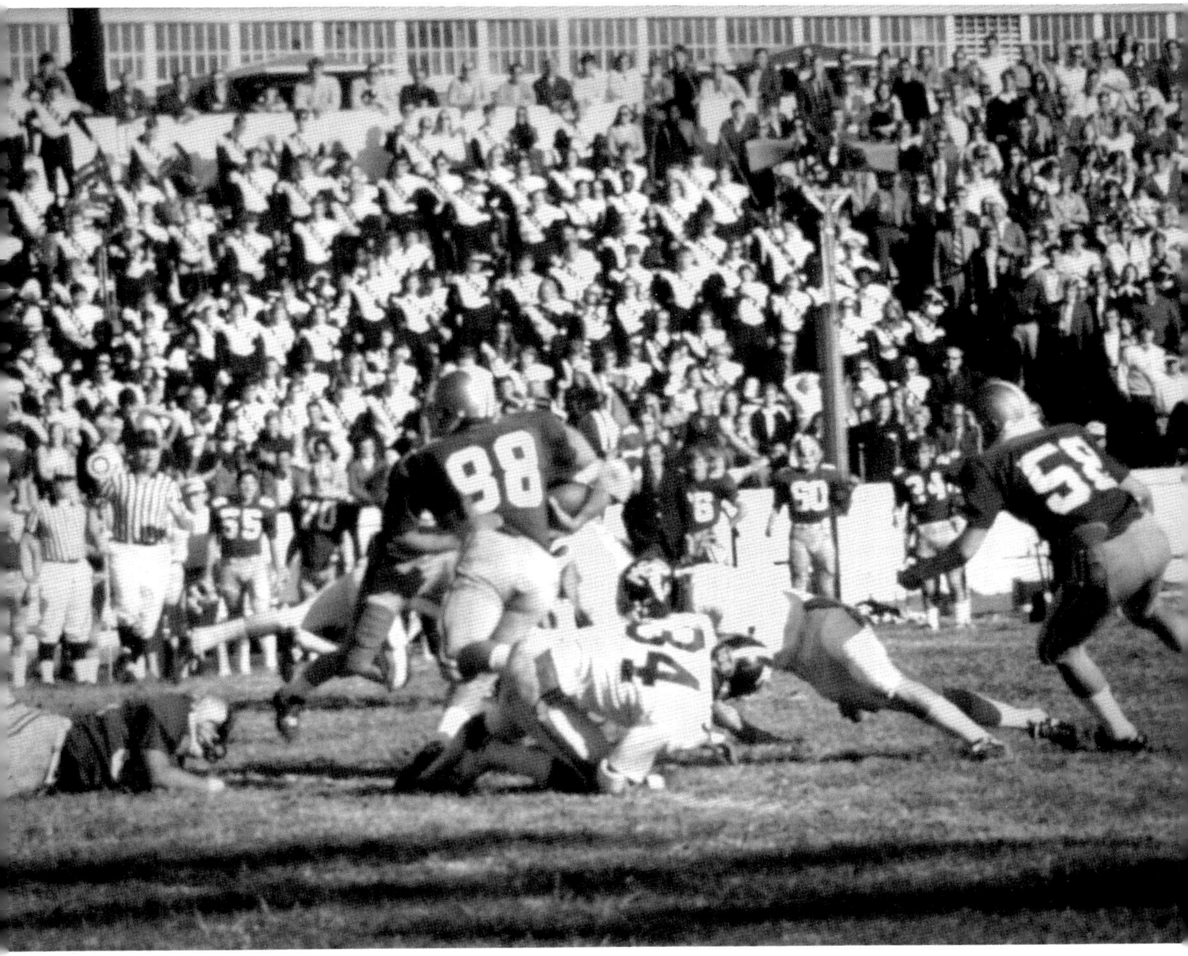

ETSU arrived in Morehead, Kentucky, on November 8 to take on the Morehead State University Eagles. After pulling off six interceptions and setting a new OVC record of 30 in the process, they left on the winning end of a 27-7 pounding. Bill Casey had three of the picks, which gave him the ETSU record for a season at 10, breaking Ron Overbay's mark of 9 the previous year. Al Guy also had two picks, which gave him nine for the year. (Photograph courtesy Buc Football and Friends Foundation.)

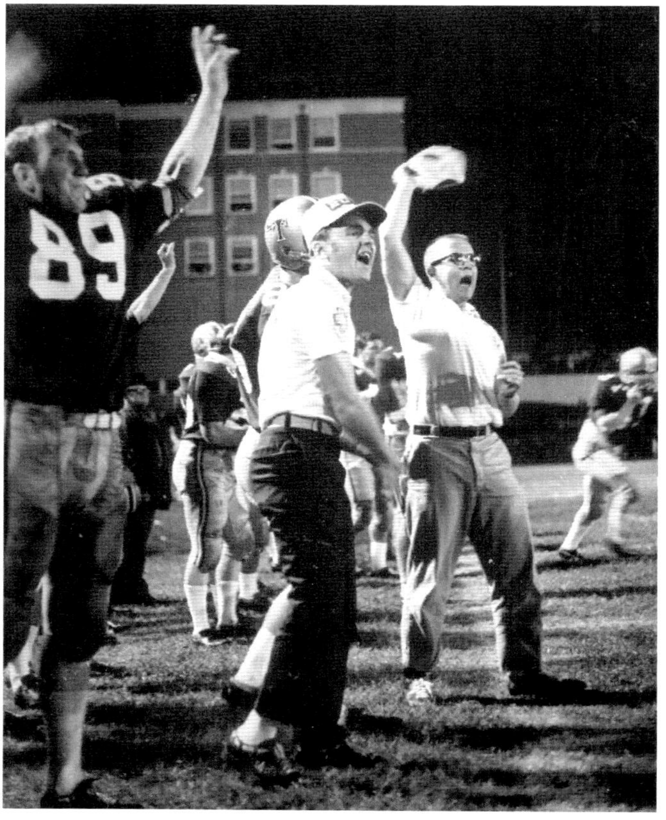

The Blue Raiders of Middle Tennessee State challenged the "Battling Bucs" but were turned away by a score of 27-21 in front of a chilled home crowd of about 3,000 fans who braved 21-degree weather. The win clinched the outright OVC crown for the Bucs, a first. From left to right, Ron Mendheim (89), Jay Shoop, and head trainer Jerry Robertson celebrate a score. (Photograph courtesy Buc Football and Friends Foundation.)

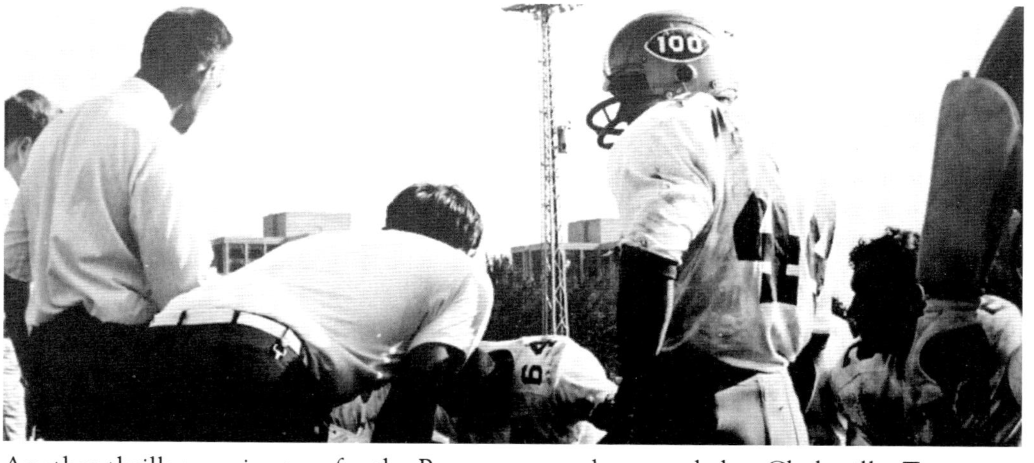

Another thriller was in store for the Buccaneers as they traveled to Clarksville, Tennessee, on November 22 to play the Austin Peay Governors. This was the homecoming game for the Governors, who stayed close the entire game despite a 1-6-1 record entering the game. The Bucs would finally prevail by a "razor-thin" two points and a final score of 14-12. During the week leading up to the game, the Bucs accepted the invitation to play in the Grantland Rice Bowl. (Photograph courtesy Buc Football and Friends Foundation.)

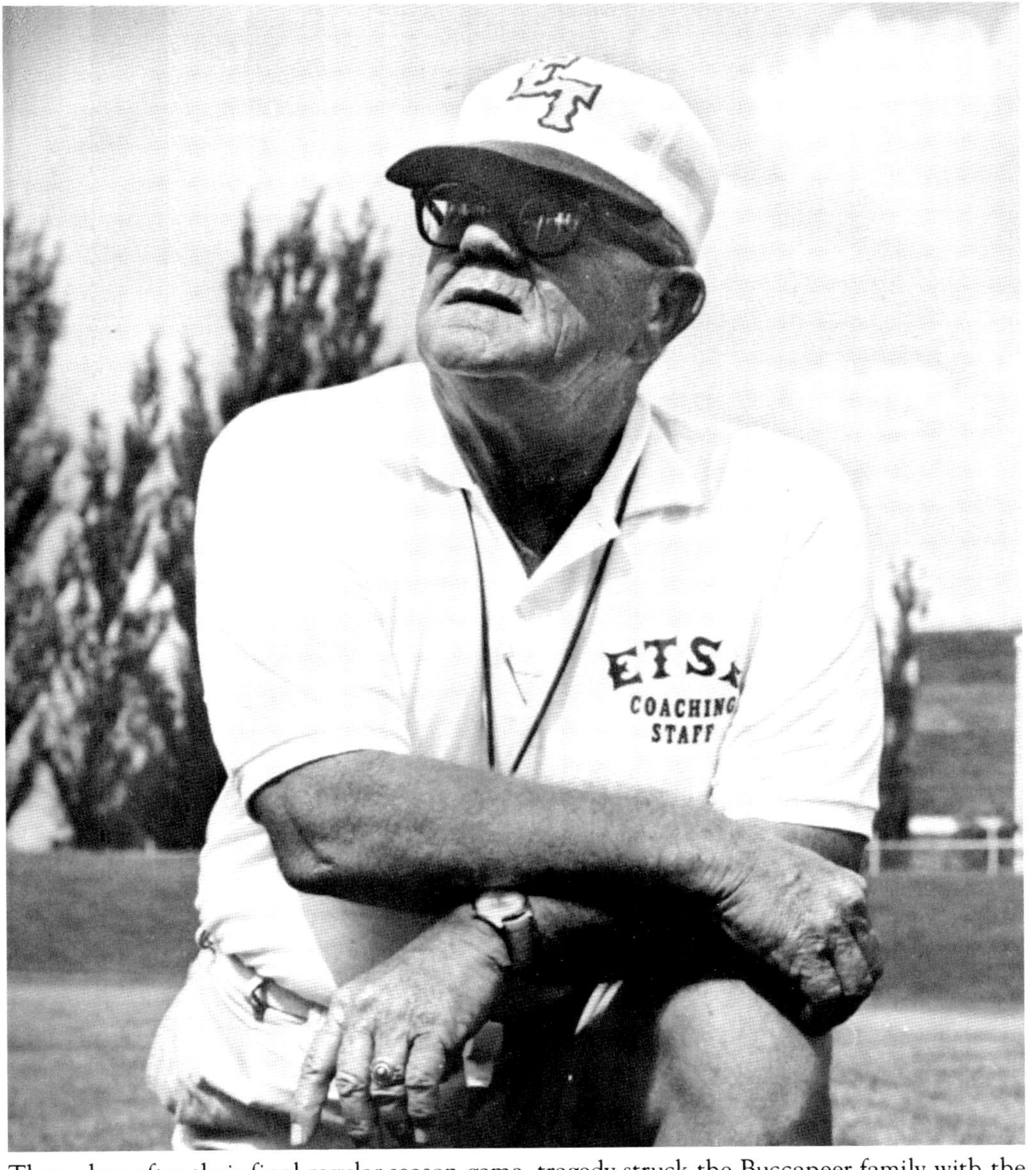

Three days after their final regular-season game, tragedy struck the Buccaneer family with the death of Calvin C. Frey. He was affectionately called "Shorty" by those who knew him, and he had served as an assistant coach with the Bucs since his arrival in 1955 from TPI. To honor their fallen coach, Buc players wore a black cross on their helmets for the Grantland Rice Bowl game. (Photograph courtesy Buc Football and Friends Foundation.)

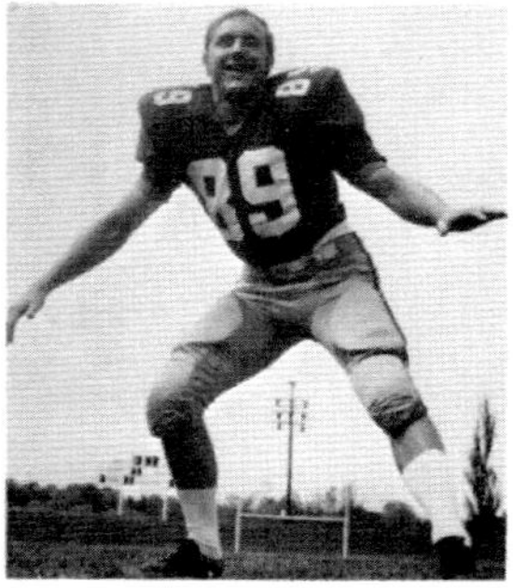

Ron Mendheim

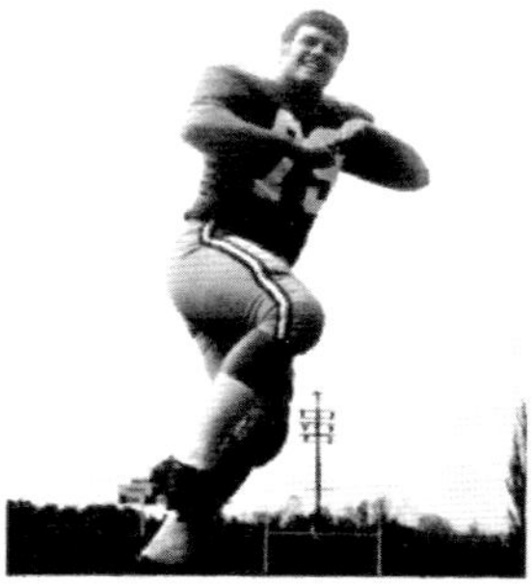

Frank Patterson

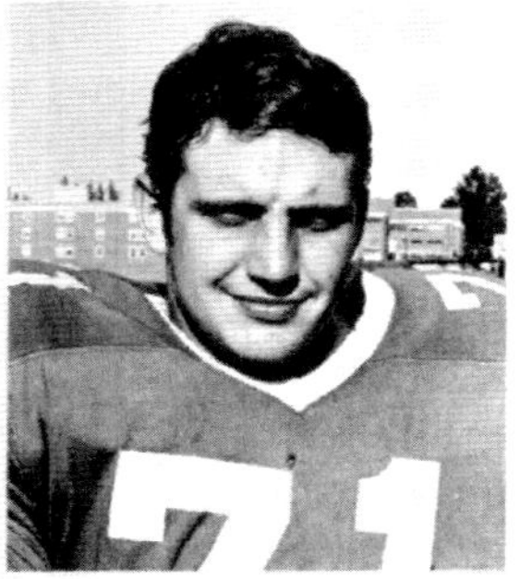

Doug Linebarger

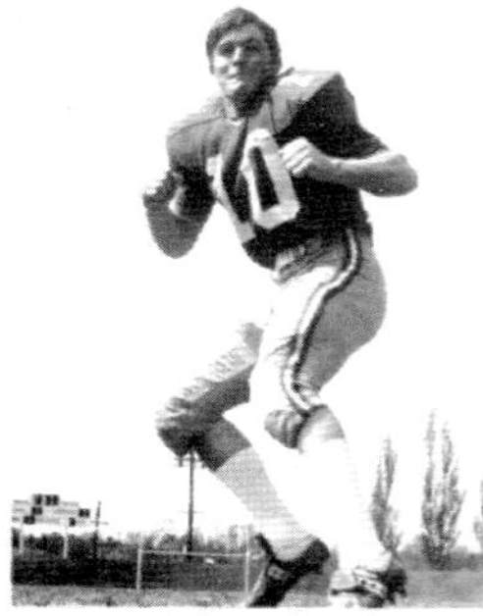

Bill Casey

ALL-AMERICAN AND ALL-OVC PLAYERS

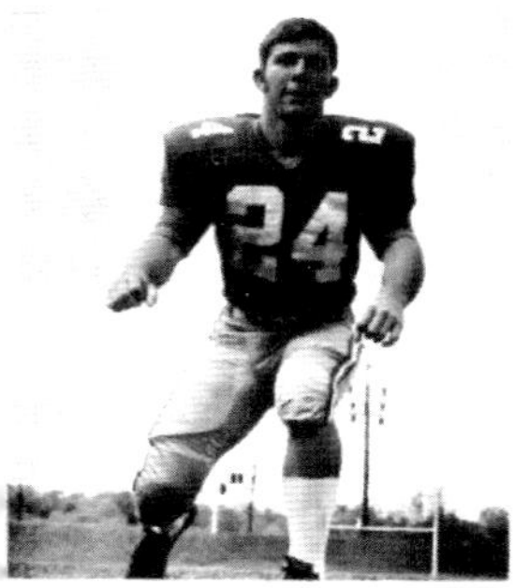

Bubba Timms

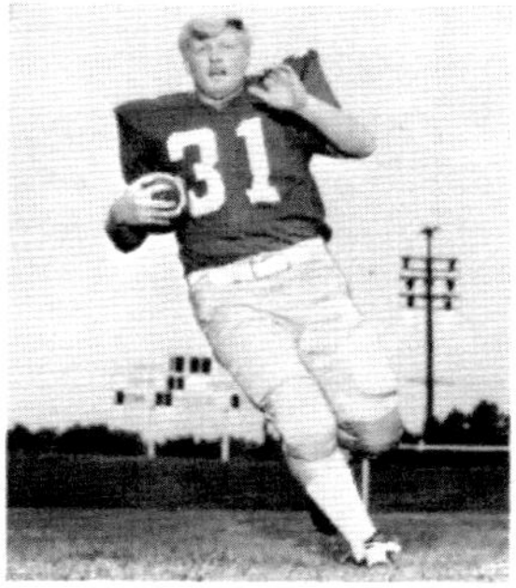

Ronnie Harrold

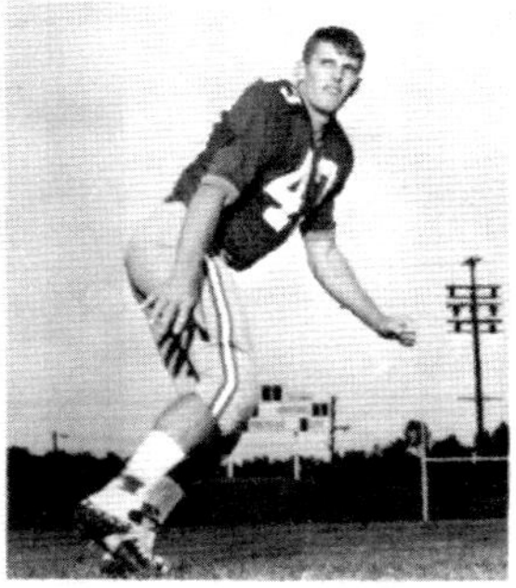

Al Guy

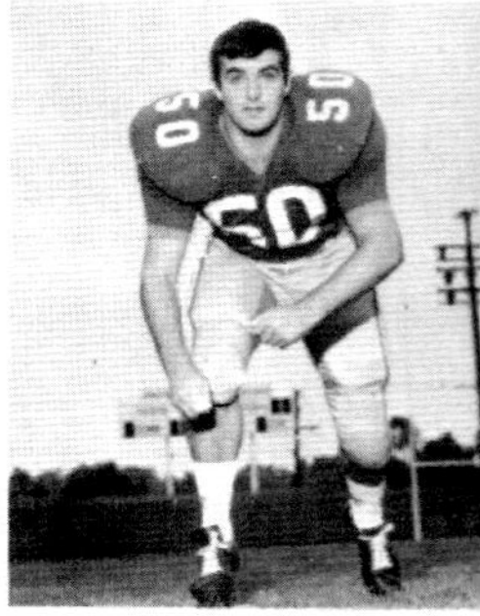

John Walton

The unparalleled success of the team was due in part to outstanding individual play. Eight players—Ron Mendheim, Frank Patterson, Doug Linebarger, Bill Casey, Bubba Timms, Ronnie Harrold, Al Guy (brother of pro punter Ray Guy), and John Walton—were honored for the quality of their play by selection to the All-Conference Team. Two of the eight, Linebarger and Walton, were selected to the All-American Team, and Casey would make All-American the following year. (Photograph courtesy Buc Football and Friends Foundation.)

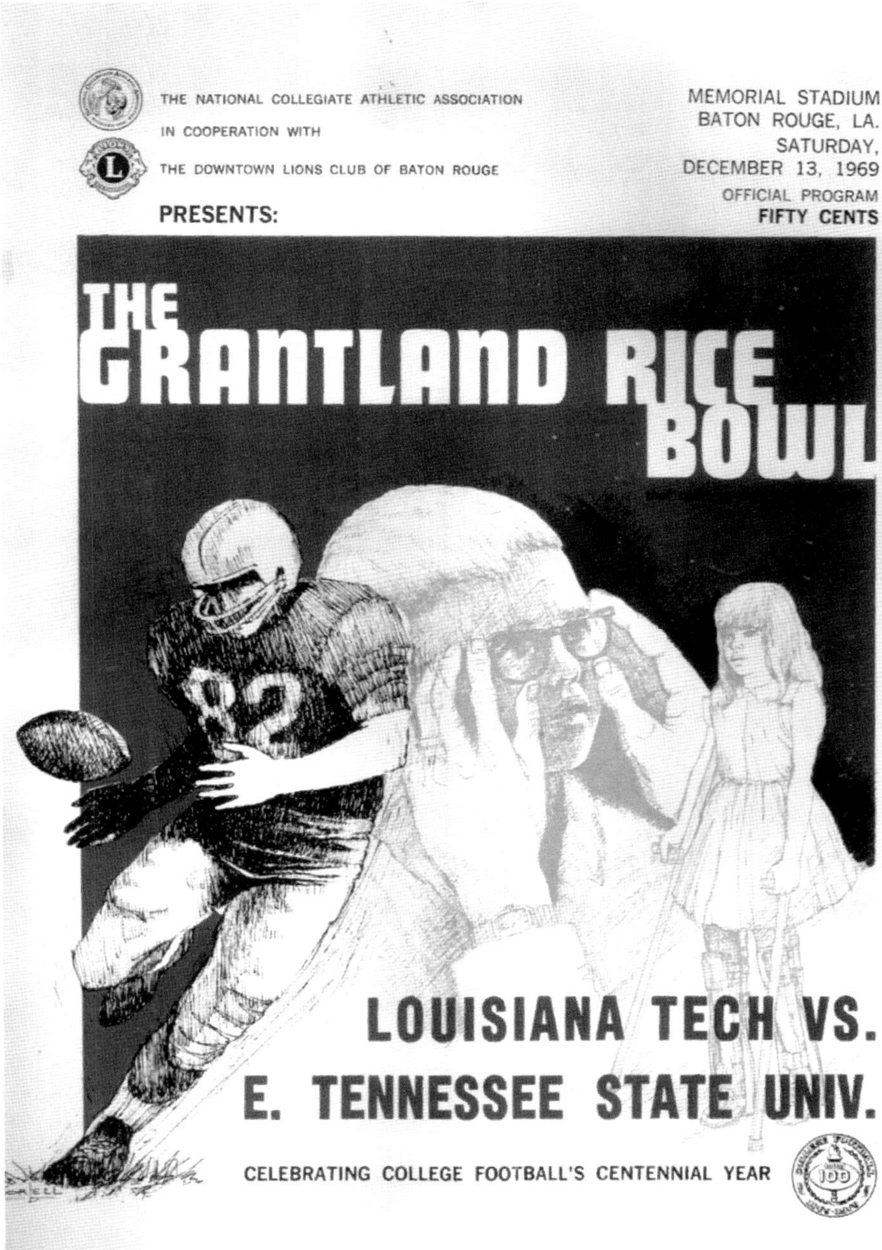

The Grantland Rice Bowl, played annually, was one of four regional NCAA college division championships from 1964 to 1972. From 1964 to 1968, the game was played in Murfreesboro, Tennessee, but the regional alignments shifted in 1969, and the game was moved to Baton Rouge, Louisiana, where it remained until 1975. In 1973, under the newly restructured college division playoff system, the game became the national Division II semifinal. With the formation of the NCAA Division I-AA and the modern playoff structure, the game ceased to exist after 1977. (Photograph courtesy Buc Football and Friends Foundation.)

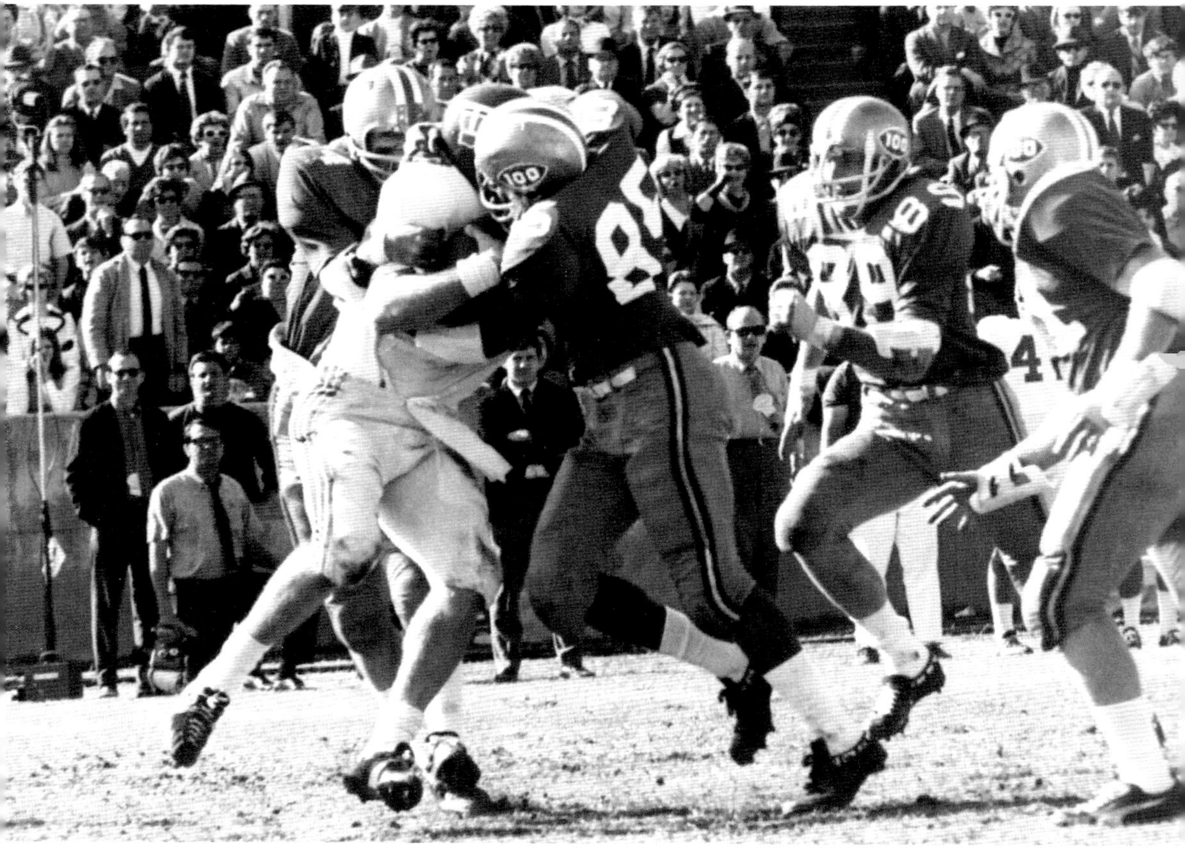

The NCAA College Division football game that garnered the most attention in 1969 was the Mideast Championship. All the attention and excitement was due to the star attraction of the game, Terry "The Blonde Bomber" Bradshaw of Louisiana Tech University. Bradshaw, a strong-armed quarterback from Shreveport, had 2,314 yards of total offense, ranking third nationally, and 136 pass completions. Coached by Maxie Lambright, the Bulldogs won the Gulf States Conference with an 8-1 record. (Photograph courtesy of ETSU Photo Lab.)

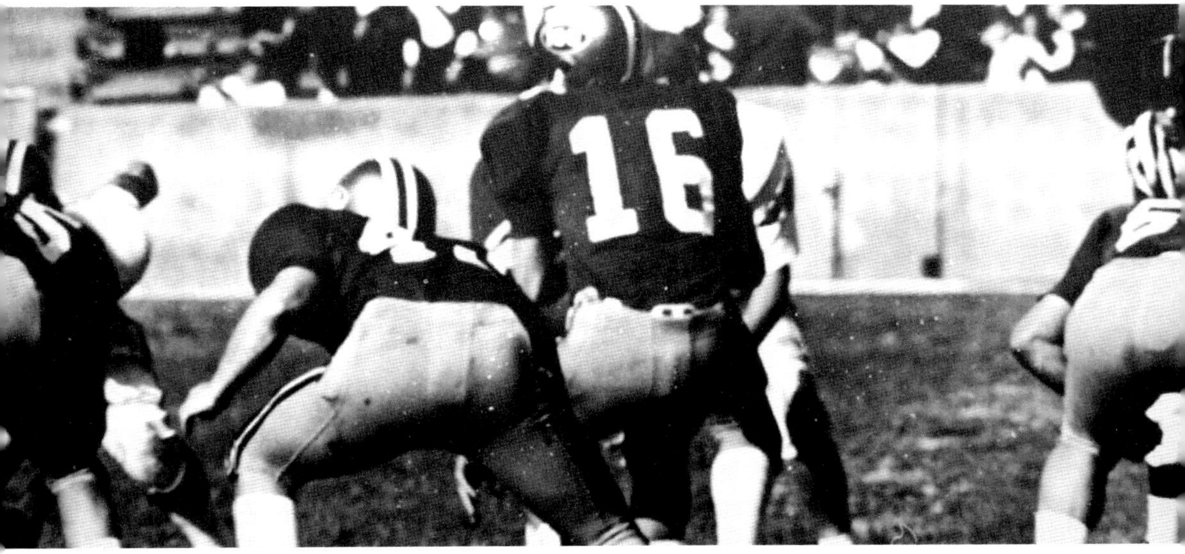

The Bucs entered the game as the 16th-ranked small college team in America by UPI. Although Larry Graham (16), pictured, had thrown only three fewer touchdown passes (11) than Bradshaw (14), Coach Bell still wanted to keep the ball away from Tech as much as possible. To do this, the Bucs needed to keep a balance between rushing and passing combined with the defense's penchant for interceptions (34 in the year). (Photograph courtesy Buc Football and Friends Foundation.)

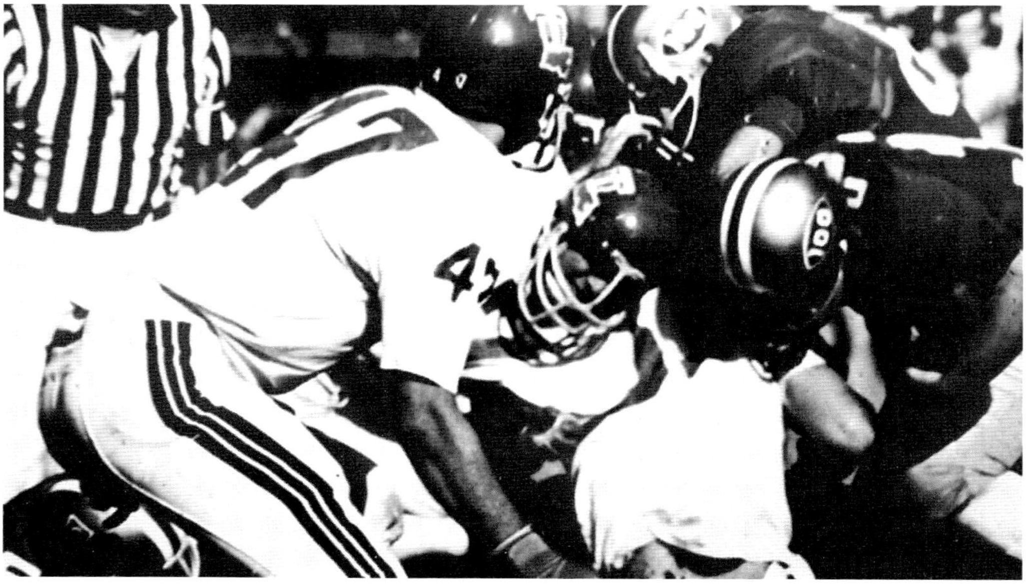

As Louisiana Tech's opponent in the Grantland Rice Bowl, the Bucs got little pre-game publicity. According to John Cathey, the ETSU SID, no one really took the Bucs seriously for three and a half months. Rival OVC coaches kept saying that offensively the Bucs left something to be desired, and despite them leading the conference in defense, it was thought that there were better defensive teams as well. However, on December 13, the Buccaneers made believers out of rival coaches, the media, and television viewers by defeating the vaunted Bradshaw and his Bulldogs 34-14. The tone for the entire game was set on the first play of the game when the "hardrocks" threw Bradshaw for a 14-yard loss, the first of 12 sacks on the day. When Bradshaw's nightmare ended, he had been thrown for losses totaling 143 yards, and the Bucs annihilated the Bulldog offense into minus 43 yards for the game, still a team record. (Above, photograph courtesy Buc Football and Friends Foundation; Below, photograph courtesy of ETSU Photo Lab.)

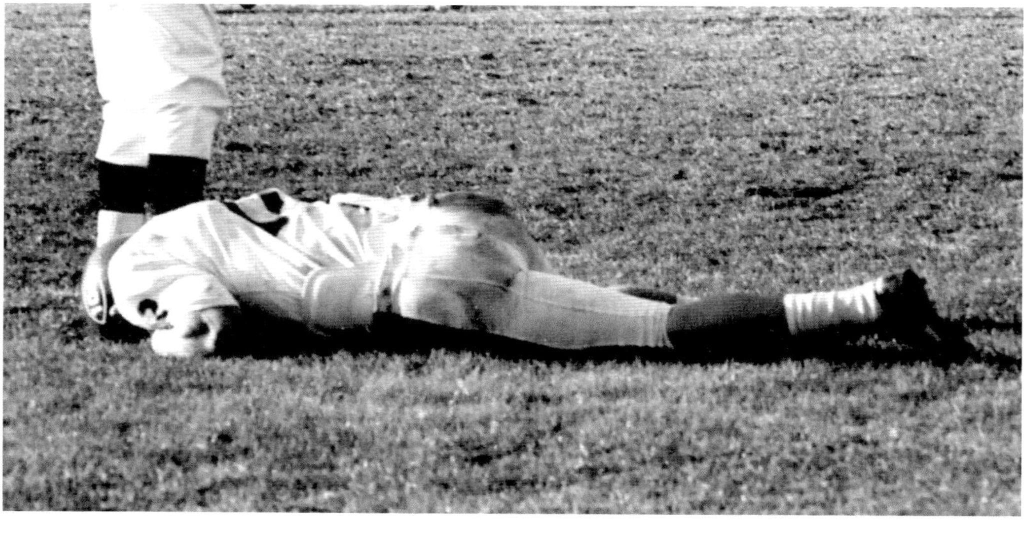

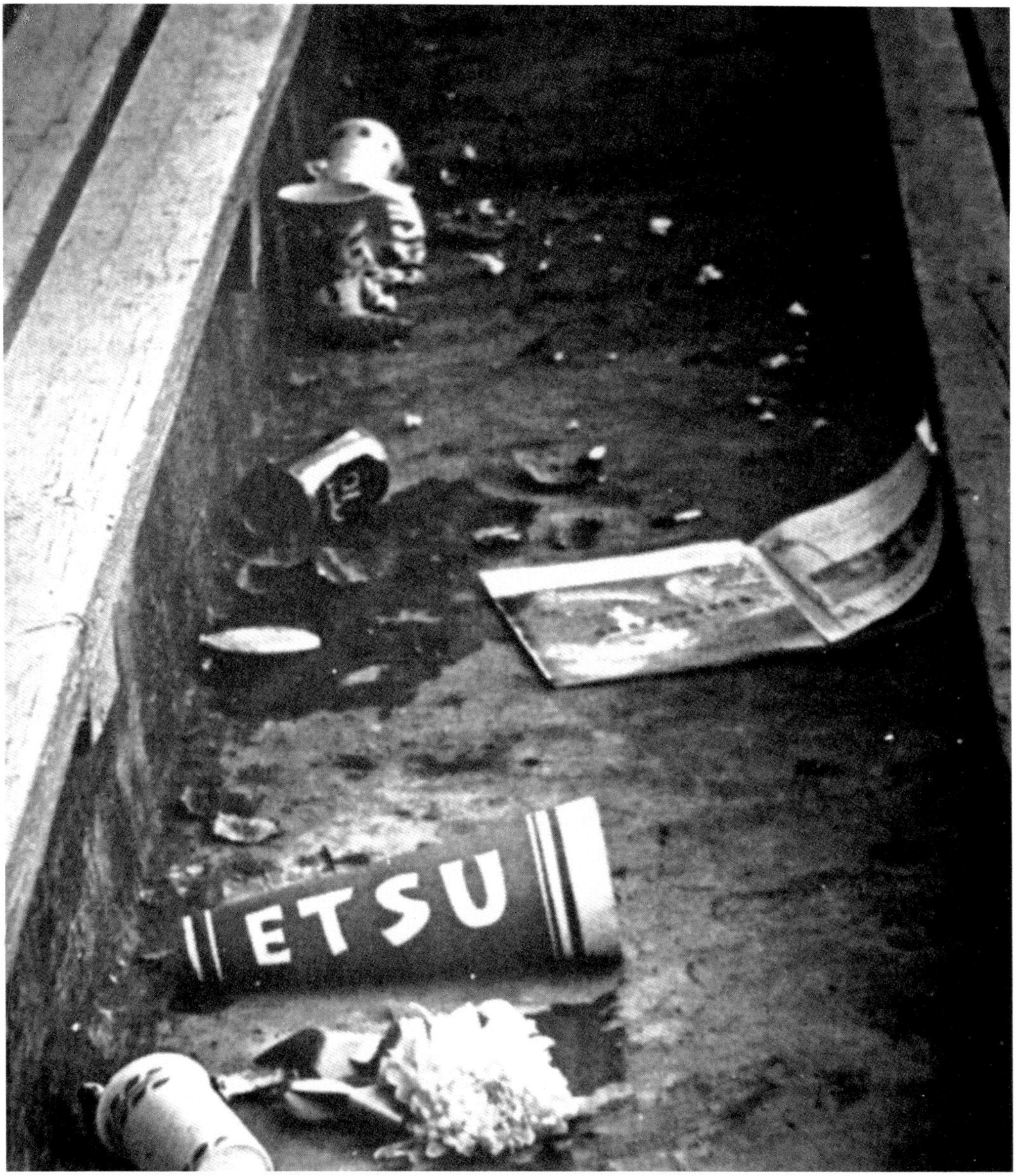

The whirlwind of Buccaneer football has passed. Will it only leave footprints of cherished moments to be relived in the minds of all who were there, or will there be something more in 2010? (Adapted from a photograph and caption in the 1965 *Buccaneer*.)